☑ SO-AHM-546

Origins of Modern

Japanese Literature

√ 10/00

ON LINE

OCT 20 2000

Post-Contemporary Interventions

Series Editors: Stanley Fish and

Fredric Jameson

Karatani Kōjin

Origins of Modern Japanese

Literature

translation edited by Brett de Bary

Duke University Press Durham and London   1993

Designed by Cherie Holma Westmoreland

Typeset in Palatino by Tseng Information

Systems, Inc.

Library of Congress Cataloging-in-Publication

Data appear on the last printed page of

this book.

"In the Mirror of Alternate Modernities" by Fredric

Jameson first appeared in the *South Atlantic*

Quarterly, Spring 1993.

Contents

Foreword: In the Mirror of Alternate Modernities

Fredric Jameson

I have high hopes that the publication of Karatani Kōjin's book—one of those infrequent moments in which a rare philosophical intelligence rises to the occasion of a full national and historical statement—will also have a fundamental impact on literary criticism in the West; and this in two ways, which are rather different from its effects in Japan itself. For *The Origins of Japanese Literature* has some lessons for us about critical pluralism, in addition to its principal message, which turns on that old and new topic of modernity itself.

I take it that any reflection on modernity—it is a little like the question about the self, or better still, about the nature of language, when you are inside it and cannot be expected to imagine anything which is outside—has known three renewals, three moments of an intense and speculative questioning. The first is presumably the moment in which the thing appears, which we call Enlightenment or Western science or industrialization, and which we might also call the last illness of God or the onset of the secular market, or capitalism and commodification. But in this first moment, the definition of science is at one with its defense, and the antediluvian Enlightenment heroes, like Auden's Voltaire, remain alert to the grim possibility of mythic regression:

> And still all over Europe stood the horrible nurses
> Itching to boil their children.

The philosophers are thus still bathed in the triumphalism of a conquest of nature that also promised to be a conquest of the self and a reconstruction of the social order in the human image and on a human scale.

Few statues to those heroes remained when the second period of a renewed interrogation of the nature of modernity rolled around: the fin de siècle, the period of positivism, of Simmel and Durkheim, the end of the Gründerzeit and of the heroic age of the establishment of the bourgeois republics, and the beginning of a long doubtful future constellated by immense working-class suburbs as well as the points of light of hysteria and neurosis, from the midst of which the more grimly stoic were able to "see how much they could bear" as Freud and Weber asked themselves unpleasant questions about the instinctual repressions and renunciations which "civilization" demanded in payment.

This second Enlightenment, or era of suspicion and demystification, was characterized by a wave of technological innovation which signed itself as irrevocable: its theorists had to confront a fundamental change in their experience, about which they had begun to be able to doubt that it was to be called progress, but were otherwise quite unable to imagine that it might ever again disappear. In fact, of course, it was still about the future that they were thinking, since outside the big cities (of the "Western" or "advanced" countries), the new science-and-technology was socially in the minority: aristocratic governments and countrysides, precapitalist colonies, still largely surrounded these "modern" industrial islands or enclaves (the spaces of Baudelaire and Zola).

In a third moment, however—our own—those vestiges of different noncapitalist pasts, if they have not everywhere disappeared, have at least receded to the point where they are objects of nostalgia. Today, therefore, a fully "modernized" life-world can be experienced as well as imagined as a realized fact: we call this fact postmodernity, at least in part because of the radically new technology that has accompanied the new global standardization, but mainly, I think, because what had previously been thought of as modernity, with its various modernisms, has now been revealed to us as a peculiarly old-fashioned and outmoded historical stage compared to our own (modernism thus paradoxically proving to be the result of incomplete modernization). Yet that older modernity could be the object of avant-garde excitement and affirmation (as the first forms of Western science were for the Enlightenment philosophes): the futurists dramatized that for us from within that industrial latecomer which at the same time inspired the thought of Gramsci; while a profound *Kulturpessimismus* offered another option, another affective or libidinal investment, with respect to the modern fact and the modern self. Postmodernity has relegated its enthusiasms and affirmations to science and technology (that is to say, to the consumption of the new gadgetry of a communications age), but is equally innocent of any Wagnerian or metaphysical global pessimism, despite the precise information it has about atomic energy, endemic famine, A I D S, and global warming. Instead, the theorization of the postmodern has seemed to billow and eddy around a new project: namely, that "overcoming of the modern" which the Japanese were the first to conceive of and name in the 1930s (when, to be sure, for some of them it meant something as simple as "overcoming" the United States and the West).

In Japan these three stages, separated in the West by two hundred years, have been compressed into a century. This is why Karatani's vision of the modern leaps out at us with such blinding force. It is indeed well known in the sciences how the "outsider principle" explains the capacity of non-card-carrying unprofessional tourists and visitors-to-a-given-discipline to deduce impending fundamental paradigm shifts; so also in the arts, where modernism is scarcely dreamed of in the British industrial core, but makes its claims in more recently "developed" areas and even more intensely in "semiperipheral" ones such as Nicaragua and Uruguay, St. Louis, Idaho, and Lisbon or Alexandria (where experience is focused and heightened by the burning glass of the metropolis).

Here, however, it is as though—even more paradoxically science-fictional than the "inversions" (tentō) with which Karatani will perform a whole series of theoretical prestidigitations—it is as though his book itself, written in the Japanese 1970s and 1980s had, lost and forgotten, somehow preceded all the other earlier theories of modernity that now look like so many commentaries on it. This is the first reason for its claims on us: it is not even an "alternate history" which is offered us by this "postmodern" analysis of the institutions of the modern self, writing, literature, and scientific objectivity that were constructed and imposed by the Meiji Revolution. Rather, it is as though that great laboratory experiment which was the modernization of Japan allows us to see the features of our own development in slow motion, in a new kind of form (which might be compared to an older traditional history or sociology as the cinema to the novel, for example, or animation to documentary).

Karatani's references are, to be sure, local and unfamiliar to many of us, although he makes it clear how immensely a figure like Natsume Sōseki (1867–1916) ought ideally (along with Rabindranath Tagore or Lu Xun) to loom on a truly global map of literary production. I find that, as with certain kinds of music criticism or theory, an account of the initial situation of production itself, with its raw materials and specific form problems, allows one to imagine the structure of the work more purely and abstractly than any distracted ad hoc audition might do; that is, certain kinds of analyses—

like those of Karatani here—are analogous to creative works themselves, insofar as they propose a schema which it is the reader's
task to construct and to project out onto the night sky of the mind's
eye; and this is in fact, I believe, the way in which a good deal of
contemporary theory is read by artists, who do not in fact read such
books primarily for their perceptive contributions to the analysis of
this or that familiar work of art, the way an older criticism was ap-
pealed to by readers of belles lettres. These younger "postmodern"
readers, as I understand it, look at the theoretical abstractions of
post-contemporary books in order to imagine the concrete referents
to which those abstractions might possibly apply—whether those
are artistic languages or experiences of daily life. Here, the analysis
produces the absent text of what remains to be invented, rather
than modestly following along behind the achieved masterpiece
with a running commentary. It is—to use the expression again—
science-fictional (as befits a culture like ours, just catching up with
science fiction, not merely in its content, but in its form): the new
abstractions model the forms of a reality that does not yet exist, but
which it would be interesting to experience.

But in Japanese literature and culture we have just such a
reality; and whether or not Sōseki and the other names in Karatani's
pages are as yet familiar to us even in the (translated) flesh-and-
blood of their *écriture*, it can be a satisfying experience to imagine
the literary situation and the multiple form-problems which Sōseki
(as Karatani presents him) is the name for.

Now let us take a closer look at Karatani's modernity, that is to
say, at ourselves and those otherwise invisible scars of our modernization that here briefly light up like an infrared flare: subject and
object, to be sure; the old "centered self" and the old "real" world of
scientific objectivity; but also—wonder of wonders!—the novel (is
it so modern, let alone socially so important?) and also landscape,
and even disease (the kind you write about in the newspapers),
children, and "depth"—for are not children a kind of depth? but
a depth rather different from Freud's unconscious or Marx's infra-
structures, which Karatani will surprise us by locating at the very
surface of our modernity.

None of these symptoms can be made visible to the naked eye
without reckoning in the effects of Karatani's "inversion" (*tentō*),
which as the Formalists, Brecht, Barthes, and so many others taught
us, turns the historical into the natural, and generates an illusion

tell the story that way, and suggest (as Karatani sometimes seems to do) that literature—the new institution of the literary as such— *causes* that reorganization called Meiji to fall into place around it. Or we can more modestly retain literature as a privileged object in which that reorganization can be analogically observed: the form of the narrative is at this point of self-consciousness not now very important (although we will return to its political consequences in a moment). There are, to be sure, other versions of the narrative as well: Masao Miyoshi's classic *Accomplices of Silence* marks the gap between the raw material of Japanese social experience and these abstract formal patterns of Western novel construction that cannot always be welded together seamlessly. (Meanwhile a similar account, which tests the imported technology—the Western form of the novel—against the content or social experience of the non-Western importing country, thereby also allowing us to measure the systematic modifications, or *Unfunktionierung* of the former in the context of the latter—can also be found in Menakshee Mukerjee's study of the origins of the Indian novel, *Realism and Reality*.) Nor will the Western reader forget the lessons of Raymond Williams, in *Keywords*, about the slow emergence of the word "literature," or of Foucault about the slow formation of that related thing he calls "humanism": slow is here the watchword for those related experiments, the measurement time is too long, the graphs in the laboratory oscillate idly over too many empty periods. The new experiment and the new laboratory equipment allow us to reproduce the same thing in a more compact set of equations, and as a more vivid event.

But there is a more basic reversal of causality at work in Karatani's *Darstellung* which is crucial insofar as it tries to strike at the most fundamental of our social and psychic illusions (at precisely those objective illusions for which literature in this sense is responsible): this is the notion of interiority, the centered subject, the psychological, indeed the Self in its intolerably Western sense (Karatani has observed elsewhere that the Japanese never needed deconstruction because they never had a centered subject to begin with: here, at least, he documents a tendency and a kind of formation). What we call interiority, however, and think of in terms of psychological experience (and by way of a great deal of imagery) is, however "simply," the effect of the literary institution as such, which by inventing a new kind of "unspeakable sentence" (Ann Banfield's name for the related phenomenon of *style indirect libre*) slowly causes a new "experience" to come into being as what that kind of sentence "expresses" (or would express if it were possible to speak it in the first place). The pages on narrative in Japanese, and in particular about the drama of Sōseki as he glimpses the radical difference of the Western novel and then produces a host of very different and unique generic experiments as a way of approximating that condition and avoiding it all at once—these pages have very little equivalent in Western criticism; only the remarkable density of Barthes's pages in *Writing Degree Zero* are comparable (and indeed, were those epigrammatic pronouncements of Barthes developed in the direction of the social and the psychoanalytic, the result would be a statement of the dimensions of Karatani's for Japan).

Now, however, we can also move in two directions: if it is not romanticized as a pre-anything, or as a form of more authentically primitive and primal writing-cum-experience, a certain approximation to what literature destroys can be attempted—it is simply the *figure,* as Chinese characters (but also the related forms of Chinese and Japanese landscape, and also the fixed forms of narrative and poetry and the like) can dramatize:

> My own concern . . . has been to consider the kind of inversion of semiotic constellation which makes transcription possible. In order for us to assume it to be natural that things exist and the artist merely observes them and copies them, "things" must first be discovered. But this requires the repression of the signification, or figurative language (Chinese characters), that precedes "things," as well as the existence of a language which is supposedly transparent. It is at this point that "interiority" is constituted.

Once such interiority is constituted, however, we can begin to work in the other direction and trace out some of the more surprising consequences: that of "disease," for instance, and of the medical in general. Karatani's striking chapter on literary tuberculosis is in fact preceded by a very interesting series of reflections on the role of Christianity in Japan as the "ideology," so to speak, of a "repression of the diversity of polytheism," and thereby the production (or "discovery") of the "natural body"—a discovery which is at one with Western sexuality and Western sexual guilt. Meanwhile, medicine builds on the production of that new body to achieve a host of new kinds of effects: it was indeed, in most non-Western countries, the first and primary form of Western science, an "agent of modernization" whose symbolic value cannot be underestimated. Any reader of Lu Xun, for example, will remember the simultaneously personal and national meaning of his decision to study medicine (in Japan), as well as the even more pointed meaning of his resolution to convert a practice of physical medicine into that of cultural production (see the preface to *Na Han* [*A Call to Arms*]). Medicine is thus all of Western science, as well as being *a* science: it is "thoroughly political, constituting one form of centralized power," and it also produces, in this case, not only the medical body but "disease" itself in its various theories. Karatani proposes something like a medical version of the James-Lange theory of the emotions in which what we sometimes think of as disease is the production of disease theory (in this case, the theory of "germs"), such that the appropriation of diseases for social and ideological purposes (as in Susan Sontag's *Illness as Metaphor*) cannot properly be the object of an ideological critique, which would imply that there existed an objective, nonideological reality of "disease" as such out there which the appropriation denatured and deformed. But for Karatani disease is always already "infected" with the literary: the illusion of an objective physical reality to which "science" and "medicine" were supposed to turn their nonideological attention is itself part of that ideology. The production of "childhood" and also of the "primitive" (or the object of anthropology and the ethnological gaze—here the inhabitants of the internally colonized Japanese "west" or the frontier of Hokkaido Island) is then an extension of this interiorizing process in a different direction. We reach the analytic climax of this line of inquiry with Karatani's discussion of "depth" as the abstract pattern and paradigm of all these ideological productions or acts of constitution. The Western reader, already bombarded with any number of post-Marxisms and revisions of Freud, will find much to ponder in Karatani's reversals of the stereotypes of those figures:

> While the theories of Marx or Freud . . . are often described as discoveries of a kind of substratum or base, what they actually accomplished was a dismantling of precisely that teleological and tran ental perspective configuration that produces the concepts of substra. and stratification: it was the surface level, rather, that commanded their attention.

The literary debate over plot versus surface provides the vehicle for this discussion, anchoring it back into the literary institution with which the book begins and recirculating its fundamental insights through the codes and thematics of nationalism and of aesthetic construction, bringing these issues down to the present of Karatani's writing (which corresponds to the postmodern self-consciousness of the rich and prosperous corporate Japan after the end of the postwar, and leaves open the fate of these structures and the questions about them in a future in which, among other things, Karatani's own book exists). I am reminded a little of Henri Lefebvre's call for a new spatial dialectic, a reconstruction of the dialectic in different terms from Hegel's old temporal ones, terms more consistent with the synchronic nature of contemporary thought. Karatani's discussions also reflect these contemporary constraints (as must everyone's), and it is not always clear whether the choice of even that minimal figure of depth versus surface does not, in its last shred of content, plunge you back into the very episteme you sought to analyze (and above which you imagined yourself somehow at least momentarily to float). But by the time this is over a reversal has taken place in which the reader—having begun by observing Japan—now finds Japanese theory observing him, and waiting for his own drawing of the consequences: as those emerge from the vague questions as to how you would do something like this in a Western context and what "application" this kind of thinking and reading might have for our own (even more "modern," modernized, and modernist) texts. This is an excellent and healthy geopolitical reversal, in my view; but any discussion of it needs to be preceded with a remark about Karatani's own political agenda.

For now we need to complicate our discussion of the dilemmas of historical representation (*Darstellung*) in an analysis like this (causality as a form, etc.), and in particular revise our suggestion that the novel or literature was at one with Meiji, and that its choice as an allegorical resonator or condenser for the historical narrative was relatively optional. For Karatani also simultaneously projects a historical narrative which stands outside this one, and which has determinate political consequences: this is the notion that what we are here calling "Meiji"—that is to say, modernization and modernity, literature, interiority, "Westernization"—is itself the result of defeat and failure. There were in this view *two* Meiji revolutions, one that succeeded and one that failed. The successful one is the constitution of the Japanese modern state as we know it; the failed revolution was contemporaneous with the Paris Commune, the popular uprisings that arose in millenarian fashion at the "dawn smell" of a new era and at the collapse of the old structures (like Bakhtin's moment of Rabelais, at the end of the Middle Ages; or

Imamura's apocalyptic and utopian film, *Eijanaika* [1981], about this same period). These needed to be repressed in order for power to be consolidated by the clique around the new emperor, but it is their repression and defeat which is accompanied by a massive popular disillusionment that can alone enable the setting in place of the new authoritarian structures: "[T]o speak in Freudian terms, the libido which was once directed towards the People's Rights movement and the political novel lost its object and was redirected inward, at which point 'landscape' and 'the inner life' appeared."

We here fleetingly glimpse an alternate world alongside our own historical one: a world in which modernity in the current coinage did not occur, without our being able to discern clearly the outlines of what, equally supplanting precapitalist forms and relations, took its place. But this alternate world, outside our own history, also lies beyond the boundaries of our explanatory and narrative systems. It is at the least, however, a rather different vision from that of Lévi-Strauss, for whom the "West" (Greek philosophy, abstract reason, science) need never have happened. Lévi-Strauss's attractive nostalgia, rooted in the experience of and commitment to "cold" or tribal societies, evokes an aleatory moment, an effect of chance, of the recombination of historical molecules, which fatally leads, or not, to the infernal machine we know as modernity or capitalism; it is a peculiarly fatalist view of the inevitability of historical development as a roll of the dice or a chance lightning strike, and then the rigid stasis of the irremediable! (This is not to suggest that history might not really be like this. . . .)

In Karatani, however, a notion of popular struggle survives which is not nostalgic, since it eventuated in failure and does not seem to imply any particular optimism about current Japanese conditions, from which all radical initiative seems to have evaporated in the years since the onset of their *Wirtschaftswunder* (the economic miracle of the early 1970s). We must remember, also, that we are ourselves trying to think this notion of a collective creativity that preempts institutions during a period of national stasis and disillusionment in the United States today which is doubled by a virtually global one: our difficulty in imagining any other narrative paradigm than a deterministic one—the slow, fateful, irresistible Foucauldian encroachments of systems and institutions—may thus be a historical symptom as much as an epistemological problem.

But I want to add something about the relationship of thought and disillusionment, which seems consistent with this glacial back-

ward look at an unfinished project that was also a missed opportunity. We are, indeed, more than familiar with the conception of
an expressive relationship between a thought system and the social
fate of its class fraction: Lucien Goldmann's picture, in *The Hidden
God*, of the way in which Jansenism's Augustinian pessimism articulated the failure of the *noblesse de robe*, from which it issued,
to become something like a mandarin ruling class, is suggestive
for a range of other moments as well. But we need to kick this
static notion of relationship into historical motion, if only in the
past tense, and to restore to this litany of class failures the fresh-
ness of opportunities, even and particularly of the missed ones. It
is a way of thinking that might even let us look differently at our
own time, which so many people seem intent on reading as the
triumph of the market, if not indeed of the nationalisms and religious fundamentalisms, over socialism. What if it were the other
way around, however? What if it were the failures of socialism,
better still, of socialists and communists, which left in their wake a
universal disillusionment in which only consumption and narrow
fanaticism seem possible, at least for the present?

The national question, then, brings me to my conclusion, which
also has something to do with the lessons of Karatani's book for
North American theory and criticism in the present conjuncture.
I suggested that a formal and suggestive way of reading about
unfamiliar literary works was possible, and sometimes, although
surely not always and not even often, recommended. Now we
need to see that something analogous can be said about unfamiliar criticism and theory, on the occasion of a book in which no
little attention is paid to classic Japanese debates most of us have
never suspected the existence of. There are also ways of reading
the form, as well as the content, of theoretical debates and critical
moves and countermoves: indeed, for anyone interested in the procedures called *mapping*, current scientific fashions show computers
at use, not in solving substantive problems, but, by way of so-called
"phase space," in matching up the abstract shapes and rhythms of
a variety of different scientific hypotheses and results, as well as in
measuring the abstract rhythms into which certain complex forms
of movement seem to break down. We don't need to extrapolate the
metaphysical slogans (the way humanists once did with Einstein-
ian relativities): it is the nature of this mapping procedure which is
suggestive, and not for predictive purposes either, or with a view
toward identifying recurrent paradigms. Rather, Karatani sets us

moderator Kawakami Tetsutarō as a response to Japanese intellectuals' shocked realization, brought on by the early "successes" of the war, that "our Europeanized intellects and Japanese blood were at odds with each other."[4] Yet, as Takeuchi observed, throughout these discussions the relationship between a decadent modernity and what, in the Japanese context, has long been called *bummei kaika* (a term loosely describing technological, scientific, and political "progress" in post-Meiji Japan) was vexing. While some ideologues took the extremist position that science and technology be included in a thoroughgoing rejection of the modern, Japanese Romanticists, an influential group of nationalistic critics affiliated with the journal *Nihon Roman-ha* (*Japanese Romanticists*, 1935–38) found they had reached a logical impasse when they attempted to condemn Western imperialism. As Takeuchi noted, "some kind of universal values had to be posited in order to judge imperialism," yet "any system of universal values subsuming East and West could not be admitted" by the Japanese Romanticists because they saw it as "divorced from tradition."[5] Other thinkers, such as the philosopher Shimomura Torajirō, insisted that since "the West was no longer the Other" for Japan and it was therefore impossible to reject modernity, it was "a new spiritual outlook" which should be the focus of efforts. Influential Kyoto School philosopher Nishitani Keiji, similarly acknowledging that "the modern in Japan is based on European elements," identified as problematic only the *manner* of "piecemeal importation, without coordination, of the various aspects of modern culture," and advocated Japan's development of a synthesizing, "spiritual outlook."[6] As Nakamura Mitsuo observed, however, "even the notion that the task of the present is to 'overcome modernity' was developed by a group of contemporary Western philosophers." To "borrow Western concepts as a way of rejecting the West is an absurd contradiction."[7] The logical bankruptcy of wartime efforts to identify and locate "pure" and indigenous elements of Japanese culture was perhaps most strikingly illustrated in Yasuda Yojūrō's 1940 essay, "The Originality of Japanese Culture" (*Nihon bunka no dokusōsei*), which ultimately and ironically could only conclude that it was the ability to adapt, even to imitate, that constituted the uniqueness of Japanese culture.[8]

As the boldest revisionist critique of modern Japanese literary history to appear since the end of the Pacific War, *Origins of Modern Japanese Literature* shares with efforts of the 1930s and 1940s the impulse to resist hegemonic narratives which, blatantly or subtly, reinforce the notion of the West as center, origin, and arbiter of modernity while marginalizing, suppressing, and depriving of self-respect the cultural productions of the non-West. It was no doubt recognition of an impassioned articulation of such an impulse that made the opening chapter of Karatani's book arresting for many Japanese readers, a chapter in which Karatani strikingly reverses the conventional evaluation of the Meiji literary giant Natsume Sōseki (1867–1916), typically credited with refining Japanese techniques of modern, psychological narration in his depiction of rootless, urban characters. For Karatani, what was significant were the tragic failures of Sōseki's career—his despair over mastering English, the book of literary theory abandoned before it was completed and which—despite the supposed universality of "literature"—Sōseki correctly suspected would not be taken seriously beyond the borders of Japan. Born just a year before the Meiji Restoration of 1868 and steeped as a child in the study of Chinese classics, Sōseki never overcame his sense of estrangement from, and skepticism toward, conceptions of literature that later modern writers saw as utterly natural.

This was because at the time of the Meiji Restoration in 1868, the inclusive term "literature," or *bungaku*, did not yet exist in Japanese, and different genres were referred to by their specific names. Karatani therefore emphasizes Sōseki's relationship to *kanbungaku*, a modern Japanese term we have carried over into the English translation to emphasize its specificity in the Japanese context. Literary Chinese, much like Latin in Europe prior to the seventeenth century, was the common written language of the Chinese, Japanese, and Korean intelligentsia into the late nineteenth century. This written language came to be generally referred to in Japanese as *kanbun*, referring to the practice of writing texts in Chinese ideographs accompanied by annotation in the phonetic syllabary enabling the Japanese reader to reconstruct Chinese sentences according to Japanese grammatical patterns. As Karatani notes in chapter 1, the modern term *kanbungaku* does not only refer to Chinese literature, but most precisely to any text that could be read in *kanbun*: the broad corpus of canonical *kanbun* texts an educated Japanese reader of Sōseki's time would have been familiar with, therefore, could in no way be seen as having constituted a "national literature." *Kanbun* texts, however, could be said to have been canonical insofar as they were the basis for the education of the Tokugawa elite. Such texts included Chinese Confucian classics; Chinese poetry,

the use of such terms as "Edo liter   " "Meiji literature," o⌐
"Taisho literature," but to use numeral   ℩ the Western caler
for specific dates and other chronologi⟨   ⟩rences. Yet in ⌐   ⌐s
of Modern Japanese Literature, Karatani b⟩   ⟩ith this c⌐ ⟩e⟩tion,
using Japanese imperial reign names to s   ⟩any developments
chronologically. For example, in stressi⟩   the firm establishment of Japanese literary realism took pl   ⟩nly after the leaders
of the Meiji Restoration had suppressed a⟩   ely supported movement for the establishment of representa⟩   political institutions
(the Movement for Freedom and People's 1⟩   ⟩hts, referred to here-
after as the People's Rights movement, init⟩   ed in 1874), Karatani
repeatedly calls attention to "the third decac⟩   of the Meiji period,"
instead of using the more conventional "189⟨⟩   ⟩ In order not to di-
lute the polemical force of these deliberate u⟩   ⟨es, we have often
translated Karatani's references to the year-p⟨   ⟩ds literally rather
than using the Western calendrical references t⟩   would have been
more familiar to non-Japanese readers.

About the Translation

The original translations of chapters 4, 5, and 6 v⟩   ⟩ prepared by
students in a graduate course on postwar Japane⟩   ⟩iterature and
criticism that I taught at Cornell University in f⟩   1989. Subsequently, I edited and revised each of these chaptei⟩   My aim was
not only to maintain continuity in the style and ter⟩   ⟩ology used
throughout the book, but also to attempt to make   ⟩re that the
movement of Karatani's argument, and the conceptu⟩   ⟩sonances
between different parts of that argument, would eme⟩   as clearly
as possible for readers of the English text. Final resp⟨   ⟩bility for
errors of translation or interpretation, therefore, is mi⟩   . Also, to
make the rich intertextuality of Karatani's book more e⟩   ⟩ly accessible to non-Japanese readers and scholars, we have ⟨   ⟩ensively
annotated the text, providing sources for all citations. (1⟩   cause of
differences in Japanese publishing conventions, these so⟩   ⟩ces and
annotations do not appear in the original book.)

After reading the translated manuscript, Mr. Karatan⟩   repeatedly expressed his concern that his book, intended for ⟩   Japanese audience, would not be accessible to non-Japanese i⟩   ⟩ders.
Although he would have preferred to substantially revise ⟩   d re-
structure his argument, we were anxious about further de⟩   ⟩ing

the appearance in English of the book. Mr. Karatani therefore confined his revisions to the explanatory "afternotes" that we have appended to each of the chapters. These notes help to provide historical context for the chapters and also suggest directions in which Mr. Karatani hopes to develop related arguments in the future. At the urging of Fredric Jameson and Reynolds Smith (our editor at Duke University Press), I have also added a glossary to the text. There, at the risk of considerable oversimplification, I attempt to identify proper names and other important terms.

I am grateful to Ayako Kano for her assistance in the time-consuming process of annotation, and to Reynolds Smith for astutely suggesting that I provide explanations for a number of other terms in the text that might be confusing for nonspecialist readers. In the course of bringing this project to completion, the support of family and friends was also crucial. I would like to thank Asai Kiyoshi, Karen Brazell, William Theodore and Fanny de Bary, Fredric Jameson, Masao Miyoshi, Victor Nee, Naoki Sakai, Etsuko Terasaki, and Phyllis Granoff and Koichi Shinohara for their encouragement. James Fujii and William Haver provided penetrating insights into Karatani's text in the guise of anonymous reader's reports. Coraleen Rooney saw the word processing of the manuscript through to the end, despite the interruption of major surgery. Finally, I would like to express my appreciation to Karatani Kōjin— first, for his patience with a project that extended longer than both of us had foreseen and, second, for the uncommon turn of mind that enabled him to peruse the final translation, less with a proprietary sense of accuracy than with a philosopher's willingness to be led to consider new interpretations of the "original."

Brett de Bary
Ithaca, New York, 1992

1 The Discovery of Landscape

1

Natsume Sōseki published the notes from his lectures on English
literature at Tokyo University under the title *A Theory of Literature*
(*Bungakuron*) in 1906, just three years after returning from London.
By that time he had already attracted attention as a novelist and
had immersed himself in the writing of fiction. Since he initially
conceived of *A Theory of Literature* in terms of a ten-year plan, its
publication at this point in time signaled his abandonment of that
plan. *A Theory of Literature* as we know it today, then, is just one
small part of Sōseki's original, ambitious conception. Sōseki expressed mixed feelings in the preface he attached to the work: a
sense of estrangement, as one who had become absorbed in creative writing, toward these "vague, impractical speculations," as
well as a feeling that he really could not give up his vision. Certainly both these sentiments were genuine; they were, in fact, the
very basis for Sōseki's creative activity.

To state the problem in different terms, we might say that
Sōseki's preface reveals an awareness that readers of his time would
be unprepared for the appearance of his *Theory of Literature* and
that they would find it somewhat odd. This surely proved to be the
case, not only in Sōseki's time, but in our own. Even if we grant
that Sōseki as an individual was compelled by some necessity to
produce such a work, there was nothing inevitable about its appearance in Japanese (or even Western) literary history. The *Theory
of Literature* was a flower that bloomed out of season and therefore
left no seed—Sōseki himself must have been keenly aware of this.
Looked at in either the Japanese or the Western context, Sōseki's
vision was an abrupt and solitary one which he himself must have
found disorienting. In his preface he explains, just as Sensei, in the
novel *Kokoro* (The heart, 1914), did in his "Last Testament," why
this unusual book had to be written. For this reason his preface is
written in an extremely personal style which contrasts strikingly
with the formal style of the work itself. Sōseki felt compelled to
explain his own passion and what had given rise to it.

I was determined, in this work, to solve the problem of defining the nature of literature. I resolved to devote a year or more to the first stage of my research on this problem.

I shut myself up in my room in my boarding house and packed all the works of literature I owned away in my wicker trunk. For I believed that reading literature in order to understand the nature of literature was like washing blood with blood. I vowed to probe the psychological origins of literature: what led to its appearance, development, and decline. And I vowed to explore the social factors that brought literature into this world and caused it to flourish or wither.[1]

"What is literature?" was the question Sōseki wanted to address, yet this was the very thing that made his passion so private, so difficult to share with others. The question itself was too new. For British readers of the time, literature was literature. Insofar as "literature" was something that encompassed them, the kind of doubt Sōseki harbored could not arise. Of course, as Michel Foucault has observed, the concept of "literature" itself was a relative newcomer to European civilization in the nineteenth century. Sōseki, although his very life was encompassed by "literature," could not escape from his doubts about it. They were doubts that seemed all the more iconoclastic in Japan of 1908, where "literature" had just firmly established itself. Sōseki's view was seen, not as an anachronism, but as an eccentricity. Certainly this response must have dampened his ardor for theory. We might at first glance take *A Theory of Literature* to be literary theory. It appears, that is, to be something written about literature from the inside. But a number of essays in the book (the one on "Evaluating Literature," for example) suggest that Sōseki originally conceived of something much more fundamental.

The first notion that Sōseki subjected to doubt was that of the universal character of English literature. Of course, by this I do not mean to imply that Sōseki's aim was simply to relativize English literature by juxtaposing it to *kanbungaku*, that diverse corpus of texts written in Chinese ideographs (or *kanbun*) in which he had immersed himself while growing up. His real concern was to point out that that universality was not a priori, but historical. It was, moreover, a universality premised upon the concealment of its own origins. "When I appeal to my own experience, I learn that the realm of poetry created by Shakespeare does not possess that universality that European critics ascribe to it. For us as Japanese it requires years of training to develop a proper appreciation of Shakespeare, and even then this is only a dim appreciation based on a deliberate adaptation of our sensibilities."[2]

Let me expand on Sōseki's statement. To the poets and playwrights trained in Latin, the "universal tongue" of their time, Shakespeare's work was beneath consideration. It continued to be ignored until the nineteenth century, when the German romantic movement discovered Shakespeare along with "literature." It was at this juncture that the image of Shakespeare—individual of genius, self-conscious artist, poet at once realist and romantic—was born. But Shakespeare's drama was quite different from realism; it was closer, one might say, to the work of Chikamatsu Monzaemon.* This was pointed out by Sōseki when he wrote about the translations of Shakespeare by Tsubouchi Shōyō. Shakespeare was not a realist, and he was not attempting to represent what was "human." When the notion of universality was established in nineteenth-century Europe, its own historicity had to be concealed.†

Sōseki had no choice but to reject such notions as the history of literature (bungakushi) because he was aware of the historicity of the very term "literature." History, like literature, was established and came to prominence in the nineteenth century; to view the past in a historical framework meant to take the existence of universals as self-evident.

Sōseki reacted against the "history of literature." But he was not therefore saying that Japanese could be permitted a unique way

---

*Chikamatsu Monzaemon (1653–1724) was the author of plays for the jōruri (puppet) and kabuki theatres. While his historical plays (jidaimono) dealt with military campaigns such as the Battles of Coxinga (Kokusenya Kassen, 1715), his most affecting works explored the tragic dimensions of the subject matter of popular sewamono (gossip) dramas: domestic conflict, events in the pleasure quarters, love suicides. Meiji critics often described Chikamatsu as a Japanese parallel to Shakespeare.

† Throughout this chapter, Karatani differentiates between the Japanese terms "rekishisei," which I have translated as "historicity," and "rekishishugi," which I have simply translated as "history." Karatani's concept of "rekishishugi" seems close to the notion of "history" (or "traditional history") described in Michel Foucault's essay, "Nietzsche, Genealogy, and History." According to Foucault, "history," as it emerged in nineteenth-century Europe, insisted upon linearity, "dissolving an event into an ideal continuity—as a teleological movement or a natural process." See p. 154 and passim in the English translation of this essay in Michel Foucault, Language, Counter-Memory, Practice, edited by D. Bouchard (Ithaca: Cornell University Press, 1977).

of reading literature. It was his questioning of the concepts of "literature" and "history" that were dominant in his own time that led him to develop his concept of "autonomy" (*jiko hon'i*).

> Whether it be social mores, customs, or emotions, we must not recognize the existence only of those social mores, customs, and emotions that have manifested themselves in the West. Nor should the attainments reached, after many transitions, by Western civilization at this point in time set the standard, however much it may set a standard for them. This is particularly true in the case of literature. It is commonly said that Japanese literature is immature. Unfortunately, I, too, hold this view. But to admit that one's literature is immature is quite a different thing from taking the West as a standard. If the immature Japanese literature of today develops, we cannot categorically declare it will become like the literature of contemporary Russia. Nor will it follow stages identical to those whereby modern French literature produced Hugo, then Balzac, then Zola. Since no one can logically maintain that there is only a single path a developing literature can follow, or a single point it should attain, it is rash to assert that the trends of Western literature today will be those of Japanese literature tomorrow. We should not leap to the conclusion that developments in Western literature are absolute. Perhaps, where the physical sciences are concerned, we may say that a certain idea is "new" or "correct." But since the path of progress twists and turns, branching off at many different points, it is impossible to say that what is "new" in the West is necessarily correct for Japan. If we set aside abstractions and examine the actual situation of literature in many different countries today, we can easily see that there is no orthodox path of development. . . .

> For that matter, we might say that it was a very precarious tight-rope act which brought Western painting to where it is today. A moment's loss of balance would have resulted in a very different history. I have perhaps not developed this point sufficiently, but it can be deduced from my earlier remarks that there are infinite possibilities in the history of painting: Western painting has followed one line, and Japanese genre painting another. I have used painting as an example, but there are many others. And it is the same with literature. Therefore, to take Western literature as we have been taught it as the sole truth and constantly appeal to that in determining our own affairs is terribly limiting. I don't deny that there is a factual basis for history. But what we have been taught is "history" can be assembled in many different ways within our minds and, given the right conditions, these other visions are always capable of being realized. . . .

In the preceding sections I have discussed three problems which arise when history is seen as a continuous development. One is a tendency to abandon the old and indiscriminately pursue the new. Another is the tendency to affix the label of an "ism" to a work which has appeared spontaneously and as a result of treating the work as representative of this "ism," to mistake it for a whole which cannot be broken up, despite the inappropriateness of such an approach. Finally, we have the confusion which arises when, in response to changing times, the meaning of the "ism" itself changes.

The methodology I wish to propose now, while not unrelated to history, nevertheless does not hinge on a notion of historical development. Rather than classifying literary works on the basis of an "ism" (which, in turn, is based on the notion that a specific period or individual can be identified in terms of distinguishing characteristics) we should look only at characteristics of the work itself, quite apart from its author or the age in which it was written. We should approach all works—ancient or modern, Eastern or Western—in this way. They should be analyzed on the basis of formal and thematic criteria alone.[3]

As the foregoing quote makes clear, Sōseki took exception to the view that history was continuous and inevitable, as well as to the hidden ethnocentrism of the "history" that emerged in nineteenth century Europe. Moreover, he rejected the idea that a literary work could be reduced to a whole called "the spirit of the age" or "the author," and emphasized "only those characteristics manifested in the work itself." Sōseki's approach here may be seen as a kind of formalist analysis, but of course it preceded the appearance of the formalist movement and formalist theory. Sōseki's F+f formula,* which he elaborates in *A Theory of Literature*, is also implicit in the approach he advocates in the cited passage.[4]

"Romanticism" and "naturalism," for example, are products of history, and they appeared in historical sequence, but Sōseki insists that they be seen, rather, as "elements" in a work:

I've already defined the two types of literature and the ways in which both are important. It is a superficial view to maintain that one school should be expelled from the literary world and the other should domi-

* Sōseki's "F+f formula" is presented in the opening passage of his *Theory of Literature* and represents an attempt to probe the psychological basis of literary expression. Following British psychologist Lloyd Morgan, Sōseki describes consciousness as a constantly fluctuating "wave" characterized by the coexistence of "focal" (F, or intensely vivid) and "marginal" (f) emotions or ideas. See the notes to this chapter for further discussion.

nate it. Because the two schools have different names, some people assume that they are in fierce opposition, that the Romantic School and the Naturalist School glare at each other from within sturdy fortifications and across deep moats. But in reality it is only the names which are contending with each other, content passes back and forth freely between the two schools and there is a great deal of commingling. We can expect this to give rise to some works which, depending on the reader's viewpoint or interpretation, could be considered Naturalist as well as Romantic. Even if one tried to draw a firm line between the two schools, countless mutations would emerge out of the grey zone between the perfect objectivity attributed to the Naturalists and the perfect subjectivity of the Romantics. Each of these strains would combine with other strains to produce new breeds, which would in turn produce a second order of changes, until ultimately it would be impossible to distinguish the Romantic from the Naturalist. We can escape from the erroneous tendencies in contemporary criticism by carefully dissecting each work, identifying which passages are Romantic, and in what sense, and which are Naturalist, and in what sense. And no matter which way we identify a passage, we should not be content with simply applying one label or the other, but we should point out the admixture of "foreign elements" each contains.[5]

Sōseki is obviously expressing a formalist perspective here. His theory identified metaphor and simile as basic patterns in linguistic expression; the former characterizing the romantic style and the latter the naturalist. He expressed this insight well in advance of Roman Jakobsen, who proposed that the "tendency" of a literary work be identified on the basis of whether metaphorical or metonymical elements predominated. The experience of living in Europe as an outsider attempting to come to terms with "literature" in the West, however, was shared by both men. Since it was necessary for a critique of ethnocentrism from within Europe to arise before the contributions even of Russian formalism were properly recognized, we can imagine just how isolated the efforts of Sōseki, as a Japanese critic, were. But it was not simply because of his sense of isolation that Sōseki finally abandoned his *Theory of Literature*.

Sōseki could not accept what Michel Foucault defines as "the principle of identity" in European thought. For Sōseki, structures were entities which were interchangeable and capable of redefinition. Once a certain structure has been selected and identified as universal, history, of necessity, comes to be seen as linear. But it was not Sōseki's intention to set up an opposition between Japanese literature and Western literature and thereby to assert their differences and relativity, for he was skeptical of identity in the case of Japanese literature, as well. It was simply that once he had discovered that structures could be assembled and reassembled, Sōseki was led immediately to question why history should be defined in one way and not another, and even (with Pascal) why "I" should be "here rather than there." Formalism and structuralism, of course, do not address themselves to these problems.

Perhaps it is relevant to note here that Sōseki was sent out for adoption by his parents as an infant and grew to a certain age believing that his adoptive parents were his real parents. Having seen himself as an interchangeable existence, he must have conceived of the bond between parent and child as not at all a natural but an interchangeable one. The child of natural parents may not immediately perceive an element of cruel gameplaying involved in this. For even if Sōseki had an intellectual understanding of his childhood situation, he would have been compelled to doubt why he was "here" rather than "there." It was very likely this doubt which sustained his creative life. In this sense we might say that it was not because he had given up on theory that Sōseki became involved with creative writing—but rather that his theory that gave birth to his fiction. I do not, of course, mean to imply that Sōseki was at heart a theoretist or that his real aim was to write a theory of literature. What I am saying is that there was no other mode of existence possible for him except as theoretician—that is, as a person who maintained a certain distance between himself and "literature."

2

The strongly personal tone of Sōseki's preface to the *Theory of Literature* suggests that the role of theoretician was something he embraced reluctantly and as if perforce. He explains how he came to entertain the question "What is the nature of literature?"

> As a child I enjoyed studying the Chinese classics. Although the time I spent in this kind of study was not long, it was from the Chinese classics that I learned, however vaguely and obscurely, what literature was. In my heart, I hoped that it would be the same way when I read English literature, and that I would not necessarily begrudge giving my whole life, if that were necessary, to its study. I had years ahead of me. I cannot say that I lacked the time to study English literature.

But what I resent is that despite my study I never mastered it. When I graduated I was plagued by the fear that somehow I had been cheated by English literature.[6]

There was a basis for Sōseki's fear that he had been "cheated" by English literature. Only those who have come to accept "literature" as natural cannot detect this "cheating." Nor should we invoke vague generalizations about the identity crisis of one who confronts an alien culture. To do this would be to assume there was something self-evident about "literature" and to lose sight of its ideological nature. Sōseki had some inkling of the ideological nature of literature because of his familiarity with *kanbungaku*. Of course, *kanbungaku* as Sōseki knew it was not simply the "literature of China," nor was he attempting to compare it with Western literature. Sōseki was in no position to pursue idle comparisons between *kanbungaku* and Western literature. In point of fact, Sōseki himself could not even grasp *kanbungaku* as a tangible existence, for by his own time it had already become something uncertain and irretrievable, something which could only be imagined on the other shore, as it were, of "literature."

Sōseki uses the term *kanbungaku* in a manner very similar to the way in which the word *sansuiga* (literally, "mountain-water pictures" or "landscape paintings") was used in Meiji Japan to denote paintings of natural scenes done in traditional styles. It was only after the Japanese had been introduced to Western landscape painting that the word *sansuiga* became widely used. As Usami Keiji wrote in an essay on a recent exhibit of such paintings:

> The word *sansuiga* was not actually used in the period when the works exhibited here were painted. At that time they were referred to as *shiki-e* or *tsukinami* (seasonal paintings). Ernest Fenollosa, who played a leading role in Japan's modernization during the Meiji period, coined the term *sansuiga* and established it as a descriptive category for paintings. The very concept of traditional "landscape paintings" arose out of the disjuncture between Japanese culture and modern Western consciousness.[7]

The same may be said of *kanbungaku*. Although Sōseki uses the term to differentiate certain practices from those of modern literature, it is itself rooted in the consciousness that produced the category "literature" and has no existence apart from it. Literature makes the objectification of *kanbungaku* possible. In this sense to compare *kanbungaku* and English literature is to ignore the histo-

something *sansuiga* has in common with medieval European painting. In the former, the transcendental place is an ideal realm to which the enlightened sages awakened; in the latter, it is the realm of Scripture and the divine.[8]

In *sansuiga* the painter is not looking at an object but envisioning the transcendental. Similarly, poets like Bashō and Sanetomo were not looking at "landscapes." As Yanagita Kunio has said, there is not a single line of description in Bashō's *Oku no hosomichi* (Narrow road to the deep north, 1694).* Even what looks like description is not. If we can follow the subtle yet crucial distinction Yanagita has drawn here, we will be able to see both the process of the Japanese discovery of "landscape" and the literary "history" that paralleled that transformation of perception.

In literature, for example, it was only when Japanese naturalism (and the rejection of Bakin) had become a mainstream trend that Saikaku was discovered to be a "realist." But it is doubtful that Saikaku's writing conformed to our contemporary definition of realism. Saikaku did not "see things as they are" any more than did Shakespeare, whose dramas were based on classical models and written within the framework of the morality play.† Similarly, the Meiji poet Shiki praised Buson's haiku for being almost like paintings. But Buson's haiku were in no way related to the sensibility of Shiki and his "sketches"; they were closer in spirit to his own *sansuiga*. This is not to deny that Buson was different from Bashō. But what differentiated them was not what we perceive it to be today. Shiki himself acknowledged this. He described, for example, the "painterly" quality of the poetry produced by Buson's bold incorporation of Chinese compounds into his poetry. The following poem, Shiki held, is enlivened by an intense dynamism because the characters (大河) are not given their Japanese reading (*ōkawa*) but the

---

*This text is the travel diary recording the poet Matsuo Bashō's journey to the remote northern provinces of the island of Honshu in 1689. The text includes, along with its narrative sections, many famous haiku about sites associated with Japanese literature and history and, allusively, with Chinese poetic and historical texts.

† Karatani alludes to two representative writers of early and late Edo literature. Ihara Saikaku (1642–93) developed a genre of prose fiction known as *ukiyo zōshi* (books of the floating world), dealing with the lives of merchants and samurai and their doings in the pleasure quarters. Takizawa Bakin (1767–1848) was perhaps the most widely read author of late Edo prose fiction. The long historical romance *Nansō Satomi Hakkenden* (1814–42, *Satomi and the Eight Dogs*) was his most popular work.

Sinicized reading "taiga." But what this example really reveals is that Buson was fascinated, not so much by landscape, as by the written word.*

> Early summer rains!
> Facing the swollen river
> Two houses

> Samidare ya
> Taiga o mae ni
> Ie niken

さみだれや
大河を前に
家二軒

The concept of Japanese literature (*kokubungaku*) took firm root during the third decade of the Meiji period. Needless to say, this was both made possible by and interpreted in terms of the newly institutionalized literature. It is not my aim in this essay to discuss the concept of "the history of Japanese literature." But I do want to point out that this very concept of a history of Japanese literature, which seems so self-evident to us today, took shape in the midst of our discovery of landscape. Perhaps it was only Sōseki who regarded this development with suspicion. Yet it is precisely because our discovery of landscape was the type of phenomenon I have described that I cannot refer to it in terms of the chronological sequence of a so-called "history of Japanese literature." "Meiji literary history" certainly appears to progress according to a temporal sequence. But it is only by distorting this temporal sequence that we can perceive the inversion we have repressed from our memories: our discovery of landscape.

3

What I am referring to as "landscape" is an epistemological constellation, the origins of which were suppressed as soon as it was produced. It is a constellation which appeared in nascent form in the literary trend of realism in the 1890s. Yet the decisive inversion

---

* In this passage Karatani refers to the late Edo poet Yosa Buson (1716–84) and to the Meiji poet Masaoka Shiki (1867–1902). Buson was a leading *haikai* poet as well as an accomplished master of *bunjinga* (literati) painting. He developed a form of unconventional, abstract brush-painting known as the *haiga* (haiku-painting). Shiki was a poet and critic who advocated the "reform" of haiku through the technique of "sketching" (*shasei*). See the note on *shasei* in this chapter.

had not yet occurred. The realistic s̱   ˌs time was basically
an extension of Edo literature. ᴵ   ᴋunikida Doppo's works—
The Musashi Plain (Musashiˬ   ˌ *Unforgettable People* (Wasureenu
hitobito), published in ₁ᶜ   ᵥhich embodied a fundamental break
with the past. *Unfˬ   ˌte People*, in particular, offers convincing
evidence that "ᴵ   ˌscape" was an inversion of consciousness before
it became a representational convention.

The novel is structured around the visits of an unknown scholar
named Ōtsu to an inn along the Tama River, where he tells tales of
"unforgettable people" to Akiyama, a man he has gotten to know
during his stays at the inn. Ōtsu takes out a manuscript he is writing which opens with the line, "The people I have been unable to
forget are not always those I *should* not have forgotten," and tells his
friend about it. The people he "should not have forgotten" include
"friends, acquaintances, and others to whom I am obliged, such as
teachers and mentors"; the "unforgettable people" are those whom
"I have not been able to forget, although it made no difference if I
remembered them or not." By way of example, he describes something he experienced when he took a steamer from Osaka across
the Inland Sea.

> Because of my state of health, I must surely have been depressed. I
> remember, at least, that I daydreamed about the future while I roamed
> the deck, and thought of the fate of men in this life. I suppose this is
> the sort of thing all young men do at such times. I heard the pleasant
> sound of the ship's hull cutting through the water, and watched the
> soft glow of the spring day melt into the sea's oil-smooth, unrippled
> surface. As the ship advanced, one small island after another would
> rise out of the mist on either side of us, then disappear. The islands,
> each draped in a thick brocade of yellow flowers and green barley
> leaves, seemed to be floating deep within the surrounding mist. Be-
> fore long the ship passed not fifteen hundred yards from the beach of
> a small island off to the right and I stepped to the rail, gazing absent-
> mindedly at the island. There seemed to be no fields or houses, only
> groves of small, low pine scattered over the hillside. It was low tide.
> The damp surface of the hushed and deserted beach glistened in the
> sun, and now and then a long streak—perhaps the playing of little
> waves at the water's edge—shone like a naked sword, then dissolved.
> From the faint call of a lark high in the air over the hill, one could tell
> that the island was inhabited. I remembered my father's poem, "The
> soaring lark betrays a farm behind the island's face," and I thought
> there must certainly be houses on the other side. And as I watched

I caught sight of a lone figure on a sunlit beach. I could tell it was a man, not a woman or a child. He seemed to be picking things up repeatedly and putting them into a basket or pail. He would take two or three steps, squat down, and pick something up. I watched carefully as he wandered along the deserted little beach beneath the hill. As the ship drew further away, the man's form became a black dot, and soon the beach, the hills, and the island all faded into the mist. Almost ten years have passed, and I have thought many times of this man at the edge of the island, the man whose face I never saw. He is one of those I cannot forget.[9]

I have included this long quote as a way of demonstrating that the man on Doppo's island is not so much a "person" as a "landscape." As the narrator says, "At such times, it is these people who flood my mind. No, it is these people standing in the midst of scenes in which I discovered them." The narrator, Ōtsu, offers many other examples of "unforgettable people," but they are all people-as-landscapes, as in the passage above. Although there may seem to be nothing particularly odd about this, Doppo calls our attention to the eccentricity of this narrator, who is haunted by people-as-landscapes, in the final lines of the novel.

At the conclusion of the novel, two years have passed since Ōtsu and Akiyama chatted at the inn:

Two years had passed.

Circumstances had brought Ōtsu to make his home in Tōhoku. His acquaintance with the man Akiyama, whom he had met at the inn in Mizonokuchi, had long since ended. The time of year was what it had been then in Mizonokuchi. It was a rainy night. Ōtsu sat alone at his desk, lost in thought. On the desk was the manuscript of "Unforgettable People" that he had shown to Akiyama two years before. A new chapter had been added, "The Innkeeper of Kameya." There was no chapter called "Akiyama."[10]

In reading *Unforgettable People*, then, we have a sense, not simply of landscapes, but of a fundamental inversion. I might even go so far as to say that it is in this inversion that we discover Doppo's landscape. For landscape, as I have already suggested, is not simply what is outside. A change in our way of perceiving things was necessary in order for landscape to emerge, and this change required a kind of reversal. Here, again, is the protagonist of *Unforgettable People*:

I am not a happy man. Always I am tortured by life's great questions and by my own overwhelming ambitions. In the deepening hours of a night such as this, alone, staring into the lamp, I experience unbearable sorrow. At these times my inflexible egoism seems to shatter, and the thought of others touches me deeply. I think of my friends and of days long past. But more than anything else, images of these people I have described to you come streaming into my mind. No, I see not the people themselves. I see the figures in the background of a much larger scene. They are part of their surroundings, part of a moment. I remember these people and from deep within me the thought wells up: How am I different from anyone else? Part of the life we share is from heaven, and part of it is from earth. All of us are returning, hand in hand, along the same eternal track, to that infinite heaven. And when this realization comes to me, I find myself in tears, for there is then in truth no Self, no Others. I am touched by memories of each and every one. Only at these times do I feel such peace, such liberation, such sympathy towards all things. Only then do worldly thoughts of fame and the struggle for fortune disappear so utterly.[11]

This passage clearly reveals the link between landscape and an introverted, solitary situation. While the narrator can feel a solidarity such that "the boundary between myself and others" disappears in the case of people who are of no consequence to him, he is the very picture of indifference when it comes to those in his immediate surroundings. It is only within the "inner man," who appears to be indifferent to his external surroundings, that landscape is discovered. It is perceived by those who do not look "outside."

4

Paul Valéry has described the history of oil painting in Europe as a process of permeation and domination by landscape painting. He writes:

Thus, the interest of painters in the landscape was gradually transformed. What started as complementary to the subject of the painting took on the form of a new realm of fantasy, a land of marvels . . . and finally, impression triumphed: matter or light dominated.

Within a few years, painting was inundated by images of a world without human beings. Viewers were content with the ocean, the forests, the fields . . . devoid of human figures. Since our eyes were far less familiar with trees and field than with animals, painting came to offer greater scope for the arbitrary; even gross distortions were acceptable. We would be shocked at the sight of an arm or a leg depicted in the same way that a branch might be in these paintings. Our ability to distinguish between the possible and the impossible is far less astute in the case of vegetable and mineral forms. The landscape afforded great conveniences. Everyone began to paint.[12]

Valéry is clearly critical of landscape painting and saw its prominence as leading to "a diminution of the intellectuality of art" and a loss of the sense of art as "an activity of the total human being." But he also wrote, "What I have written about painting applies, with astonishing accuracy, to literature. Literature was invaded by description during the same period that painting was invaded by landscape; it went in the same direction, and with the same results."

The practice of "sketching" (*shasei*) developed by Masaoka Shiki in the 1890s exemplifies almost perfectly the type of process described by Valéry.* Shiki adopted and advocated the practice of going out into nature with notebooks and making "sketches" which were actually haiku poems. It was at this point that he abandoned the traditional subject matter of haiku. The subjects of Shiki's "sketches" were ones which could not have been incorporated into poetry before that time. This is not to say that we find in his work the kind of twisted malice that we see in *Unforgettable People*. Rather, Shiki's works appear to be monotonously realistic. Yet there is latent within "sketching" the same type of inversion we find in Doppo, and this cannot be overlooked. We might also cite Takahama Kyoshi's poetry as exemplifying this inversion. The influence exerted on Takahama by "sketching" is, in a sense, the secret of his poetry. "Description," as practiced by these writers, was something more than simply portraying the external world. First, the "external world" itself had to be discovered.

*The technique of "sketching" (*shasei*) was developed by Masaoka Shiki, a practitioner and teacher of verse-writing in the *tanka* (a five-line verse containing lines of 5-7-5-7-7 syllables respectively) and *haiku* (5-7-5) forms. Asserting that these "traditional" forms were in crisis by the late nineteenth century, Shiki advocated their reform in a series of controversial articles published in the newspaper *Nippon* in 1893. (A translation of one of many passages in which Shiki elaborated his notion of "sketching" may be found in the glossary.) By the mid-1890s the closely related term *shajitsushugi* (literally, "copy reality-ism") was widely used to refer to the growing acceptance of conventions of Western-style realism. Despite its close association with realism, we have consistently translated *shasei* as "sketching" and have used the term "sketching literature" to denote the genre of prose writing (*shaseibun*) that was stimulated by Shiki's early experiments with poetry.

I am not here talking about a matter of vision. This inversion, which transforms our mode of perception, does not take place either inside of us or outside of us, but is an inversion of a semiotic configuration.

As Usami Keiji has suggested, medieval European painting and landscape painting share something in common that differentiates them from modern landscape painting. In both, *place* is conceived of in transcendental terms. For a brush painter to depict a pine grove meant to depict the concept (that which is signified by) "pine grove," not an existing pine grove. This transcendental vision of space had to be overturned before painters could see existing pine groves as their subjects. This is when modern perspective appears. Or more accurately, what we call modern perspective had already emerged at some point before this in the form of a perspectival inversion.

Despite the similarities I have pointed out, it was only European medieval painting that contained elements that evolved into landscape painting; brush painting did not. The nativist scholar Motoori Norinaga's criticism of "place" in Japanese brush painting as being dominated by a "Chinese sensibility" is relevant here. Claiming that the Japanese could only "see" things in terms of perceptions conditioned by their reading of Chinese literature, Motoori asserted that a different type of perception, "of things just as they are," could be found in the *Tale of Genji*. We should bear in mind that Motoori already had some awareness of the modern West and that his criticism might be seen as analogous to a type of thinking emerging in the West. But Motoori's speculation by no means led him to a "discovery of landscape." Tsubouchi Shōyō's *Essence of the Novel* linked Western "naturalism" and Motoori's writings on Genji. But "landscape" emerged neither in Tsubouchi's writings nor in Motoori's.*

---

* Motoori Norinaga (1730–1801) was perhaps the leading nativist scholar. Critical of the "artificial" qualities of Chinese writings which were a pervasive influence in Japanese culture, Motoori wrote extensively on early Japanese poetry and narrative. Motoori's major work was a forty-four volume translation and commentary on Japan's oldest chronicle, the *Kojiki*. Motoori translated the *Kojiki*, originally written in thousands of Chinese ideographs, all with many possible pronunciations, into the Japanese phonetic syllabary or *kana*. Tsubouchi Shōyō (1859–1935) was a playwright, novelist, and literary theorist whose treatise, *The Essence of the Novel* (Shōsetsu shinzui) elaborated a sustained critique of late Edo prose and advocated the adoption of conventions of Western realism. Tsubouchi claimed that Motoori Norinaga had affirmed certain principles of modern psychological realism in the latter's celebration

Thus, Western landscape painting, as an inversion of medieval painting, had its source in that painting and arose out of something distinctive to European culture. I will say more about this later, but let me here point to one blind spot in the passages by Paul Valéry quoted above. Valéry overlooks the fact that he himself is part of the history of Western painting. He depicts Leonardo da Vinci, for example, in idealized terms as a "total human being," yet from the perspective of a Shiki Da Vinci's works would surely appear to be landscape paintings. In fact, in order to understand why "invasion by landscape painting" inevitably took place on a worldwide scale, we must take up the relationship of Da Vinci to landscape painting.

The Dutch psychiatrist Jan Hendrik Van den Berg, for example, suggests that it was in Da Vinci's "Mona Lisa" that we find the first European depiction of landscape as landscape. Van den Berg prefaces this comment by calling attention to Martin Luther's "The Freedom of the Christian," written in 1510. He finds in Luther's work the notion of an "interior man" who is brought to life solely by the word of God and who rejects everything external. Interestingly enough, Da Vinci died the year before Luther wrote this work. But as Rilke has pointed out, the inner self captured in the Mona Lisa's enigmatic smile did not arise out of the Protestant spirit but was rather a forerunner of it. Van den Berg, commenting on similarities between the Mona Lisa and Luther's draft, wrote:

> At the same time the Mona Lisa inevitably became the first human person (in painting) to be alienated from the landscape. The scene which lies in the background of the figure is, of course, renowned. This is because it was truly the first landscape to be depicted as such because it was a landscape. It is a pure landscape, not simply a backdrop for human action. Here we have a "nature" unknown to the medieval mind, an external nature sufficient unto itself, and from which human elements have been excluded as a matter of principle. It was the strangest landscape that could be seen by human eyes.[13]

Of course, what we see in the Mona Lisa is merely a nascent form of the type of landscape painting that became dominant in the nineteenth century. But Van den Berg has accurately analyzed the process whereby an alienation from the external world—or what we might call an extreme interiorization—led to the discovery of

---

of Heian court writing (particularly the *Tale of Genji*) in its difference from Chinese Confucian texts.

landscape. It was with romanticism that this trend emerged in full bloom. Rousseau, in his *Confessions*, describes his sense of oneness with nature when he was in the Alps in 1728. Although the Alps at that time were regarded simply as an annoyance and obstruction by Europeans, they began to flock to Switzerland to discover what Rousseau had seen. The Alpinist was a virtual creation of literature. Needless to say, it was Europeans who discovered the Japan Alps and initiated Japanese into the sport of mountain climbing. Yet as Yanagita Kunio has pointed out, the existence of mountain climbing as a sport in Japan is predicated on a qualitative transformation and homogenization of space which had traditionally been held as "separate" on the basis of religious values and taboos.

In the very moment when we become capable of perceiving landscape, it appears to us as if it had been there, outside of us, from the start. People begin to reproduce this landscape. If this is "realism," it has actually emerged from an inversion of romanticism.

It is clear, then, that realism in modern literature established itself within the context of landscape. Both the landscapes and the "ordinary people" (what I have called people-as-landscapes) that realism represents were not "out there" from the start, but had to be discovered as landscapes from which we had become alienated. Shklovsky proposed the view that defamiliarization was the essence of realism. Realism should make us see that which, through force of habit, we have been unable to see. Thus realism has no specific method. It is a relentless defamiliarization of the familiar. In Shklovsky's view, even supposedly antirealist works like those by Kafka can be termed "realist." This type of realism does not describe landscape but always creates it. It brings into existence landscapes which, although they had always been there, had never been seen. Shklovsky's realist had always to be an "interior person."

Now let us consider what the Japanese literary theorist Kitamura Tōkoku wrote in 1894.

> I endorse realism (Tōkoku uses the term *shajitsu*, with the gloss "riarizumu" in the phonetic syllabary, ed.) completely, but each person has a different notion of what realism is. Some depict only the ugly side of human life, while others focus on the dissection of an unbalanced mind—but all of these emphasize a very narrow aspect of realism; they do not benefit humanity or move our universe forward in any way. Although I do not dislike realism, I cannot say that realism based on such vulgar objectives is attractive. At the root of

realism there must be passion; without passion it is hard for there to be anything more than description for the sake of description.[14]

Tōkoku had already elaborated on the nature of that "passion" he saw as the basis of realism. This was his "inner world" (*sōsekai*); and he was asserting that genuine realism had to be based on the preeminence of the inner self. This was the crucial ingredient that Shōyō's theory lacked.

In this light it appears meaningless to set up a functional opposition between romanticism and realism. Insofar as we are captivated by this opposition, we will be unable to discern the conditions that produced it. Sōseki tried to describe the "proportion" of romantic and realistic elements. While this is a formalistic viewpoint which disregards the historicity of the romantic-realist opposition, Sōseki at least avoids thinking in terms of a universal "history of literature."

Nakamura Mitsuo has written that naturalist literature in Japan had a romantic character; the role played by romanticism in European literature was accomplished in Japan by the naturalists. Yet it is foolish to debate whether a writer like Kunikida Doppo is a romantic or a naturalist. The ambivalence we find in Doppo's writing is merely a very blatant manifestation of the inner link between romanticism and realism. Of course, if we take Western "literary history" as our basis, Meiji Japan, which absorbed Western literature in such a brief period of time, appears as nothing more than a jumble. Yet in fact, Meiji Japan offers us a key to the nature of that inversion which was specific to the West yet was concealed (since it took place over a much longer period of time) under the facade of linear development.

The concepts of realism and romanticism must be discarded when we try to interpret the situation of Japan in the 1890s. Even today Meiji literature is discussed in terms of the very categories Sōseki tried to negate. One exception is the essay "Sources of Realism" (*Shinchō*, October 1971) by critic Etō Jun. Etō attempts to analyze developments in this decade of Meiji by focusing on the "sketching" of Shiki and his disciple, Takahama Kyoshi. According to Etō's interpretation, "description" (*byōsha*) in Meiji literature should not be understood as a process of describing something, but as the emergence of the "thing" itself," and hence, of an entirely new relationship between "words" and "things."

It was an effort of consciousness, a bold attempt to name that which they had no way of naming—the new "things" which had appeared in the wake of disintegration. "Description" expressed the thirst for a new, more vital relationship between human sensibility, or language, and "things." Meiji artists did not become realists because realism was imported from the West. As Shiki wrote, "Perhaps no one realizes this, but we struck out in new directions hoping to add a drop of oil to a lamp that was about to sputter out." What Shiki is asserting here is that it was because he was in a situation where this direct encounter with "things" was ineluctable, that he had "struck out in new directions." Accordingly, Kyoshi and Hekigotō had no choice but to make a break with "the old stale *haiku*" and turn to "sketching." It was a time when both the Edo weltanschauung and the world of *haikai*,* which had been brought into being by Bashō and flowered under Buson, seemed on the verge of extinction. Shiki must have cross-examined his disciples desperately about whether there was any other way, short of this, to bring *haiku*—in fact, writing itself—back to life.[15]

Of course, as Etō has pointed out, the views of Shiki and Kyoshi did not concur entirely. Shiki sought to develop an objectivity in sketching which was close to the natural sciences; he wanted to "strip language of its autonomy as language, to move ever closer to a kind of transparent sign." The real differences between Shiki and Kyoshi were made apparent only on the basis of and simultaneous to the emergence of "landscape" (or what Etō would term the emergence of "things").

That Kunikida Doppo was influenced by "sketching literature" (*shaseibun*) is indisputable. Yet if we stand back from conventional literary historical concepts like "influence," it becomes clear beyond any doubt that what all of the writers of the 1890s encountered was "landscape." What Etō calls the "well-spring of realism" was also the wellspring of romanticism. I have chosen to describe this encounter as "the discovery of landscape," not only in an effort to overcome the biased view implicit in conventional histories of literature and histories of the *bundan*, but also because I wish to investigate the source of our own accommodation to the epistemological configuration brought into existence through landscape.

As I have stated in the foregoing, both realism and romanti-

---

* It was Masaoka Shiki himself who began the practice of using the word *haiku* to refer to an independent three-line verse of seventeen syllables. The word *haikai*, used in the Edo period, refers this practice to its origins in the group composition of linked verse, in which a second poet would wittily respond to the lines of verse composed by the previous poet in such a way as to "finish it," creating a complete, 31-syllable *tanka*.

cism must be seen as products of a certain historical situation, and because of this cannot be objectified as "stages" in literary history. Harold Bloom has argued that we live in an era of romanticism, when the very effort to reject romanticism is essentially romantic. According to Bloom, T. S. Eliot, Sartre, and Lévi-Strauss can all be considered part of the romantic movement and we have only to look, for example, at Wordsworth's "Prelude" or Hegel's *Phenomenology of Spirit* to understand why even an antiromantic stance was part of a larger romanticism. Both these works record an "experience of consciousness" or "maturation" according to which romantic subjectivism evolved toward objectivity. They suggest that we remain caught up in the "romantic dilemma," which renders even the antiromantic position a romantic one. Yet by the same token we could also call this the "realist dilemma." Once realism is defined as a ceaseless movement toward defamiliarization, antirealism becomes another manifestation of realism.

In the case of *Unforgettable People*, for example, the narrator forgets all the people who seem to be important and remembers the ones who don't matter. This process is quite similar to that by which landscape, which had been the background, came to supersede religious and historical themes. With Doppo, people who had been seen as ordinary and insignificant appeared imbued with meaning. Similarly, when the ethnologist Yanagita Kunio* began to use the term *jōmin* ("ordinary and abiding folk") in the early Showa period (1926–89), he was not at all referring to "ordinary people," but to a kind of landscape which had become visible to him through the type of inversion of values I have just described. It was in such a context, indeed, that Yanagita Kunio discarded his earlier terms *heimin* (commoner) and *nōmin* (farmer), which had had very specific referents in Meiji society.

Nakamura Mitsuo has correctly pointed out that "there was a common concern linking Yanagita Kunio, who aspired to study folklore because he sensed poetry in the 'lore of the common folk' and Doppo, who cried, 'What is the history of the family in the

---

*Yanagita Kunio (1875–1962) was involved as a young man in the intellectual movement surrounding the emergence of Japanese naturalism (*shizenshugi*), which established the dominance of realism in prose fiction in the early 1900s. As an official of the Ministry of Agriculture, Yanagita recorded details of the agricultural life which had begun to be irrevocably transformed under the onslaught of modernization. One of the most influential modern Japanese thinkers, Yanagita is credited with "founding" Japanese ethnology.

sian pl   sophy, for example, can be seen as a product of principles
of persp   ve. For the subject of Descartes's "cogito ergo sum" is
confined,   ictably, within the schema established by the conventions o   spective. It was in precisely the same period that
the "object"   ught came to be conceived of as a homogeneous,
scientifically .   irable entity—that is, as an extension of the
principles of   ctive. All of these developments paralleled
the emergence   'ground" as a dehumanized "landscape" in
the Mona Lisa.

In her work, *Pi.*   *in a New Key*, Suzanne Langer described
the cul-de-sac of mc   ropean philosophy, which is still preoccupied with the phi   cal issues posed by "landscape."

> After several cen   s of sterile tradition, logic-chopping, and
> partisanship in philoso   , the wealth of nameless, heretical, often
> inconsistent notions born   f the Renaissance crystallized into general
> and ultimate problems. A l ew outlook on life challenged the human
> mind to make sense out of l   bewildering world; and the Cartesian
> age of "natural and mental" pl losophy succeeded to the realm.
>
> This new epoch had a mig y and revolutionary generative idea:
> the dichotomy of all reality into i *er experience and outer world*, subject
> and object, private reality and pub. truth. The very language of what
> is now traditional epistemology be ays this basic notion; when we
> speak of "the given," of "sense data " "the phenomenon," or "other
> selves," we take for granted the imme liacy of an internal experience
> and the continuity of the external worl . Our fundamental questions
> are framed in these terms: What is actue ly given to the mind? What
> guarantees the truth of sense-data? Wha 'ies behind the observable
> order of phenomena? What is the relation f the mind to the brain?
> How can we know other selves?—All the are familiar problems
> of today. Their answers have been elaborate into whole systems of
> thought: empiricism, idealism, realism, pheno nenology, *Existenz Phi-
> losophie*, and logical positivism. The most comple and characteristic of
> all these doctrines are the earliest ones: empiricisi and idealism. They
> are the full, unguarded, vigorous formulations of he new generative
> notion, Experience: their proponents were the enth siasts inspired by
> the Cartesian method, and their doctrines are the obv ous implications
> derived by that principle, from such a starting point. E ich school in its
> turn took the intellectual world by storm. Not only uni rsities, but all
> the literary circles, felt the liberation from time-worn, o| ressive con-
> cepts, from baffling limits of inquiry, and hailed the new v rld-picture
> with a hope of truer orientation in life, art, and action.

After a while, the confusion and shadows inherent in the new vision became apparent, and subsequent doctrines sought in various ways to escape between the horns of the dilemma created by the subject-object dichotomy, which Professor Whitehead has called the "bifurcation of nature." Since then our theories have become more and more refined, circumspect, and clever; no one can be quite frankly an idealist, or go the whole way with empiricism; the early forms of realism are now known as the "naive" varieties, and have been superseded by "critical" or "new" realisms. Many philosophers vehemently deny any systematic Weltanschauung, and repudiate metaphysics in principle.[17]

But will contemporary philosophers, who are trying to break out of a Cartesian weltanschauung even as they operate within it, really succeed in making their escape? Modern artists, when they studied primitive art, or thinkers like Claude Lévi-Strauss, in his work on the "savage mind," faced the same dilemma. Sophisticated technology and Rousseauian romanticism are paradoxically intertwined in Lévi-Strauss's thought. But both these elements had their origins in the modern "landscape." It is the historicity of that landscape that must be exposed.

In Western Europe it was Marx, Nietzsche, and Freud who, albeit from differing perspectives, first exposed the problematic nature of the European conception of landscape. Nietzsche, for example, claimed that European epistemology itself was "an illusion based on the principles of linear perspective." As a product of interiorization, according to Nietzsche, the very notion of linear perspective was "an illusion of itself." The "self," the "inner," "consciousness," and "cogito" in Cartesian philosophy were all based on an inversion of subjectivity.

In order to expose the historicity of European culture Sōseki did not need to look back to ancient Greece, as Nietzsche did. Rather, he maintained within himself a certain attitude toward life that had existed prior to "landscape" and "modern Japanese literature." Sōseki was able to do this because he lived through the discovery of "landscape." We Japanese witnessed with our own eyes and within a limited period of time the occurrence in condensed form of a process which, because it had extended over many centuries, had been repressed from memory in the West.

Various institutions of the modern nation-state were consolidated, in preliminary form, during the third decade of the Meiji period, starting with the promulgation of the Meiji constitution. As Nakamura Mitsuo has written, "if we see the second decade of the Meiji period as one of turbulence, the third was one of unification and stability." In the eyes of those born after the Meiji Restoration, this order appeared to be something that had already solidified. What had been malleable possibilities just after the Restoration now appeared shut off to them. In his *Meiji Literature*, Nakamura Mitsuo describes the People's Rights movement* of the 1880s as follows:

> For the movement was a logical extension of that great reform which was the Meiji Restoration, and it had been entrusted with the great hope that this social revolution had awakened in the people. It was through the People's Rights movement that the spirit of the Restoration which until that time had been the sole possession of the warrior class gradually came to infiltrate the popular consciousness. The setback of the movement, therefore, meant the destruction of that vital component of all revolutions, the idealism which is contained within them and which can be transformed into something else at any point in the revolutionary process. The straitened circumstances of the warrior class became a grave social problem in the early years of Meiji. For the few who found themselves in an advantageous situation there were many who had fallen into despair, yet this very fact meant that control of political and cultural life remained the uncontested prerogative of that class. But by 1885 or so, the dissolution of the warrior class became a pronounced trend, the children of commoners began to swell the ranks of students, and Meiji society began to show its true face as a mercantile state created by the offspring of the warrior class.
>
> Vis-à-vis this emerging militarist state dominated by pragmatism and the pursuit of worldly success, the phantoms of freedom and people's rights became the last ideals for which young men who were heirs of the Restoration could risk their lives. The loss of these ideals created a spiritual vacuum which could not be banished and which found expression in a form which was completely different from the political novel.[18]

*The People's Rights movement (*jiyū minken undō*) was launched by Itagaki Taisuke and other samurai disaffected with the policies of the Meiji government in 1874. Agricultural depression and popular opposition to the new uniform tax system swelled the ranks of the movement, broadening its base to include village leaders, wealthy farmers and merchants and, by the 1880s, women. In 1880, the Osaka Congress of People's Rights called for the immediate establishment of a national assembly. The government rejected this demand and imposed severe restrictions on the convening of public meetings. Itagaki's Liberal Party was dissolved in 1884.

This insight may also be applied to Sōseki. While contemporary writers like Masaoka Shiki, Futabatei Shimei, Kitamura Tōkoku, and Kunikida Doppo were agonizing over questions of artistic practice, Sōseki stood at the head of the Meiji government's corps of students of the West constantly pursued by a desire to flee from their ranks. What he wrote while he was in their midst had to be "theoretical," for it represented certain conclusions he had reached with reference to the English literature which he had already decided to study. Later, as a novelist, Sōseki appeared obsessed with the phenomenon of the "belated" nature of choice, a problem which he had confronted during this period. In this sense, *kanbungaku* probably symbolized for Sōseki not so much a corpus of texts as a certain atmosphere that existed prior to the establishment of various modern systems. This was during the same period when the political novel was at the height of its popularity. Sōseki's sense that he had been "cheated" by English literature may have corresponded to his observation that the institutions which were set up in the third decade of Meiji were nothing but a sham.

But such interpretive notions as "political disillusionment" or "the influence of Christianity" cannot be interjected into our consideration of the Japanese discovery of "landscape." These ideas suggest a psychological motivation for the process, but the concept of human psychology itself appeared at precisely this time. To treat the psychological as an autonomous sphere, as the science of psychology does, is a historical, not a timeless, phenomenon. The most significant development in the third decade of the Meiji period was rather the consolidation of modern systems and the emergence of "landscape," not so much as a phenomenon contesting such systems, but as itself a system.

Academic historians of modern literature write of the "modern self" as if it were something that existed purely within the mind. But certain conditions are necessary for the production of this "self." Freud, like Nietzsche, viewed consciousness not as something which existed from the start, but as a derivative of "introjection." According to Freud, it is at a stage when there is no distinction between inner and outer, when the outer is purely a projection of the inner, that the experience of trauma results in a redirection of the libido inward. With this, for the first time, outer and inner are separated. As Freud wrote in *Totem and Taboo*, "It is only after abstract language and thought come into existence that the perceptual residue of language links up with subjective material in such a way that we first become aware of subjective phenomena."

To speak in Freudian terms, the libido which was once directed toward the People's Rights movement and the writing of political novels lost its object and was redirected inward, at which point "landscape" and "the inner life" appeared. Let me repeat, however, that Freud himself was not aware of the historicity of psychology and of the fact that, like "landscape," it was the product of a specific historical order. The Meiji novelist Mori Ōgai, for example, created characters that appear "a-psychological" in his historical fiction. Toward the end of his life, Ōgai tried as much as possible to return to an awareness that predated modern conceptions of psychology and landscape. We may legitimately use a psychological approach in dealing with writers who emerged after the third decade of the Meiji period, but we must keep in mind that such an approach will not expose the conditions which produced the science of psychology itself.

However, what I find most significant in Freud's thought is the notion of the simultaneous emergence in the human being of the capacity for "abstract thought and language" and of "interiority" (accompanied by an awareness of the external as external). What does "abstract thought and language" correspond to in the Japanese context? Perhaps to the conception of writing which evolved in the Meiji period, known as *genbun itchi*. For *genbun itchi* was a manifestation in the linguistic realm of the establishment, around 1890, of the various institutions of the modern state. It goes without saying that the meaning of this concept was hardly that of bringing "writing" (*bun*) into conformity with "speech" (*gen*), or speech into conformity with writing, as is usually maintained. *Genbun itchi* represented the invention of a new conception of writing as equivalent with speech.

Of course, insofar as *genbun itchi* was an effort towards modernization similar to the Meiji constitution, it could not be a purely "inner" speech. Writers considered to be introverts in the third decade of the Meiji period—Ōgai and Tōkoku, for example—preferred to write in the classical style, and the *genbun itchi* movement quickly lost momentum. Interest did not revive until the end of the decade, which was already the era of Kunikida Doppo and Takahama Kyoshi.

Of course, Futabatei Shimei's novel *Ukigumo* (Drifting clouds), which appeared between 1886 and 1889, may be cited as an exception to this trend. Notions of landscape and the inner self which Futabatei could elaborate when he was writing in Russian, however, seemed to slip through his fingers when he tried to write about them in Japanese, when somehow the language of Shikitei Samba and other *kokkeibon* writers took possession of him.* The agony of Futabatei was to have discovered "landscape" without being able to locate it in the Japanese language. By Doppo's time this dilemma had disappeared. What influenced Doppo was not the style of *Ukigumo* but the translation of Turgenev's *Rendez-vous*.

For Doppo the "inner" was the word (the voice), and expression was the projection outward of that voice. In Doppo's work the concept of "expression" came into being for the first time in Japanese literature. Before this time, no one spoke of literature in terms of expression. It was the identification of writing with speech which made such a concept possible. But it was only because Doppo, unlike Futabatei, was oblivious to the fact that *genbun itchi* was a modern system that he was spared the dilemma of Futabatei. That the "inner self" was historical, that it was a system, had by that time been forgotten. Needless to say, we live today on the same soil that Doppo did. In order to know what holds us there, we must uncover its source; we must investigate further this historical period when language was simultaneously exposed and hidden.

Afternote to Chapter 1 (1991)

What I have called the "discovery of landscape" was not merely an "internal" event: it was accompanied by the discovery of a landscape that was new in actuality and not enveloped in any way by ancient texts. This landscape was that of Hokkaido, the northern island which, until the Meiji period, had been inhabited by Japanese only on its southern tip. Hokkaido became a new territory for colonists, created by driving its indigenous people, the Ainu, off their lands and forcibly assimilating them. In this way the Meiji government was able to provide large numbers of unemployed members

---

*Shikitei Samba (1776–1822) wrote in numerous genres, but is best known for two works of comic fiction (a genre given the name *kokkeibon* during the 1820s), *Ukiyoburo* (1809–13) and *Ukiyodoko* (1813–14), describing scenes from Edo's public baths and barbershops.

of the samurai class with new lives as pioneer farmers. With the agricultural school established in Sapporo as its center, Hokkaido became the prototype for the colonial agricultural policy later applied by Japan to Taiwan and Korea. At the same time, Hokkaido was a place where various types of religious reforms flourished, as émigrés lived their lives cut off from the traditions of the mainland. Hokkaido in the Meiji period might in this sense be comparable to early New England, both in terms of its climate and its political role. The first head of the Sapporo Agricultural School, Dr. Clark, who had been recruited from Amherst, for example, had greater influence in Hokkaido as a Protestant missionary than as an agricultural scientist. It was this influence that produced the prototypical Meiji Christian, Uchimura Kanzō. Kunikida Doppo, also mentioned in the foregoing chapter, spent time in Hokkaido as a Christian disciple and an émigré.

Seen in this context, the "discovery of landscape" in the Meiji period was a discovery—if we refer to Kant's distinction—not of the beautiful but of the sublime. For the vast wilderness of Hokkaido inspired awe in human beings, unlike the mainland which had been regulated for centuries and enveloped by literary texts. But in order to grasp this territory as sublime it was necessary, as Uchimura said, to take on the Christian attitude which regards nature as the handiwork of God. It was an attitude, at any rate, which was not continuous with Japanese thought as it had existed up to that point.

Unlike the Meiji Christian thinker Uchimura Kanzō, who rejected his background in the Confucian philosophy of the Wang Yang Ming School when he embraced Christianity, Sōseki remained attached to *kanbungaku*. We should not understand this, however, as a matter of literary taste. The significance of Sōseki's remarking that he "wanted to devote his life to *kanbungaku*" was that *kanbungaku* had political meaning for him. Sōseki made the comment during the second decade of the Meiji period, when the People's Rights movement flourished. By the third decade of Meiji, that movement had been suppressed. Instead the various systems of Japanese modernity were being put into place. It seems that for Sōseki *kanbungaku* was associated with an atmosphere that preceded the establishment of these systems as well as with the Meiji Restoration as a social revolution that had contained within it malleable possibilities. Interestingly, the "political novels" written by members of the People's Rights movement were not written in colloquial

Japanese but in a style of Japanese strongly influenced by *kanbun*. Thus even the People's Rights movement, while flying the banners of Western philosophy (especially the thought of Rousseau), was still grounded in Chinese literature and philosophy. This fusion of democratic thought and *kanbungaku* might appear to be paradoxical. But it was a paradox with which the Meiji Restoration itself was fraught.

The Meiji Restoration is frequently narrated in terms of the restorationism of the nativist scholars and the Enlightenment thought of those who had studied the West. But for the majority of Japanese intellectuals, Chinese literature and philosophy continued, as ever, to constitute the canon. Restoration ideology—the *sonnō jōi*, or "Revere the Emperor, Expel the Barbarian" philosophy—was actually a product of the Mito School, which was devoted to the study of the thought of the Chinese philosopher Chu Hsi. Saigō Takamori, a Restoration leader, adhered to the principles of Wang Yang Ming. Chinese philosophy, then, provided one important context of the Meiji Restoration. Moreover, for Saigō Takamori, Japan's Restoration could not be sustained without revolution in China and Korea. Somewhat like a Trotsky or Che Guevara, Saigō sought to export Japan's revolution to China and Korea. In terms of its external manifestations, this export of revolution was indistinguishable from a policy of aggression vis-à-vis other nations. Yet the Meiji revolutionary government, fearing that its own existence might be placed in jeopardy by the attempt to expand the revolution, expelled Saigō, which resulted in civil war (the Seinan Rebellion led by Saigō in 1877). However, the same government which suppressed Saigō commenced its own aggression toward Korea somewhat later. This began with the waging of the Sino-Japanese War in 1894–95. In this context, through his tragic death, Saigō became a symbol of the People's Rights movement and pan-Asianism on the one hand and of Japanese expansionism on the other.

These ambivalent attitudes remained strong throughout the Sino-Japanese and Russo-Japanese wars. It is for this reason that the two wars were widely supported by thinkers of every hue, including members of the People's Rights movement, Christians like Uchimura Kanzō, Enlightenment thinkers like Fukuzawa Yukichi, and advocates of a strong, centralized state. But the disillusionment that followed in the wake of this enthusiasm was also great. Uchimura Kanzō, for example, who fervently supported the Sino-Japanese War and wrote about its "just cause" in English, came to the real-

2 The Discovery of Interiority

1

The *genbun itchi** movement is thought to have originated with Maejima Hisoka's submission of a petition, in 1866, to the Tokugawa Shogunate entitled "Reasons for Abolishing Chinese Characters." Maejima was an interpreter at one of the shogunate's schools for Western learning in Nagasaki. He claimed that his writing of the petition was prompted by discussions with an American missionary he had met in this school, who had persuaded him that the use of "abstruse and confusing" Chinese characters for purposes of education was inappropriate. Maejima wrote, "Education of the populace is the foundation of the state and this education should be promulgated among the entire population, regardless of status. To this end we should employ words and sentences which are as simple as possible; in the most diverse fields of scholarship, no matter how lofty or profound, we should avoid obscure, roundabout methods of teaching which equate knowledge of words with knowledge of things. I submit that in all cases learning should not be other than an understanding of the thing itself."

Many features of the *genbun itchi* movement are indicated in

---

*Genbun-itchi is usually translated rather literally into English as "unifying spoken (gen) and written (bun) languages." *Bun* in the Japanese expression is an abbreviation for *bungo,* the word still used to denote the classical or "literary" Japanese employed in texts written in Japanese prior to the 1890s. In fact, in the Meiji period, as today, the term *bungo* referred to at least half a dozen distinctive styles. All of these styles, however, employed verb-endings which were not used with any frequency in colloquial speech. In standard literary histories, authors Yamada Bimyō and Futabatei Shimei, mentioned in this chapter, are seen as pioneering the use of the new style, in which the complex system of inflections used in *bungo* was abandoned. Karatani in this chapter takes issue with the prevailing interpretations: first, by noting that the new styles introduced by Yamada Bimyō and Futabatei were not in fact faithful reproductions of the speech of their contemporaries, and secondly, by calling attention to the ideological nature of the phonocentrism (according to which writing was seen as derivative of speech) which was the condition of possibility for the movement. The *genbun itchi* reforms are discussed by Marleigh Grayer Ryan in *Japan's First Modern Novel: Ukigumo of Futabatei Shimei* (Columbia University Press, 1967).

this, its earliest document. First of all, Maejima asserted that *genbun itchi* was indispensable for the establishment of the modern nation. Although Maejima's proposal was eventually ignored, it raised issues which emerged as crucial in the second decade of Meiji when the effort to establish the institutions of the modern state was getting underway. It was in the decade whose infatuation with Western ways was symbolized for the public at large by the construction of the *Rokumeikan*, or Deer Cry Pavilion,* that we note the appearance of organizations such as the Kana Society (*Kana no Kai*, established in 1884 to promote writing in the Japanese syllabary or *kana*) and the Romaji Society (*Romaji no Kai*, established in 1886 to encourage writing in *romaji*, or romanized script). It was also in this decade that movements to reform drama, poetry, and fiction emerged one after another. The *genbun itchi* movement, however, may be seen as incorporating all these other movements.

A second point of interest is that the Maejima proposal does not, in fact, make its subject that "unification of the spoken and written language" commonly understood to have been the aim of the *genbun itchi* movement, but rather the proposal that Chinese characters be abolished. This clearly indicates the fundamental nature of *genbun itchi* as a movement to reform the writing system and do away with Chinese characters, *kanji*. Maejima touched only briefly on the issue of correspondence between the spoken and written language: "Defining the national literary canon and regulating grammar does not mean returning to ancient texts and using suffixes like *haberu, keru*, and *kana*. We should take words which are widely used at the present time, such as *tsukamatsuru* and *gozaru*, and make these the general rule. It seems to me that all nations are similar in that their languages change over time. However, I believe we should avoid setting up a distinction between the flavors of the written and spoken language such that we consider spoken words colloquial and written texts literary." To take these lines of Maejima's out of context and regard them as articulating the philosophy of the *genbun itchi* movement is to mistake the nature of that movement. For Maejima it was reform of the writing system which was the crux of the matter, while the opinions expressed above

---

*The Rokumeikan, or Deer Cry Pavilion, was built in 1883 for the purpose of entertaining foreign diplomats. When a costume ball was held at the pavillion by Prime Minister Itō Hirobumi in 1887, Itō and his ministers were ridiculed as the "dancing cabinet" because of their zeal to demonstrate their knowledge of Western social graces.

were secondary. Spoken and written languages diverge because the practices of speaking and writing are different. They do not "correspond" in any language, and the Japanese language hardly represents the most striking case of their divergence. The problem, as Maejima pointed out, lies with the nature of writing as a mode of signification.

Looked at in this way, we may understand that *genbun itchi* was first and foremost a new ideology of writing. As an official interpreter for the shogunate, Maejima found himself captivated by the economy, preciseness, and egalitarian nature of phonetic writing systems. He saw Western superiority as linked to that phonetic system and believed the implementation of such a system was an urgent priority for Japan. Phonetic writing is usually seen as the transcription of speech. Saussurean linguistics, for example, treated writing as secondary and exempted it from the analysis of *langue* as a system. Maejima's proposal clearly reflects a similar notion of writing in the service of speech. It thus inevitably gave priority to the spoken language, and once this view had been established, the question of whether or not *kanji* were actually abolished became moot. Once even Chinese characters had come to be seen as subordinate to speech, the issue became simply a choice between characters and the native phonetic syllabary (*kana*). Once Maejima came to look at writing in this way it was a matter of course that he began to give priority to the spoken language and to consider the gap between spoken and written language—never a concern in the past—a "problem." We must bear in mind, then, that his conception of the spoken language was itself rooted in a preoccupation with phonetic writing.

It is noteworthy that in his discussion Maejima turned first to the matter of suffixes like *tsukamatsuru* and *gozaru*. It was perhaps inevitable, given the nature of the Japanese language, that people came to think of *genbun itchi* as having been from the start purely a question of suffixes. In the Japanese language it is impossible to leave the relationship between speaker and listener unspecified, which is also why one can know which person is being alluded to even in a sentence that has no subject. What I wish to call attention to here is not the existence of words known as honorifics (*keigo*) in Japanese but rather the phenomenon that linguist Tokieda Motoki referred to when he suggested that indication of relative status of speakers was inherent to the Japanese language itself. For Tokieda the notion of *keigo* or honorific speech could be used to describe the

Japanese language as a whole. Maejima proposal that the suffixes *tsukamatsuru* and *gozaru* be universally used was certainly linked to his own status and the types of social relationships he was involved in as a member of the samurai class.

Novelist Futabatei Shimei, in the essay "How I Came to Use *Genbun Itchi*" (*Yoga genbun itchi no yurai*), recalled his own attempts to develop a *genbun itchi* style.

> As for my opinion on *genbun itchi*—since I haven't given the matter that much study let me rather make a confession. The truth is, and my reader will surely find this shocking, that I turned to *genbun itchi* because I didn't know how to write; it was as simple as that. I don't now remember how long ago it was, quite a while back. I felt I wanted to try my hand at literature, but my style was so poor I was utterly at a loss. I decided to visit Professor Tsubouchi to ask his advice. He told me, "You know the comic storyteller Enchō, don't you? Why not write the way Enchō narrates?" I did just as he suggested. Well, as a Tokyoite, I naturally use the Tokyo dialect. So what I produced was a work in the Tokyo dialect. I took it to Professor Tsubouchi's place immediately. He studied it intently and then startled me by slapping his knee and crying, "This is perfect just as it is! Rather than doing piecemeal revisions which will leave you with a mish-mash, leave it alone." Tsubouchi's response disturbed me a bit, but since he had praised the work there was no reason to be upset about it and in fact I was rather pleased. Certainly, as an attempt to reproduce Enchō's narration the work was in the *genbun itchi* style, but there were still problems with it. Should I use the polite form of the first person pronoun, *watakushi*, with sentences ending in *gozaimasu*, or the more familiar masculine personal pronoun *ore*, as in "*Ore wa iya da*" ("I don't like it")? Professor Tsubouchi was of the opinion that there should be no honorific speech used. I was not entirely happy with this idea, but it was after all the view of the expert whom I had even contemplated asking to revise the manuscript for me. So I went ahead and finished the work without using honorific speech. This is the story of how I began writing in *genbun itchi*.
>
> Not long after that Yamada Bimyō published his *genbun itchi* manuscripts. I discovered that he had chosen the polite *watakushi* and the polite verb ending *desu:* we belonged to different schools. Yamada was of the "*desu* school," I was the "*da* school." Later I heard that Yamada had initially experimented in writing without honorifics and had tried ending sentences with the familiar *da*, but had given it up as unsatisfactory. Whereas I had been inclined to *desu* and ended with *da*. We went in opposite directions.[1]

Futabatei claims that he used the *da* style to avoid honorific speech but insofar as *da*, too, expresses his relationship to the speaker it must be considered an honorific suffix (a polite suffix), broadly speaking. For the use of *da* in conversation signals that the addressee is the speaker's equal or inferior. It is virtually a matter of indifference whether one chooses *da* or *desu*; neither is a neutral term that transcends relationality. The *da* style is assumed to have become dominant because it appears closer to a style that would avoid honorific speech, or *keigo*. Futabatei and Yamada, both attempting to incorporate the spoken language, went in "completely different directions" because Futabatei sought to abstract conversational speech for purposes of writing. Of the two, he had a better understanding of the nature of *bun*, or writing.

Nevertheless, it is reductive for us to consider *genbun itchi* merely a matter of verb endings. The experiments of writers like Futabatei and Yamada sputtered out when, for example, "The Dancing Girl" (*Maihime*) of Mori Ōgai, published in 1890 in a classical literary (*bungo*) style, was highly acclaimed. The *genbun itchi* movement is generally seen to have stagnated over the next four years. But let us examine the style of "The Dancing Girl."

aru　hi　no　yūgure narishi ga,　　yo wa　　jūen o　manpo shite, unteru,　　　den,　　　rinden　　o
或る日の　夕暮なりしが、　余は　　獣宛を 漫歩して、　ウンテル、デン、リンデンを
sugi,　　wa ga　　monbishūgai no　　　kyōkyo ni kaeran to,　　kurosuteruko no　furudera no mae ni
過ぎ、我が モンビシュウ街の　僑居に　帰らんと、クロステル巷の　古寺の　　前に
kinu.　　yo wa　kare no　tōka　no　umi o watarikite,　　kono　semaku usuguraki chimata ni　hairi,
来ぬ。余は　彼の　　燈火の海を 渡り来て、この 狭く　薄暗き　巷に　　入り、
rōjo no　obashima ni hoshitaru　shikifu, juban nado　mada toriirenu　　jinka, agohige nagaki
桜上の　木欄に　　干したる 敷布、　褐袢など まだ 取り入れぬ人家、頬髪　長き
yudayakyōto no okina ga kozen ni tatazumitaru izakaya,　hitotsu no hashigo wa tadachi ni
猶太教徒の　翁が　戸前に 佇みたる 居酒屋、一つの 梯は　　直ちに
takadono ni tasshi,　hoka no hashigo wa anagurazumai no　　kaji ga　　ie ni　tsūjitaru
桜に達し、　他の 梯は　あなぐら住まひの 鍛冶が 家に 通じたる
kashiya nado ni mukaite, ōji no katachi ni hikikomite taterareru,　　kore sanbyakunen mae no
貸家などに向かひて、凹字の形に　引き籠みて立てられる、 此三百年前の
iseki o nozomu goto ni, kokoro no kōkotsu to narite　　shibashi tatazumishi koto ikudonaru o
遺跡を望む毎に、　心の　　恍惚と　なりて 暫し　佇みしこと　幾度なるを
shirazu.
知らず。

One evening I sauntered through the Tiergarten and then walked down Unter den Linden. On the way back to my lodgings at Monbijou-strasse, I came in front of the old church in Klosterstrasse. How many times, I wonder, had I passed through that sea of lights, entered this gloomy passage, and stood enraptured, gazing at the three-hundred-year-old church that lay set back from the road.[2]

Compare this to the opening sentences of *The Drifting Clouds* which was said to have been written in the *genbun itchi* style.

Chihayafuru kaminazuki mo mohaya ato futsuka no nagori to natta   nijūhachinichi no
千早振る　　神無月も　　　最早　　跡　二日の　　　余波となった　二十八日の

gogo sanji goro ni, kandamitsuke no uchi yori, towataru ari, chiru kumo no ko to uyouyo
午後三時頃に、　神田見附の　　内より、塗渡る蟻、　散る蜘蛛の子と　うようよ

zoyozoyo wakiidekuru no wa,   izure mo otogai o kinishitamau katagata.   shikashi
ぞよぞよ 沸出で来るのは、　いづれも頤を　気にし給う 方々。　　しかし

tsura tsura mite toku to tenken suru to, kore ni mo samazama shurui no aru mono de,
熟々　　　見て 篤と　　点検すると、是れにも　様々　　種類の　あるもので、

mazu hige kara kakitatereba,   kuchihige, hohohige, ago no hige, yake ni oyashita
まず 髭から　　書き立てれば、口髭、　　頬髭、　　顎の髭、　暴に興起した

naporeonhige ni,   chin no kuchimeita bisumarukuhige, sono hoka chabohige,
拿破をん髭に、　狆の　　口めいた　比斯馬克髭、　そのほか 矮鶏髭、

mujinahige,   ari ya nashi ya no maboroshi no hige to, koku mo usuku mo
むじな髭、　ありやなしやの 幻の　　　　髭と、濃くも　淡くも

iroiro ni   haewakaru.
いろいろに生分る。

It is three o'clock on the afternoon of a late October day. A swirling mass of men stream out of the Kanda gate, marching first in ant-like formation, then scuttling busily off in every direction. Each and every one of the fine gentlemen is primarily interested in getting enough to eat.

　　Look carefully and you will see what an enormous variety of individual types are represented in the huge crowd. Start by examining the hair bristling on their faces: mustaches, side whiskers, Vandykes, and even extravagant imperial beards, Bismarck beards reminiscent of a Pekinese, bantam beards, badger's beards, meager beards that are barely visible, thick and thin they sprout in every conceivable way.[3]

Ōgai's writing is much easier to translate into English. While written in the literary (*bungo*) style, "The Dancing Girl" has the conceptual and grammatical structure of a work written in a European language and translated into Japanese. It is "realistic." *The Drifting Clouds*, on the other hand, is almost impossible to translate literally into English, and despite its array of moustaches has nothing "realistic" about it. In this sense, it is a very crude form of explanation that asserts that Futabatei abruptly abandoned his writing, leading to an impasse of the *genbun itchi* movement. *The Drifting Clouds* is permeated with stylistic elements drawn from the comic fiction of Shikitei Samba, and despite its use of the verb-ending *da*, it cannot be considered a *genbun itchi* work. It is true that Futabatei was dissatisfied on this score, and that he attempted to compose the second book of the novel in Russian which he then translated into the colloquial written style (*kōgo*), an undertaking which would be nearly inconceivable for a contemporary Japanese. But I would interpret these developments differently. First, although possessed of a kind of self-awareness produced by his reading of Russian literature, Futabatei was unable to completely resist the pull of the *ninjōbon* and *kokkeibon** styles. Moreover, since these styles were in fact a form of *bungo*, they existed in a different realm from conversational speech. Secondly, in order to write in *genbun itchi* Futabatei had to distance himself from both the existing literary and conversational forms of Japanese. The conversational speech we are supposed to discover in *genbun itchi* was already quite different from the conversational speech of Futabatei's time.

By merely changing verb endings, one can transform Ōgai's writing into a fully contemporary style. This suggests that "The Dancing Girl" was not necessarily a retreat from *genbun itchi*. When we consider the real nature of the *genbun itchi* movement, it is Ōgai's work which represents an advance, and it is his work, rather than Futabatei's, that brings the issue of *genbun itchi* to light.

2

I have asserted that it was a reform of writing, "the abolition of *kanji*," that was at stake in the *genbun itchi* movement. Of course, the issue here was not the actual abandonment of Chinese writing but rather a profound undermining of the privileged status of writing (as *kanji*), which was accomplished through advocating an ideology of phonetic speech. Since we can analyze the privileged status of writing in a number of different contexts, let me now turn to developments in an area which may initially seem unrelated,

---

* "Comic books" (*kokkeibon*) and "erotic books" (*ninjobon*) denoted two genres of writing which circulated among a mass readership in the last century of the Edo period. Futabatei, like most early Meiji readers, was highly conversant with these genres.

but which represent an extension of the *genbun itchi* movement. Consider the following passage from the *Travel Essays* (*Kikō bunshū*) edited by Japan's first ethnologist, Yanagita Kunio. The works in the anthology, according to Yanagita, are "a few works composed by distinguished travellers of the late Edo period which I read and reread as a youth, and which I knew I would want to dip into in the future if they were available." He comments,

> Works like these are all referred to as belonging to the genre of *kikōbun*, or travel literature, but grouping them in a single category gives rise to a misconception on the part of readers, since there are in fact two distinct types of works: the first consists of a string of poems and lyrical essays; the second consists exclusively of description, narrated by a traveller who is simply a discreet presence hidden in the shadows of the actual scene. In Japan, among the works known as *kikōbun*, beginning with the first travel diary written by Ki no Tsurayuki (*The Tosa Diary*, c. 935), the former predominate. This is the reason why books describing scenery which have begun to appear in recent years have so often been dismissed, and scorned as vulgar, by connoisseurs of literature, and why the efforts of those who wish to bequeath such documents to posterity have been viewed as the products of futile toil.[4]

In this passage we find Yanagita narrating the "discovery of landscape" in terms of a change in the way *kikōbun* were actually written. Let me suggest that this transformation consisted of the liberation of travel literature from the literary, from the convention of what Yanagita describes as "a string of poems and lyrical essays." Why, in fact, was it that for so many centuries Japanese recognized as landscapes only the famous places celebrated in literature and could be satisfied with "stringing together poems and lyrical essays"? It was because this was the "landscape" given to them by their encounter with Chinese literature—the Imperial poetry anthology, the *Kokinshū* (905), provided the basic model. Even Motoori Norinaga did not deviate from tradition on this point. The iconoclast was Masaoka Shiki, who exclaimed that "Ki no Tsurayuki was a terrible poet and his anthology, the *Kokinshū*, is rubbish!"[5]

Conversely, we may say that all those who were not the least bit bored with strings of poems and lyrical writings felt that way because for them literary landscapes were much more "real" than actual landscapes. I have already noted that for a brush painter to depict a pine grove meant to depict the signified "pine grove," not an existing pine grove, and that this vision of transcendental space had to be overturned before painters could see existing pine groves as their subjects. From such a topos, the concept "pine grove" was not something dull and empty but rather sensuous and vibrant.

T. S. Eliot wrote of Dante that "Dante's is a *visual* imagination. It is a visual imagination in a different sense from that of a modern painter of still life: it is visual in the sense that he lived in an age in which men still saw visions."[6] What Eliot asserts is the figurative nature of Western medieval thought, in terms of which conceptions of the transcendental belonged to the realm of the visual. We may find a parallel here with Japanese poets before the *genbun itchi* movement. However "painterly" Buson's poetry may have appeared in the eyes of Shiki, it could not have been what Shiki imagined it to be, and its visual qualities were of a different order from those produced through the process of sketching that Shiki advocated. Similarly, we must ask why even a writer like Futabatei was irresistibly attracted to the style of Takizawa Bakin, even though his teacher, Shōyō, had rejected Bakin's "didactic" allegorical writings. Although it has already become almost impossible for us to conceive of this, it was because, in the literary age dominated by Bakin, allegory, however abstract, was thoroughly visual.

Maejima, pointing out that a compound combining the characters "pine" and "plain" (松平) can be given four alternative phonetic readings (*matsutaira, matsuhira, matsuhei, shōhei*), among which it is impossible to determine which is correct, decried *kanji* as "eccentric, unwieldy, an evil without parallel in this world." But without any phonetic reading at all the characters 松平 immediately evoke a meaning. The same can be said about Buson's poem on the summer rains. We interpret it, as it were, visually. Contrary to what Shiki maintained, what makes possible the painterly effect of Buson's poem is the superimposition of sound and visual form. If Japanese words possessed what Maejima advocated, "the virtue of having one fixed pronunciation, recognizable at a glance by anyone," the effect of Buson's poem could not be achieved.

Furthermore, the movement to free Japanese poetry from figurative writing also entailed freeing it from the human voice, from rhythm. Shiki's disciple Takahama Kyoshi, for example, wrote the following in his essay, "The Origins and Significance of Sketching Literature" (*Shaseibun no yurai to sono igi*):

I think I can safely claim that today's sketching literature (shaseibun) was pioneered by members of our group, and the public would acknowledge this. Of course, I would not deny that Tsubouchi Shōyō's *The Temper of Students of Our Time* (*Tōsei Shosei Katagi*) represents the first emergence of a kind of sketching literature, but Tsubouchi's work, still fettered by the 5-7 rhythm, conveys a sense of clinging to the old forms. The Kenyūsha writers who emerged slightly later were also involved with sketching, but they were not able to escape the legacy of earlier *gesaku* writers. When we look back at the writers of the third decade of the Meiji period from a contemporary vantage point, we have the sense that, while trying to break away from the old molds they were nevertheless unable to write without them.

I think it was around this time that Western-style painters—the one that we had direct contact with was Nakamura Fūsetsu—began to advocate "sketching." The view of traditional Japanese brush-painters was that one should respect the conventions bequeathed to us by the old masters: beneath *ominaeshi* flowers one must always paint quails, with rushes, wild geese, and so forth, adhering to established traditions just as earnestly as the performers of Nō or kabuki. Western-style painters, however, opposed this, claiming that to follow the old forms just as they were was degenerate, that one should copy the natural world as one saw it with one's own eyes, and from there obtain the new.[7]

The first thing of note in Kyoshi's observations is his sense that those who were "fettered by 5-7 rhythm" were "clinging to old forms." Futabatei's *Drifting Clouds* is interesting to look at in this respect. The reason a lively rhythm predominates in that novel is because it has none of the visual quality cultivated by the sketching technique. Conversely, *genbun itchi* had to negate a certain notion of rhythm as transcendental in order to come into being. As Kyoshi suggests, the same was true of Nō and kabuki. This is the basis for my earlier assertion that the movements to reform poetry and drama were simultaneously a part of the larger *genbun itchi* movement and that it is only by considering it in this broad context that we can understand the nature of this movement.

3

If we set aside the novel-centered bias of canonical narratives of Meiji literary history, we can see that it was the movement to reform

a seemingly insignificant person. But no matter where one looks during this period, the ordinary face has begun to take on meaning.

Itō Sei describes how Ichikawa Danjūrō "struggled to create expressions that would convey a sense of psychology to his audience," but in fact it was the familiar naked ("realistic") face that emerged at this time as something that conveyed meaning, and that meaning—to be precise—was "interiority." Interiority was not something that had always existed, but only appeared as the result of the inversion of a semiotic constellation. No sooner had it appeared than it was seen as "expressed" by the naked face. In the process of this transformation the meaning of dramatic performance was reversed. That Ichikawa Danjūrō was originally thought of as a poor actor was symbolic of the change, as is the story of Futabatei Shimei, who switched to *genbun itchi* because he "didn't know how to write." Before Ichikawa audiences had found a vibrant meaning in the doll-like movements of the actors and in the masked face, the face as a figure; now they had to search for meaning "behind" the actor's ordinary face and gestures. Although they were by no means radical, Ichikawa's "reforms" were substantive enough to influence Tsubouchi Shōyō to envision the reform of the novel.

It should by now be clear that the reforms in drama and *genbun itchi* were of the same nature. I have defined *genbun itchi* as a reform of writing motivated by the aim of abolishing *kanji*. Writing and voice were originally distinct from each other, for as André Leroi-Gourhan has demonstrated, it was not painting that gave birth to writing but hieroglyphic writing that gave birth to painting. With the evolution of phonetic writing where voice and script combined, the memory of the origins of writing was lost. Moreover, in the case of Japan, there was a unique experience of the ideograph which was different even from that of the Chinese. Like the decorated face, the Chinese character has a direct, figural meaning. Once a phonocentric ideology of language had been adopted, however, even when *kanji* were used their meaning was subordinated to sound. Similarly, the conception of the face came to be that of the naked face as a kind of phonetic cipher. Meaning was then constituted as an inner voice recorded and expressed by the face. The Japanese discovery of realism and interiority was thus profoundly linked to the *genbun itchi* movement.

4

We can see the clearest articulations of a phonocentric ideology in the movement to reform poetry. Yamada Bimyō's *Treatise on Japanese Verse* (*Nihon inbunron*, 1890) is particularly noteworthy. Yamada attempted to establish a basis for Japanese verse writing by analyzing Japanese phonology. His argument, in brief, introduced a concern for stressed and unstressed syllables into an area which previously had been seen only to be a matter of *hyōshi* (often translated "rhythm"), the alternation of 5 syllable and 7 syllable lines. Yamada maintained that a composition in which stressed and unstressed syllables were not skillfully balanced could not be called verse, even if it was composed of alternating 5-7 syllable lines. It is clear that Yamada was simply trying to introduce principles of European poetry. Yet it is significant that as a result of his text a conception of poetry that up until that time had been seen as self-evident was relativized. That is to say, the body as rhythm was relativized. For if initially the "face" was the decorated face, and the "body" was the rhythmic body, what was discovered in the reform of poetry was a Cartesian conception of the body as mechanism. This is strikingly suggested by the following passage from the essay "The Future of Haiku," in Masaoka Shiki's *Talks on Haiku from the Otter's Den* (*Dassai Shooku Haiwa*, 1892).

> A certain contemporary scholar conversant with mathematics has said: "It is evident from the theory of permutations that there is a numerical limit to the tanka and haiku of Japan, which are confined to a mere twenty or thirty syllables." In other words, sooner or later, the tanka . . . and haiku will reach their limit. He says that even now it has reached the point where not a single new poem is possible. . . .
>
> Although one may place the blame on the many mediocre teachers and poets who have appeared in this age of decline, part of it must certainly be assigned to the intrinsically narrow confines of the tanka and haiku. You may ask, "If that is so, when will the end come for the haiku and tanka?" And I reply: "I can't, of course, predict the time of their total extinction, but speaking approximately, I think the haiku has already played itself out. Even assuming that the end is yet to come, we can confidently expect it to come sometime during the Meiji period. The tanka allows more syllables than the haiku and thus, from the mathematical standpoint, the number of tanka possible is far greater than that of haiku. However, only words of the classical language may be used in the tanka and since there are extremely few, the

tanka is in fact even more limited than the haiku. I conclude, therefore, that the tanka has been practically played out prior to the Meiji
period.[11]

Shiki's thesis, widely referred to as the "thesis that *tanka*'s days
are numbered" paradoxically revealed the secret of *tanka*'s long life.
This was, of course, rhythm. Short verses, whose content if rendered in prose would have been trivial, took on meaningfulness
through rhythm. To Shiki, however, this was merely a matter of
syllable count. By his time, *tanka* and *haiku* had come to be seen in
terms of a linear, phonetic script. Shiki's advocacy of sketching was
not unrelated to this, for an ideology of "copying" becomes possible
only when the human body has been liberated from the figural and
from rhythm. This is why Takahama Kyoshi, while acknowledging
that Tsubouchi Shōyō's *Temper of Students in our Times* represented
the "emergence of a kind of realism," nevertheless found it "fettered by the 5-7 rhythm." Shiki's concept of sketching, moreover,
could be extended to the prose writings called *shaseibun* because in
essence it was a liberation from rhythm, which Shiki acknowledged
in poetry only as an object to be manipulated. When Shiki turned to
traditional poetry in his "Tanka's Days are Numbered," however,
he had to pose the fundamental question of what enabled poetry
to be poetry.

And what of the relationship between the rhythm of classical
poetry and writing? Since the publication of "Eight Treatises on
Japanese Poetry" (*Kokka Hachiron*) by the National Learning scholar
Kadano Arimaro, a distinction has been drawn between poems
which were chanted aloud and written poems. Motoori Norinaga
proposed that the poetry in the *Kojiki* had been chanted and should
be regarded as the prototypical form of poetry in Japan. Yoshimoto
Takaaki, however, following the assertion of Kamo no Mabuchi,
states that far from being the origin of Japanese poetry, these poems
in the *Kojiki* represent a fairly high level of development.

One may discover many words which sound quite unfamiliar among
Shinto *norito* (prayers), for example, *iisoku, kamunaobi, oonaobi*. Initially,
these were spoken words, but as the rituals were codified Chinese
characters were applied to the words phonetically, and they were written as 言排　神直備　大直備 . These characters were, in their
turn, read as Japanese, as *iisoku, kamunaobi,* and *oonaobi*. Although
this process may seem rather insignificant, it suggests one facet of the
profound influence that Chinese characters—figures used to suggest

either meaning or pronunciation—had on early versification. *Iisoku, kamunaobi, oonaobi* were indigenous words used in formal ceremonies, at any rate until the time when the *Shukushi* was compiled. The *soku* in *iisoku* was probably a widely used familiar word. The word *naobi* referred to religious rituals, or the places in which they were performed. *Kamu* or *oo* expressed respect. In this period, it is thought that Japanese freely combined existing words into new words and ascribed them meanings. When these words were adopted for use in official ceremonies and transcribed with Chinese characters, however, the Chinese characters as graphic figures endowed them with a kind of new meaning. It was in this manner that the process of endowing indigenous words with sacred meanings began, and if we interpret this sacralization, in turn, as an impulse toward versification, we can see that we already have here the germs of poetry. Standardization of phrases and codification of laws further intensified the impulse to versification. For this involved arranging words and phrases in lines, which is a kind of versification.[12]

On the basis of this noteworthy formulation of Yoshimoto's, we may posit that it was the adoption of Chinese characters which stimulated the development of poetry and versification. The poetry in the *Kojiki* and the *Nihongi* which Norinaga saw as the prototype of Japanese verse represented, rather, an advanced stage which could only have evolved through the mediation of Chinese characters. Although it is true that these poems were chanted aloud, their composition was made possible only through the use of script. As Yoshimoto observes, "Perhaps Norinaga did not have an awareness of a qualitative difference between 'written words' and 'uttered words.' He did not perceive that vocalization of a written word and oral speech which precedes the development of writing are utterly different."[13]

Yoshimoto's observations help bring into view the topology on which Masaoka Shiki was standing. Shiki assumed that writing was phonetic in nature. The written word for him was merely a means of transcription, and Chinese characters were one kind of means. His position was therefore different from that of the National Learning scholars who attempted to expunge Chinese characters while nevertheless remaining under the sway of those characters through their concern for rhythm itself. Norinaga's work for this reason remains within the canon of classical poetics which made the *Kokinshū* the standard for poetic composition. Shiki had no interest at all in the *Kokinshū*. On the other hand, writing itself was no longer an issue for Shiki. It had been reduced to a process of transcription.

My own concern, however, has been to consider the kind of inversion of semiotic constellation which makes transcription possible. In order for us to assume it to be natural that things exist and the artist merely observes them and copies them, "things" must first be discovered. But this requires the repression of the signification, or figurative language (Chinese characters) that precedes "things," as well as the existence of a language which is supposedly transparent. It is at this point that "interiority" is constituted.

5

The theme of the exploration of the modern self, however diverse its articulations, dominates discussions of modern Japanese literature. Yet it is laughable to speak of this modern self as if it were purely a mental or psychological phenomenon. For this modern self is rooted in materiality and comes into existence—if I may put it this way—only by being established as a system. What I want to emphasize is the systematicity of the very "inner self" that is usually seen as challenging systems. In explaining literary developments from as early as 1890 on, for example, Japanese critics have relied on an opposition between "politics and literature" (*seiji to bungaku*), but since the historicity of this opposition is never questioned, it is a sterile paradigm.

Accordingly, I have attempted to reverse the assumption that it was the needs of the inner self that gave rise to the *genbun itchi* movement and to propose instead that it was the formation of the *genbun itchi* system that made possible the so-called "discovery of the self." Not to do so would be to fail to historicize, and indeed to further legitimate, a metaphysics which sees the existence of a "self" and its "expressions" as natural and self-evident. Those, for example, who discuss *The Drifting Clouds* and *The Dancing Girl* in terms of "inner struggle" and so forth disregard the issue of writing, as if it were something quite separate from interiority. I want to stress that it is *genbun itchi* that sustains this very illusion: that there is an inner self existing in and of itself.

Earlier I have described how modern landscape was discovered, not by those with an interest in the external world, but by introverts who had turned their backs on that world. I was not proposing that such introverted individuals existed *and then* discovered landscape, nor was I speaking of a psychological process. Certainly the Edo period had its full share of introverts and those who were excessively self-conscious. What I mean by the "discovery of interiority" is something different.

According to van den Berg, the first landscape painted simply as a landscape in Europe was the "Mona Lisa," in which for the first time the human was presented as alienated from the landscape, and vice versa.[14] But we must be wary of the question which seeks the meaning of the Mona Lisa's smile. We must not regard this as expressing some kind of interiority. For here, too, the case is the reverse of what we assume. It was because for the first time in the Mona Lisa the naked face, not the face as signified, appeared, that some kind of inner meaning expressed by this face has been incessantly posited. Interiority was not expressed here—the naked face, suddenly disclosed, began to signify interiority. This inversion took place contemporaneously to, and in the same manner as, the liberation of "pure landscape," from the figurative.

Da Vinci was of course a scientist, but in his case to be both a scientist and a painter was in no way contradictory. Interiority was profoundly linked to modern science. Descartes's conception of "extension," by which he referred to the object of thought, similarly conceived of the "landscape as alienated from the human." Extension for Descartes was unrelated to the medieval conception of figurative space which was assigned meaning in qualitative terms. Descartes's *cogito* belonged solely to the realm of extension. Thus the discovery of interiority must be differentiated from a concept of simple self-consciousness or consciousness of "existence." Existentialists have claimed Pascal as their predecessor but Pascal, himself a distinguished scientist, was expressing fear of the space discovered by modern astronomy when he wrote in the *Pensées* of the terror inspired in him "by the silence of infinite space." Medieval society had no conception of an infinite space. Moreover, Pascal's query, "Why am I here, and not there?" was a modern one, for such a question could not have arisen in the stratified world of medieval cosmology where "here" and "there" were qualitatively different spaces. Medieval theology could account for why one was where one was, in the same way that members of Edo society did not question their membership in the samurai or farmer class. Such a question is only possible within the context of a homogeneous notebooks to sketch they were acting as true scientists. At the same time, a certain kind of inversion was already latent in their obsession with documentation, the inversion that produced the notion of a transcendental interiority. They were not themselves "inward personalities," but their practices established a basis for interiority.

Meiji Japanese absorbed many European ideas, and I would not deny that their influence was significant. But the significance of material practices went far beyond that of European ideas. As evidence, I would like to suggest that the prototypical manifestations of Japanese interiority did not appear until the end of the third decade of Meiji, when *genbun itchi* was solidly established, indeed, so firmly entrenched that Japanese writers were no longer even conscious of it.

6

Kunikida Doppo's *Musashi Field* (*Musashino*, 1898) has become known as a text which severed the connection between landscape and "famous sites." A "famous site" was nothing other than a place imbued with historical and literary significance. However, Doppo accomplished an even more radical form of severing when he wrote about his experiences participating in the government-sponsored development of Hokkaido in 1895 in "On the Banks of Sorachi River" (*Sorachigawa no kishibe*, 1902).

> As someone who grew up in the densely settled Chūbu area in the mainland, accustomed to landscapes in which both hills and fields had been thoroughly absorbed by the products of human labor, how could I find myself gazing on Hokkaido without my heart leaping up? They say Sapporo is the Tokyo of Hokkaido, but I found its scenery completely bewitching.
>
> No sooner had dusk settled on the woods than an autumnal rain came pattering down from branches high above. It stopped as suddenly as it had begun, returning the woods to hushed silence.
>
> I gazed intently for some time into the darkened woods. Where was society, where was the "history" that humankind transmitted so triumphantly? At this moment, in this place, a person could feel only that he or she was in the charge of "life" itself, of a single breath of nature. A Russian poet once wrote that, sitting in the forest, he felt the shadow of death approach, and it is true. And also that "when the last human being vanishes from the earth it will not cause a single tree leaf to tremble." [17]

This passage by Doppo bears out Marx's observation that what we see as "nature" is always already humanized or Yanagita's insight that landscape is "a human creation." For we find in Doppo a viewpoint that discovers history, not in the realm of politics or human activity, but in what Yanagita has called "the commingling of humanity and nature." It is a viewpoint made possible by discovering landscape beyond literature. This radical scission underlies the following position articulated in *Musashino Field*.

> There are of course no bare mountains in Musashino, but the countryside undulates like the surge of the ocean. At first glance, Musashino looks like a level plain, but it is set high and here and there are shallow depressions and valleys. At the bottom of these valleys you usually find paddy fields whereas the higher spots which are normally divided between field and wood are given over to dry fields. The plain is so constructed that you might get mile upon mile of woods or fields or perhaps just a little of each so that a wood is surrounded by fields and sometimes the fields are surrounded on three sides by woods. The farmers have their dwellings scattered about over the plain and divide the fields among them. Fields and woods are so confusedly scattered that sometimes you enter a wood and come straight out into fields again. This is a special feature of Musashino. Unlike the pristine nature of Hokkaido's vast plains and great forests, here life and nature exist side by side, giving Musashino a flavor all its own.[18]

Doppo asks "Where else could one find such a pleasant mingling of wood and field, a place where life and nature are so thoroughly intertwined?"[19] What Kunikida Doppo calls "life" is what Yanagita terms "hidden reality"—the life of Yanagita's *jōmin* or common people. Yanagita's ethnology should be seen, not as the importation of ethnology from the West, but as a "discovery" sustained by the same kind of process through which Doppo discovered landscape.

"Observation" and "factual description" are two other qualities that have been noted in Doppo's *Musashino Field*. For example, Doppo delineates regional boundaries. But what is significant about the way he does this may be remarked in the following comment. "I consider that Tokyo lies at the heart of Musashino, but that we must leave out, because it is impossible to imagine what it must have been like in days of old, when now it is filled with . . . busy streets and soaring government offices,"[20] Doppo writes. For Doppo, Tokyo's political history is simply one facet of the history of Musashino as

The doctor's attit   e   rd "death" is extremely cool, but I cannot believe that tho   ou gathered here are much different. Once
one understands th   ⁀logical processes involved in the transition
from life to death   ⁀o longer mysterious. Once the cause of
the suicide is d   ₎rea   natter will have been settled and there
will be nothi⁀   to won   ₎t.

As I w   ₎king all th   had the sense that I was enclosed in
a kind o⁀   ₎brane, and th₎   y perceptions of all existence were
someh⁀   ₎tanced by that si ₎ layer of skin. My anguished self
belie⁀   ₎ven now, that if I cann₎ t confront facts and phenomena di-
re⁀   ₎ce to face, then neither go₎' nor truth nor beauty exists, they
⁀   ₎mply an empty game. This is a₎ that I can believe.[24]

⁀e find even more pronounced examples of Doppo's sense of
₎eriority in the work "Beef and Potatoes" (*Gyunikū to bareisho*,
₎901). The protagonist Okamoto has a "strange desire" to be "sur-
prised." As he puts it, "it is not a desire to penetrate the mysteries
of nature but to be astonished by mysterious nature . . . not a desire
to understand the secret of death but to be astonished by the fact
of death," not faith itself "but a desire to be so tormented by the
mysteries of life in this universe that I can never be at peace without
faith." We find in Doppo a sense that the self is severed from the
self. This gives rise to opacity, "a kind of membrane." For Doppo,
to be astonished is to break out of that membrane and arrive at
transparency. The illusion that there is something like a "true self"
has taken deep root. It is an illusion that is established when writing has come to be seen as derivative and that voice which is most
immediate to the self, and which constitutes self-consciousness,
is privileged. The psychological person, who begins and ends in
interiority, has come into existence.

7

Modern Japanese literature could be said to have attained spontaneity in writing for the first time in Kunikida Doppo's work.
This spontaneity was linked to a sense that interiority and self-
expression were self-evident. I have treated this as a product of
the writing system known as *genbun itchi*. Interiority is brought
into being through a sense of the presence of one's own voice, to
which one listens. Jacques Derrida has defined this phenomenon

in the West as phonocentrism, with its basis in a phonetic script or alphabet. Since Plato's time the written word has been devalued as a mere instrument for transcribing the voice, and the privileging of the voice as presence to consciousness has been the distinctive feature of Western metaphysics.

By now the implications of *genbun itchi* should be quite clear. As I have repeatedly stressed, it consisted in the repression of the figurative, of Chinese characters. We can now understand why Natsume Sōseki, although he was deeply immersed in Western literature, nevertheless remained stubbornly attached to *kanbungaku*—not to those forms of premodern literature represented by court poetry, which were written in phonetic Japanese. Although his whole being was submerged in an interiority from which there was no exit, Sōseki still sought a world beyond that of linear, phonetic speech, a world where the meaning of writing was polysemic and radial. It is a world that has become difficult for us even to imagine. As André Leroi-Ghouran has written, "Homo sapiens has spent the longest portion of its evolutionary history employing modes of thought which have now become remote to us. Yet these modes of thought form the basis for major areas of our behavior. Because in our lives we carry on unitary forms of linguistic activity in which sounds are transcribed according to a phonetic system of writing, we can no longer conceive of modes of expression in which thought is recorded through radial structures."[25]

By "we" Ghouran of course refers to Westerners, but this already includes us, Japanese. When we examine the literature of the third decade of Meiji, we have to imagine an "interiority" which did not really exist at the time. As a system, "interiority" was not, in fact, inside us, but rather we who were incorporated within it. Literary scholars who discuss the modern self in "The Dancing Girl" forget that it was written in the classical style. They forget that what they are discussing is first and foremost a text, not "self-expression." Indeed, the theme of interiority was not deepened by Ōgai in any fundamental way after he wrote "The Dancing Girl." In "Delusions" (*Mōsō*, 1901), for example, Ōgai made the following observations about himself. "Although I have contemplated the physical pain involved in death, it is not the pain of the annihilation of the ego as Westerners conceive of it." He writes,

> Westerners think of a culture which does not fear death as barbaric. Then I must be what Westerners conceive of as a barbarian. When I

reflect on this it also occurs to me that when I was a child both of my parents instructed me from time to time that since I was a member of a samurai household I had to be able to commit suicide (*seppuku*). I remember thinking then that it would be physically painful but that I would have to endure that pain. This must make me all the more a so-called barbarian. Yet I still cannot accept the Western view as entirely correct.

I don't mean to imply that I am completely indifferent to the fact that my ego will disappear. I regret that I will die without ever having a clear sense of what the ego is or knowing it, although supposedly I possess one. This is truly a shame! It is what Confucian scholars describe as "living in drunkenness, dying in a dream." Yet while this strikes me as a shame and regrettable I am also filled with a keen sense of emptiness. It is a loneliness I simply cannot express. This, for me, is the source of agony, the source of pain.

Perhaps Ōgai's attitude here seems similar to Doppo's "desire to be astonished." But if Doppo's opaque "membrane" can be described as somehow internal, for Ōgai it is external. In Ōgai's writing the "self" has no substance, it is an "assemblage of threads pulled together from different directions," precisely what Marx described in *The German Ideology* as "a totality of diverse relationships." Ōgai's pain is the reverse of Doppo's and derives from the fact that he has no illusion of a tangible, immediate self as conceived of in Western thought.

Ōgai's deepest desires were therefore realized in the historical fiction where he wrote of samurai characters. In these works Ōgai tried to thoroughly eliminate any trace of the "psychological." In doing this Ōgai had something in common with the later Sōseki who wrote fiction in the morning and lost himself in a world of Chinese poetry and ink-brush painting in the afternoon. For both men "literature" must have retained a certain unfamiliarity; both must have developed a perspective which rejected the concept of "expression." The mainstream of modern Japanese literature continued along lines set forth by Doppo rather than by Ōgai or Sōseki. All the germs of the literature which was to be produced by the next generation were contained in the writing of Doppo, who died so prematurely. It was Doppo who produced the first work of confessional literature in "An Honest Account" (*Azamukazaru no ki*, 1893–97). Not only was there his relationship with Yanagita Kunio, but he was spoken of by Tayama Katai in "Doppo, Man of Nature," as "Kunikida, the father of the carnal novel," and later by Akutagawa Ryūnosuke (who compared him with Strindberg, Nietzsche, and Tolstoy) as "the poet who could vividly understand the mentality of the poor laborer killed by a train."[26] Shiga Naoya, too, was clearly under the influence of Doppo when he began his career as a writer. That Doppo, like Rousseau, has seemed to speak with many voices (it is for this reason that controversy has always surrounded the issue of whether to classify him as "romantic" or "naturalist") is because Doppo was indeed standing for the first time on a new horizon. As Paul Valéry observed, the person who discovers a new way of looking at a single phenomenon will immediately discover a host of other phenomena. Edgar Allen Poe took the basic form of the detective story to its limits, yet it was his bold experiment in exploring the consciousness of poetic composition, not crime, that constituted his advance. The multiplicity of Doppo has nothing to do with which literary school he belonged to, but results from his having been the first Japanese writer to attain "transparency."

Afternote to Chapter 2, 1991

The problem of *genbun itchi* is considerably more complex than I have shown it to be here. Let me discuss just one aspect of this. I have focused only on the question of whether Futabatei Shimei, for example, chose the *da* or *desu* endings, but what was more important was that Futabatei used a fixed form, the past tense *ta*, to conclude his sentences. Of course, the Japanese *ta* form does not, strictly speaking, express a past tense. *Ta* unifies into a single form the many complex suffixes used in *bungo*, the classical literary language, to correspond to what in English would be the perfect, past perfect, as well as other tenses. In the passage from Mori Ōgai's *Dancing Girl* that I cite, for example, there is a diversity of suffixes that creates an effect quite different from a *genbun itchi* style in which all sentences conclude with *ta*.

Why was it that this diversity had to be sacrificed? *The Dancing Girl* is written in the first person, with its narrator as protagonist. This was epoch-making at the time. But this feature did not constitute the kind of third-person "objective narration" that was indispensable for the modern novel. In other words Ōgai does not here present us with a mode of fiction in which the narrator is only an implicit, rather than explicit, element in the text. The use of the *ta* form was required to bring such narration into existence. The premodern literary suffix *keri*, for example, expresses hearsay. The well-known opening line of each episode in the *Tales of Ise* (c. 950), "Mukashi otoko arikeri" (Long ago there was a man), means that "it is said that there was a man." In other words through the suffix the tale announces itself as narration and indicates the presence of a narrator. Once *ta* is used, the narrator's presence is not made explicit, even though the function of the narrator remains. Narrator and protagonist become subtly fused. It was the use of the *ta* suffix which produced this form so familiar to readers of modern fiction. Thus *ta* not only signifies the past tense, it makes the narrator a neutral feature existing on the meta-level of the text. This produces a sense of "reality" in the text. It also makes possible a temporality from which the development of events in the tale can be surveyed retrospectively from a single point. Narration takes the form of retrospection, in which the narrator and the interiority of the protagonist are subtly fused. The use of *ta* was indispensable in bringing about this neutralization, or effacement, of the narrator.

The Japanese *ta* may be compared to the use of the preterite in French. Barthes described the preterite in the following way: "Even from the depth of the most sombre realism, it has a reassuring effect because, thanks to it, the verb expresses a closed, well-defined, substantival act, the Novel as a name; it escapes the terror of an expression without laws: reality becomes slighter and more familiar, it fits within a style, it does not outrun language." [27] *Ta*, then, has to do with the nucleus of narration in the modern novel. Third-person narration could not emerge until the narrator had been neutralized by the use of *ta*.

Sōseki deliberately resisted the use of this *ta*. He perceived the use of *ta* for sentence endings as the basic posture of the modern novel. Sōseki's fictional writing began with the composition of "sketching literature" or *shaseibun* writings, which generally employed the present progressive tense and which featured an overt narrator. This type of writing was pioneered by Masaoka Shiki, but I would like to make some broad amendations to the discussion of Shiki presented in the foregoing chapter.

The concept of "sketching" or *shasei* developed by Shiki should not be confused with a notion of "realism" that had already become conventionalized by Shiki's own time. The originality of Shiki was to have discovered a kind of realism in that shortest of Japanese verse forms, the haiku. Shiki himself tells us that he studied sketching when learning to paint (oil paintings). But everything Shiki describes as "like sketching" (as "realistic") or as "painterly" in haiku has to do, in fact, with language. For example, Shiki praised the painterly quality of haiku by Buson and of *waka* poetry by Mina-moto Sanetomo (1192–1298), but what he meant by this was that we find many Chinese ideographs in their verses and that nouns pre-dominate while particles are few. Shiki discussed the decadence of *waka* thus: "The decadence of waka is due to its failure to develop a new style, and this failure to develop a new style is due to a paucity of vocabulary." [28] For this reason Shiki advocated that "elegant dic-tion, vulgar diction, Western words, and Chinese words should all be used as necessary." [29] It is clear that for Shiki, what was more im-portant than sketching as a concept was language and linguistic di-versity. This is really the basis of "sketching literature," or *shaseibun*. Sōseki alone, composing in multiple and diverse genres, demon-strated an awareness of this. But for the most part "sketching" was understood in terms of an orientation toward "realism" (*shajitsu*) based on a monotonous language. It was Takahama Kyoshi, who had originally aspired to becoming a novelist, who encouraged this tendency.

It was extremely significant that Shiki's point of departure was haiku. Sōseki had similar views on haiku, such as the following: "Although it is regrettable that no literature exists that adequately represents the Japanese people, in some senses we might say that, contrary to expectation, a literature which uplifts and refines human beings to an even greater extent than Western literature is not lack-ing here: this is that haiku literature which is unique to Japan and which is also a literature of the common people." [30] The search for a literature "worthy of the Japanese people," a "literature of the com-mon person", and furthermore the discovery of these very qualities in haiku, was common to both Shiki and Sōseki, who had been close friends since their university days. Shiki started out attempt-ing to reform haiku and subsequently became involved in reforming *waka* and prose writing. His criticism of *waka*, however, already emerges in the book *Principles of Haiku* (*Haikai taiyō*), which he pub-lished in 1895. Actually, the very fact that Shiki proposed that haiku poetry be seen as representing the Japanese poetic tradition since the *Manyōshū* constituted a critical stance. But Shiki was not ob-sessed with the specificity of haiku. "Haiku is one part of literature. Literature is one part of art. This is why the standard for art should be the standard for literature, and the standard for literature should be the standard for haiku. In other words, we should use the same standard in evaluating painting, sculpture, music, drama, poetry, and prose narrative."[31] What Shiki asserts here is that haiku is "one part" of art (or beauty) and that as an artistic practice—regardless of whether it is Eastern or Western—it adheres to the same principles. Furthermore, although each haiku is rooted in a discrete feeling, it is susceptible to intellectual analysis and thus capable of being criticized. Especially in the case of something like haiku, there is a tendency for people either to abandon it in its particularity or to privilege it through the development of exclusionary attitudes on the part of haiku poets themselves. This has also been true of *waka*, which Shiki later criticized even more vehemently. Practitioners of *waka* will probably defend it against its critics by claiming that it possesses a subtle, mysterious quality that cannot be analyzed. But this kind of argument is not only made in relation to *waka* and haiku. Many speak broadly of Japanese literature itself as that which cannot be analyzed or which rejects analysis because it is of a different nature from Western literature. What Shiki asserted was that for the time being this difference should be left behind. It was probably only Sōseki, trying quite literally in his *Theory of Literature* to inquire into the "standards for literature old and new, Eastern and Western," who carried on the legacy of Shiki, who died at the age of thirty-five while Sōseki was in London.

Yet it is in no way contradictory to aspire to the universal while adhering to that which is extremely specific. The two are interdependent. Nevertheless, why did Shiki choose haiku? It was not only because haiku, unlike *waka*, had its origin in what is often called the "early modern" (*kinsei*) Edo society and was an art of the common people. It was because haiku is doubtless the shortest poetic form in the world. To write in the haiku form is to probe to its very limits the poetic nature of language itself. In this sense Shiki's methodology as a critic is a formalist one. This is because the brevity of haiku makes it impossible to critique it purely in terms of meaning or content. In fact, in the West at this time there was no critic who brought language into focus as sharply as Shiki did. Thus it was that the Japanese practice of haiku composition, in its very specificity, could provide a point of departure for inquiring into the nature of the universal.

3 Confession as a System

1

Modern Japanese literature may be said to have come into existence together with the confessional literary form. Literary confession, however, should not be confused with an act of confession, for in this case it is the form itself that produces the "inner life" that is confessed. For this reason, no matter how often Japanese literature has tried to reject or transcend confession in the narrow sense of the word, the form itself has survived intact and has even thrived on criticism. A binarism persists according to which the inner life that the novelist expresses is seen as independent from the content of the work. Criticism of the "I-novel," for example, has not negated the notion of confession in and of itself. Rather, Japanese critics have objected to the conflation in the Japanese I-novel of the "I" who confesses and the subject of confession. According to their view, although the literary work is a form of self-expression on the part of the author, it should create a world which is different and autonomous from that of the author's "I"; by conflating the author's "I" and the "I" of the work, the Japanese I-novel has failed to create a self-sufficient fictional world. On the basis of such criteria, Futabatei's *Drifting Clouds*, although written as early as the late 1880s, has been deemed to have succeeded far better than many later works in realizing the novel form as it had been defined in the West. Shimazaki Tōson's *Broken Commandment* was another step in the right direction, but the development of the Japanese novel was thrown off course by Tayama Katai's *Futon*—this schema has attained the status of a truism in Japanese literary history.

Yet this schema is premised on several assumptions. One is that there is a "self" in need of expression whose existence precedes that of expression—in other words that a binary distinction can be made between the self that expresses and the content of expression. By now we have extended this binarism to our discussions of premodern literature. We characterize poets of the *Manyōshū* (c. 750) as "naive" yet "direct" in expressing themselves. But it is pure anachronism to find self-expression in these early poems. Poets of the become? Would the "normal" evolution of the Japanese novel that critics have fantasized have been truly normal? Or is the Western normality they have taken as a standard abnormal? And what if this were the source of the abnormality of the Japanese novel?

Shimamura has said that Katai wrote of feelings but not of events. The kinds of feelings that Katai described, however, had not existed from the start but were brought into existence by a process. In the Christian New Testament, for example, it is written that "You have heard it said, 'Thou shalt not commit adultery,' but I say unto you that whoever looks at a woman with lust in his heart has already committed adultery in his heart." This statement contains a frightening inversion. All religions, including Judaism, have prohibitions against adultery. But in Christianity we find an inversion unprecedented in any other religion, for adulterous feelings, rather than acts, become the object of prohibition. To maintain this kind of conscience requires one to exercise constant surveillance over one's inner thoughts. One must keep watch over one's "interiority" at all times. One must scrutinize the passions that surge up "within." It is this surveillance, in fact, that produces interiority. In the process the body and sexuality are discovered.

It is a body which has already been diminished. The body laid bare by the naturalist writers was a body subjected to repression. All the efforts of the naturalist writers to liberate the body and sexuality from Christianity took place within the framework of this prior repression. Antonin Artaud wrote of the Balinese theatre: "The actors assisted by their costumes form moving hieroglyphs. These three dimensional hieroglyphs are in turn ornamented by prescribed gestures and mystical signs. The mystical signs correspond to a dim, fantasmatic reality that we Westerners have completely repressed." Artaud was speaking here of the Western repression of the body, of which even the naked body in European culture must be seen as a product. Unlike Artaud, we do not have to seek an alternative far off in the distance. We have only to look at Edo theatre.

Why did Katai's *Quilt* create a sensation? It was because "sexuality" was written of for the first time in this novel. It was the sexuality brought into existence by repression, a sexuality which had been unknown prior to that time in Japanese literature. The novelty of this sexuality was shocking to readers in ways that Katai never anticipated. Although Katai was seen as confessing what had been hidden, it was the reverse. The institution of confession led

Katai to discover "sexuality." As Michel Foucault observed in *The History of Sexuality*,

> From the Christian penance to the present day, sex was a privileged theme of confession. A thing that was hidden, we are told. But what if, on the contrary, it was what, in a quite particular way, one confessed? Suppose the obligation to conceal it was but another aspect of the duty to admit to it (concealing it all the more and with greater care as the confession of it was more important, requiring a stricter ritual and promising more decisive effects)? What if sex in our society, on a scale of several centuries, was something that was placed within an unrelenting system of confession? The transformation of sex into discourse, which I spoke of earlier, the dissemination and reinforcement of heterogeneous sexualities, are perhaps two elements of the same deployment: they are linked together with the help of the central element of a confession that compels individuals to articulate their sexual particularity—no matter how extreme. In Greece, truth and sex were linked, in the form of pedagogy, by the transmission of a precious knowledge from one body to another; sex served as a medium for initiations into learning. For us, it is in the confession that truth and sex are joined, through the obligatory and exhaustive expression of an individual secret. But this time it is truth that serves as a medium for sex and its manifestations.[3]

Foucault's analysis suggests why *The Quilt* had more influence on the development of modern Japanese literature than did Shimazaki Tōson's *Broken Commandment*, which in its form was much closer to a Western novel.

2

The system of confession had been well established before Katai and Tōson began to write confessional literature. Interiority, produced through an inversion, had already come into existence. One concrete manifestation of this inversion was the practice of Christianity. We must bear in mind that both Katai and Tōson had practiced Christianity for a time. Although their involvement was so brief we might dismiss it as something like catching a case of the measles, it was significant for that very reason. For the influence of the type of inversion associated with Christianity comes into being when its relationship to Christianity has been repressed. Masamune Hakuchō wrote

I was struck by the power of Christian⸝ ⸝s I travelled through different countries of Europe. I had known ⸝   ⸝ literature and art of
the European past could not be understoo⸝   ⸝rom Christianity,
but this came home to me much more keenly ⸝   ⸝⸝s on the spot.
Although it is often said that humanity was libera⸝   ⸝⸝perstition
with the development of science, I wonder if this is⸝   ⸝d the
impression that, with the exception of a small group⸝   ⸝en-
tsia, traces of religion were cherished deep in the hearts⸝   ⸝.
Many popular films I saw seemed to smack of religiosity⸝
the theatre religious nuances were striking to a foreign obs⸝
myself. In the Japanese literary world, however, which is stri⸝
emulate the West, Christianity seems to have come and gone wit⸝
leaving a trace. The Japanese literary world did not accept philosoph⸝
like Tsunashima Ryosen, who advocated "the experience of beatifi⸝
vision." A lukewarm humanism with a vaguely Christian hue appears
in the work of various writers—that is all. . . . Or so I thought in the
past. Recently, as words like "doubt," "remorse," and "penance" have
begun to issue from the mouths and even preoccupy the minds of
writers of the era of Naturalism, such as Tōkoku, Doppo, and Roka,
I have begun to reconsider and to wonder whether this is due to the
impact of Western religions. It is my opinion that the psychological
phenomena of doubt and remorse would not arise in men who were
liberated from religion.[4]

In this passage Masamune, looking back in a detached manner,
finds himself unable to deny that an encounter with Christianity,
however ephemeral, was the point of departure for many Meiji
writers. For Masamune, moreover, while Western societies may
have appeared superficially to have moved away from Christianity,
they remained shaped by it in even the smallest details. What I am
arguing here is that the perspective of literary scholars is greatly
limited by the practice of looking for the "influence" of Christianity
in the life of a particular writer. Modern European literature as
a whole was formed within the discourse of confession, and the
writers who succumbed to the contagion of this literature were incorporated within it, whether they ascribed to Christianity as individuals or not. It is not a matter of identifying specific literatures as
Christian or Christian-influenced.

Consider, for example, Kitamura Tōkoku's claim that in the fiction of Kōda Rohan (1867–1947) and moreover, in Edo literature in
general, there is no such thing as romantic love (ren'ai), only the
sensibility of iki or elegance. In his essay, "A Consideration of Iki,

extended to *The Aloes-wood Pillow*," Tōkoku maintains that the ideal of *iki* evolved in the pleasure quarters and that "the writers of that time were, on the whole, dreamers who whiled away their lives in the pleasure quarters, faithfully recording what transpired within its confines." Accordingly, one did not lose oneself in *iki* as one did in romantic love.

> Another way in which *iki* should be contrasted with romantic love is that it is not monogamous. I have the sense that it is a rule that the possessor of *iki* pursue amorous relations (*koi*) without becoming carried away with them—one does not lose one's senses even if one causes one's lover to do so. There is the feeling that to lose control is already to compromise the value of one's *iki* a bit. To become carried away is a sign of foolishness and the fool can never attain real *iki*. To become carried away is to dissipate the wisdom of *iki*—the inelegance of falling in love is precisely what is said to disqualify one from being *iki*. Therefore, anyone with even the slightest degree of fastidiousness in pursuing *iki* must make it an ideal to seduce a lover whom money cannot buy, keeping the emotions hidden all the while, and to abandon that lover after sexual union has been consummated. To have a love affair during which neither oneself nor one's lover become carried away is *iki*; to remain unperturbed when one's lover becomes carried away is still *iki*—when both become carried away it is no longer true *iki*.[5]

Yet, we may ask, is what Tōkoku calls "love" natural? While the ideal of *iki* is certainly not a natural one, the same can be said of romantic love. There was *koi* in premodern Japan, but not romantic love (*ren'ai*).[6] Nor did such an ideal exist in classical Greece and Rome. The ideal of romantic love originated in Western Europe. While not persuasive in every respect, Denis de Rougemont's *Love in the Western World* demonstrates convincingly that despite certain anti-Christian aspects the ideal of passionate love was a "sickness" with its origins in Christianity. When those already afflicted with romantic love analyze its psychology as "natural," they unwittingly accept the naturalness of Christianity's inverted world. In point of fact, as was the case with Kitamura, the notion of romantic love began to be diffused into Japanese society from within Christian churches and their environs, so much so that it is difficult to know whether the young men and women who assembled there did so out of a concern for faith or for romance. Yet Western literature in and of itself promulgated the notion of romantic love throughout Japan. Readers of Western literature gradually replaced Christian congregations as a locus of actualization of the ideal. The literary youth described in *The Quilt* illustrate this. Far from being natural, romantic love was for them a kind of religious fever. This fever was communicated through literature even to those who had had no direct contact with Christianity. People became obsessed with a strange problem which was called *ai*, not *koi*. Even Sōseki, who disliked Christianity, became entangled in the problem of *ai* in attempting to deal with love.

But it is possible to define Christianity in an even more direct sense as a source of modern Japanese literature. The affiliates of the journal *Bungakkai*, as well as Tayama, Doppo, and others, were believers in Christianity. As Hakuchō has suggested, Christianity was as significant an intellectual force in the third decade of Meiji as Marxism came to be in the early Showa period. Nietzsche insisted, "Christianity *needs* sickness just as Greek culture needs a superabundance of health—to make sick is the true, secret purpose of the whole system of redemptive procedures constructed by the church."[7] In examining Meiji literary history, we discover the sudden appearance of "illness" after 1890. Illness was not dealt with in Tsubouchi's *Essence of the Novel* nor in the writings of Fukuzawa Yukichi. This is because modern Japanese literature had its sources in something altogether different from the so-called "will to modernize." The Christian church functioned, quite literally, as one such source.

3

Let me emphasize again that I am not concerned here with the "influence" of Christianity. In the absence of that psychological attitude which is predisposed to being influenced, there can be no question of influence. The issue I wish to address is rather why Christianity, specifically Protestant Christianity, was able to wield such influence during this time. In order to do so, it will first be necessary to consider what kinds of people were attracted to Christianity.

Hiraoka Toshio, in *The Beginnings of Modern Japanese Literature*, opens his discussion by citing Yamaji Aizan's observation that "spiritual revolutions begin on the margins of an era." Aizan noted that Meiji converts to Christianity such as himself, Uemura Masahisa, Honda Yōichi, Ifuka Kajinosuke, and others were all the children of former vassals of the Tokugawa shogunate. "Those who write about the history of our era should not overlook the fact that the young men who professed the new religion and resolved to take on the whole world for it were without exception those who were not advancing on the currents of the time. They had no hopes of sating themselves with prestige. Their expectations of attaining status in the real world were minimal."[8] Hiraoka stresses that the young men who dedicated themselves to spiritual revolution were descendants of samurai who had supported the Tokugawa shogunate against the forces of restoration and were not ordinary citizens. The Christian spiritual revolution, in other words, originated among former samurai whose new status was no better (and sometimes worse than) that of commoners, but who were not able to think of themselves as such. This is an important observation.

Uchimura Kanzō, for example, declared that "only Christianity, of all religions, works from within the heart. Christianity is what other religions have searched for, weeping streams of tears." Those moved from within by Christianity, however, happened to be former samurai who were alienated from the Meiji establishment. Those who responded empathetically to Christianity were members of the social class that could no longer live as samurai and yet had no other basis for its sense of identity and self-respect. It was into such hearts, filled with impotence and resentment, that Christianity made its inroads. It is no accident that, beginning with Nitobe Inazō, bushidō* had been seen by the samurai class as having a direct link to Christianity. By becoming Christian adherents, these youths were able to secure for themselves an identity as warriors. By the same token, Christianity failed to become a popular religion.

The following is the testimony of Yamamoto Taijirō in *How I Became a Christian*:

> It was only after a long and fearful struggle that I gave in and decided to become a student of theology. As I have already indicated, I was born into a samurai family. The samurai, like any other man of action, scorned those who dallied their time away in scholarship or

---

*By the Edo period, the term *bushidō* (literally, the way of the warrior) had come to refer broadly to the ethos and codes of behavior considered appropriate for the ruling samurai class. This ethos had been variously and elaborately codified since the establishment of the first Kamakura shogunate in 1192. Karatani refers to the influential English presentation, *Bushido, the Soul of Japan*, published by Nitobe Inazō in 1900. Nitobe was a Christian and later became the first Japanese citizen appointed to serve in the Secretariat of the League of Nations in 1919.

tude that constitutes the inversion which accompanies confession. Because the system of confession appears to stand in opposition to external authority, rather than having been imposed by it, it has proven resilient to criticism. Furthermore, although contemporary writers have turned away from confession in the narrow sense, it remains inherent in modern literary practice.

4

The life of Uchimura Kanzō may be seen as prototypical of the dynamics of the establishment of subjectivity in modern Japan. As a student in the Sapporo Agricultural College, Uchimura was forced by upperclassmen to join other students in signing a "covenant of believers in Jesus." Despite the fact that his participation had been forcibly obtained, Uchimura discovered that in signing the covenant he had liberated himself in one stroke from a problem which had long preoccupied him. A deeply religious child, he had striven to be faithful to the prohibitions of the gods. But "since the gods were so diverse and prolific, their demands contradicted each other. A person who had to satisfy more than one of these gods faced tragedy. With so many gods to appease and mollify, I developed into a timid, irritable child. I created a general-purpose, one-line prayer which could be offered to any god."[12] For a youth such as this, the so-called "practical advantages" of a belief in monotheism were indeed desirable.

> Up until that point, as soon as a shrine came into view, I had interrupted my conversations to pray silently, but now I was able to walk to school chatting happily all the way. I was not distressed that I had been forced to sign the "covenant of believers in Jesus." Through monotheism I had become a new person. I began to eat beans and eggs again. The thought that there was just a single God was so exhilarating that I felt I had understood the whole of Christian doctrine. My body and soul were brought back to health by the spiritual freedom conveyed on me by this new creed, and I intensified my efforts in my studies. Ecstatic over the vitality with which my body had been newly endowed I wandered through fields and hillsides, as the spirit moved me, marvelling at the birds soaring through the skies, and at lilies blooming in the vallies: through nature I attempted to converse with the God of nature.[13]

I know of no other document which describes the conversion from polytheism to monotheism so dramatically. Through monotheism, for Uchimura, nature became for the very first time "simply nature." Uchimura felt he had attained a freedom of spirit—in fact, spirit itself—through his conversion. Taken out of context, the passage above seems more evocative of Old Testament spirituality than of Christianity. One has the sense, moreover, of a discovery of landscape here. Nature, formerly veiled by diverse prohibitions and significations, becomes "simply nature" when it is seen as the creation of a single God. Yet this kind of Nature (or "landscape") exists only by virtue of the existence of the spirit or of an inner world. Uchimura's discovery of landscape may be compared with that of Kunikida Doppo, another Christian believer. For it was on the basis of a kind of spiritual revolution that landscape was discovered in modern Japan. Thus the debate over whether Kunikida Doppo was a romantic or a naturalist involves a merely superficial distinction made on the basis of Western literary history. The pantheistic spirit of the romantic movement may have appeared as the converse of monotheism, but it was fundamentally different from indigenous polytheism. While Uchimura's paean to the "God of nature" appears to verge on pantheism, it was made possible by his conversion to Christianity.

Monotheism was of decisive significance in the conversion of Uchimura Kanzō. Although Christianity, divided as it was into many competing factions, was not that dissimilar from Shinto with its conflicting gods, Uchimura overcame this difficulty through his belief in monotheism. It was for this reason that Uchimura's Christianity, which was independent of any sect, resonated with the spirit of the Old Testament. He was more drawn to the prophet Jeremiah than to Christ.

> The human Jeremiah, who did not perform a single miracle in the course of the book, was revealed before me in a form in which all the strengths and weaknesses of humanity were exposed. I whispered to myself, "Should all great men be called prophets?" I recalled all the great men of my homeland, a heathen land, and by comparing their words and deeds with Jeremiah's reached this conclusion: the same God who spake to the prophet Jeremiah spake to some of my compatriots.[14]

Uchimura's book *A Typical Japanese* (*Daihyōteki nihonjin*) is written from the same perspective. His writings on pacifism begin with the announcement that Uchimura has learned how to defend the homeland from the Old Testament prophets. By taking the position of a man facing the one and only God, Uchimura attempted to maintain his independence from both Japan and Christian nations. In other words the militantly independent spirit with which Uchimura rejected every form of subordination was made possible by the absolute subjectivity which he achieved in subjecting himself to a single god. In Uchimura's case inversion took a particularly dramatic form. This explains why Uchimura's was the most influential version of Christianity among the next generation of Japanese.

As we have seen in Japanese literature of the 1890s, it was only by means of inversion that the modern subject came into existence. It is in the very natural way in which we now take for granted the opposition in modern philosophy of subjectivity (the subject) and objectivity (the object) that this inversion is disguised. The subject, and subjectivity, as Uchimura Kanzō has shown, is established through the repression of the diversity of polytheism. This is nothing other than a repression of "the body." It is through this repression, we must not forget, that the body as simply body, the "natural body," was discovered. No wonder, then, that Japanese who had become Christians in the 1890s and early 1900s soon turned to naturalism. The flesh and the sexual desire that they explored had been produced by the repression of the body.

One exception was Shiga Naoya* (1883–1971). Interestingly, Shiga had been a disciple of Uchimura Kanzō, and it was in the process of a confrontation with Uchimura that he emerged as a novelist. Shiga described this process in his essay, "An Impure Mind" ("*Nigotta Atama,*" 1911).

> I had been an easy-going child, both physically and psychologically, until my encounter with Christianity. I loved athletics of every type . . . baseball, tennis, boating, gymnastics, lacrosse . . . and I was only lazy when it came to studying. I would come home from school at night so hungry that I would consume six or seven bowls of rice; I then retired to my room in a state of exhaustion. Sitting at my desk was a pure formality, since I fell asleep immediately. Most of my days were spent like this.

* Shiga Naoya's works included many short prose narratives and the long *Anya koro* (*A Dark Night's Passing,* tr. 1976). Donald Keene notes that although not all of Shiga's work was in the *watakushi-shōsetsu* vein, he was best known for this type of writing and it was "to his writings that authors who chose the genre most often turned. . . ." (Keene, *Dawn to the West,* p. 459.)

All this changed completely when I came into contact with Christianity.

What prompted my conversion was a very simple matter. One of the tutors in our household had become baptized while participating in an evangelical movement and this provided all the motivation I needed. My life, however, was completely transformed by the event. I stopped participating in sports. There was no specific reason for this. On the one hand, such things had simply come to seem insignificant to me, and on the other, I began to want to distinguish myself in some way from "all the others."

On the very evening of my conversion I went to the secretary of the Academic Reform Committee and asked to withdraw from the committee. I reiterated the phrases of a social reformer whose speech I had once heard. The esprit de corps of a school, I told him, was not something which could be enhanced through the centripetal force of reform measures which originated purely externally (like the resolution we had passed that day)—rather, change should be impelled by the natural centrifugal force generated by concentration at the center. I finally persuaded him to let me withdraw from the committee. I was delighted with myself. I experienced a kind of pride I had never known before. I, who at that time had not a single wound that needed to be healed through religion, was the recipient of this one and only benefit thanks to Christianity. The activities of my friends came to seem more and more absurd in my eyes. I began to read when I returned home from school. Biographies, poetry, sermons—I read broadly in these areas. Of course I had to some extent cultivated a habit of reading before this, but my interests were exclusively in fiction and I had abhorred serious books.

All was well for a time. Then I began to suffer. I became oppressed by sexual desire.[15]

Some readers of this passage may conclude that Shiga's encounter with Christianity was purely superficial. But is it not also possible that only the all-too-healthy Shiga grasped what constituted the world of Christianity, a Christianity which could reduce those sound in mind and body to a state of sickness and enfeeblement? As Nietzsche observed in *The Anti-Christ*, "Christianity would become master over *beasts of prey*: its method is to make them *sick*; enfeeblement is the Christian recipe for *taming*, for 'civilizing.' "[16]

For Shiga it was Christianity's prohibition against "adultery" which alone proved to be a serious problem. He did not see the

Christian conception of adultery as pertaining only to sexual pro-miscuity, but also to homoeroticism which was, in fact, commonly accepted in Japan at that time. Within the framework of Christian thought, homosexual relations were defined as a perversion for the first time. When Freud, for example, characterized the sexuality of children as polymorphous perversity, he relied on a notion of perversion which was produced by the Judaeo-Christian tradition. Psychoanalysis is rooted in this notion. In Christian dogma, which recognizes only one body—that which is the opposite of spirit— the body itself is seen as a perversion. Thus Shiga's antagonism to Christianity did not develop on logical grounds. What he perceived in Christianity was an absolutism which sought to centralize the diverse and polymorphous body (desire). Shiga perceived that to become a subject in the Christian sense entailed violent repression. While Shiga's literary colleagues were striving to ground their work in "self-consciousness," Shiga knew that that consciousness was at best "an impure mind." Insofar as self-consciousness, the uni-fied self, and subjectivism are seen as the points of departure for modern Japanese literature, Shiga represents a reaction against the perversion upon which they were based. His literature grew out of the doubts he harbored toward the notion of a unified self. In "The Diary of Claudius" (*Kuroodeiusu no nikki*, 1912), for example, Shiga describes an astonishing murder. The first-person narrator (*jibun*, or Claudius) sleeps beside his brother one autumn night when they are out hunting. Although he had not been remotely conscious of a desire to murder his brother, he had the following dream.

> I lay in bed thinking, but I was so exhausted from the day that be-fore realizing it I had dropped off to sleep. It was at just the moment when one is poised between dream and waking. Before I had reached a deep slumber I was startled by a strange voice. I opened my eyes to find that the lamp had gone out and that my brother was groaning. I realized in an instant that he was having a nightmare. He let out a horrible, chilling scream, as if he were being strangled. I, too, was terrified. Thinking to wake him I began to get out of bed again and was halfway out from under my quilts when a strange fantasy floated into my mind. I was shocked. For in this fantasy I was the person strangling my brother in his dream. As soon as I began to imagine it, I felt as if I could see myself taking shape—vividly, terrifyingly—in the darkness of the room. At the same time, I experienced the sen-sations of the murderer. I saw myself as a fiendish being. I had done

something fiendish. . . . At the moment when I thought the deed wa. done I intensified my stranglehold on my brother's neck like a man half-crazed. . . . this was the vision of myself that I perceived quite clearly. . . .

I felt somehow uneasy about all of this the next morning, but my brother began to discuss our plans for hunting that day as if he had no recollection of having had a nightmare. This reassured me. Still, from time to time the fantasy came back to me, and when it did I felt disturbed.[17]

To have a dream of killing one's brother is not unusual, nor even to take such a dream for reality. But Shiga is describing a different phenomenon: the lack of a clearly differentiated boundary between his own personality and his brother's. The nature of the phenomenon Shiga is describing has been discussed by Merleau-Ponty.

It is the case of a little girl, who, when seated beside her maid and another little girl, seemed uneasy and unexpectedly slapped her companion. When asked why, she answered that it was her companion who was naughty and who hit her. The child's air of sincerity ruled out any deliberate ruse. We have here a manifestly aggressive child who gives an unprovoked slap and explains herself right afterward by saying that it is the other child who slapped her. . . . The child's own personality is at the same time the personality of the other, that indistinction of the two personalities that makes transitivism possible; this presupposes an entire structure in the child's consciousness.[18]

The quality that Merleau-Ponty describes may be the basis for the frequent characterizations of Shiga's work as having a childlike or primitive aspect. What I wish to call attention to, however, is the way in which Shiga's work displays a bodily sensibility which precedes the distinction between the self and the other. Ichikawa Hiroshi has defined that site called the body as a "knot in a web of relationships generated simultaneously in many different directions." He states that "to posit a dualism of substance between body and spirit is to transform the relationship between the two (as well as the relationship between the self and matter or other persons) into a purely external one which disguises the fundamentally relational nature of personal existence."[19]

While many novelists who have adapted the theme of Shakespeare's *Hamlet* have interpreted it as a drama of self-consciousness, Shiga turned such interpretations inside-out. He understood intuitively that Shakespearean tragedy had nothing to do with Greek tragedy, that it could only have been a product of Christian theology. He saw clearly the inversion involved in making a subject of God the autonomous subject. Shiga's relationship with Uchimura Kanzō was not "a brief case of the measles." Nor was he simply ignorant of Christianity—he was engaged in a fundamental struggle with it. He perceived a kind of absolutism in Uchimura's thought which was directed, first and foremost, toward the body. For Uchimura's autonomous subject existed as a form of absolute domination over the polymorphous body of polytheism. As Nietszche wrote,

> The assumption of one single subject is perhaps unnecessary; perhaps it is just as permissible to assume a multiplicity of subjects, whose interactions and struggle is the basis of our thought and our consciousness in general? A kind of aristocracy of "cells" in which dominion resides? To be sure, an aristocracy of equals, used to ruling jointly and understanding how to command?[20]

Also,

> The body and physiology the starting point: why?—we gain the correct idea of the nature of our subject—unity, namely as regents at the head of a communality (not as "souls" or "life forces"), also of the dependence of these regents upon the ruled and of an order of rank and division of labor as the conditions that make possible the whole and its parts. In the same way, how living unities continually arise and die and how the "subject" is not eternal. . . . The danger of the direct questioning of the subject *about* the subject and of all self-reflection of the spirit lies in this, that it could be useful and important for one's activity to interpret oneself *falsely*. That is why we question the body and reject the evidence of the sharpened senses: we try, if you like, to see whether the inferior parts themselves cannot enter into communication with us.[21]

Nietzsche's words might be seen as summarizing the essence of Shiga's rejoinder to Uchimura. Yet even Shiga's consciousness, like that of Nietzsche, was grounded in the "disease" of Christianity. Shiga's writings are confessions, and they have often been attacked for that very reason. But those Japanese writers who have described Shiga as "the supreme egotist" are off the mark. Shiga's is a world of plural selves. How ironic that his writings, which have nothing in common with the concept of a unitary self or subjectivity, have been labeled the products of an I-novelist! Shiga, no whit different from those who have tried to banish confession from Japanese fiction while participating in that system themselves, had to struggle against the system of confession from within the confessional form.

The inversion of semiotic constellation that took place in the third decade of the Meiji period emerges in relief when we view it from Shiga's perspective. For it was in tandem with the consolidation of the modern state that the subject of modern Japanese literature and religion was established. Thus, the contradictions within polytheism that troubled the young Uchimura had their parallels in other areas. As Uchimura wrote, "Lord, father, and teacher: these constitute a trinity for the young man of today. He never thinks of one as superior to the other. Nothing causes him more anguish than to try to decide, if all three were about to drown and he had the power to save only one, which one he would save."[22] In the feudal period, however, such things were seen as merely formal contradictions. In the Tokugawa power structure, where emperor, shogun, and *han* daimyo coexisted, precisely the same problem might have arisen. Although the Mito scholars attempted to resolve the contradiction by elaborating a philosophy of reverence for the emperor which clarified the hierarchical relationship between the three, in practice the distinction was left a highly ambiguous one. Although contradictions existed, they did not generate actual conflict.

It was after Perry's arrival that the potential contradiction between these forces was actualized; through the Meiji Restoration a government was established which proclaimed the supreme authority of the emperor. The Satsuma-Chōshū oligarchy maintained control over this government in actuality, while other groups opposed them. In this sense (although one very different from Uchimura's) there was a kind of "conflict among gods" competing for the loyalty and identification of the early Meiji population. It was not until the third decade of Meiji that the implementation of policies of homogenization and centralization led to the establishment of a modern state. Naturally this state was the creation of the already existing power structure. But during the very same period, from among those who opposed this power structure, emerged the formations of the subject and interiority. From the start they were mutually implicated.

When contemporary scholars of literature speak of the struggle of Meiji writers to establish a modern self, they merely confirm an ideology in which we are already thoroughly steeped. They set up an opposition between the state, or political power, and faithfulness to interiority, or the self, unaware that "interiority" is itself politics and that it is a manifestation of absolute authority. Those devoted to the state and those devoted to interiority complement each other.

It was in the face of the overwhelming dominance of the West that the establishment of both the modern state and interiority in the third decade of Meiji became ineluctable. That these developments took place should not be the focus of our critique. What we can criticize are contemporary modes of thought which accept these products of an inversion as natural. In every case scholars go back to the Meiji period to establish their foundations. While the images such scholarship constructs often conflict with each other, in conflicting they also complement each other, working together to camouflage their real origins. It is not enough for us now to revise our histories of literature. We must seek to expose the historicity of that very "literature," of literature as a system which ceaselessly reproduces itself.

Afternote to Chapter 3

Uchimura Kanzō presents us with an example of the dialectical process through which the "subject" emerges in the condition of "being subject to the Lord." Uchimura replaced the feudal loyalty of retainer to lord with loyalty to the Christian Lord. The modern Japanese subject, however, emerged through the conflation of this subject, whose historical origins had been forgotten, with the psychological ego. In actuality almost all the representative writers and intellectuals of modern Japan abandoned Christianity for an Emersonian transcendentalism or humanist socialism. As I discuss in chapter 5, Japanese Christianity in the Meiji period did not penetrate into the masses as did the Jesuit Christianity of the sixteenth century, but merely spread among the intelligentsia together with a general atmosphere of modernity and Westernization. If, nevertheless, we assert that Christianity was indispensable to the formation of modern Japanese literature, it was because of the influence of Uchimura Kanzō. Only in Uchimura do we find a thoroughly consistent Christian subjectivity. For Uchimura to be a subject meant to reject the authority of anything (including the state and the church) other than God. This attitude made Uchimura doubly isolated: first in his dramatic confrontation with the emperor system and imperialism, and secondly (in his later years) in his critical position vis-à-vis modern humanism and socialism.

Many of the leading modern writers—Arishima Takeo, Masamune Hakuchō, Osanai Kaoru, Shiga Naoya and so forth—spent a period of time studying with Uchimura. Their rejection of Christianity was a betrayal of Uchimura as a person. It required not that they simply move along with shifting intellectual currents, but that they engage in a fundamental, philosophical confrontation with Uchimura's thought. Among these writers who rejected Christianity, Shiga Naoya's role has been largely ignored. This is because Shiga appears to be a writer who lacked a basic understanding of Christianity. In Shiga's writings the Japanese word *kibun* (which might be translated as mood, feeling, or, in German, *Stimmung*) predominates and appears to exist quite independently from the ego. When Shiga writes, in Japanese, "*to omou*," this should not be translated as it usually is into the English "I think," but rather as "I feel," or, even more accurately, as "It thinks in me," or "It feels in me." Although mood is often seen as being arbitrary and capricious, in Shiga it entails a coercive force. For Shiga subjectivity only exists as "being subject to It." This "It" might be analogous to the Freudian Es (the id) or to that impersonal subjectivity "Es," the term Heidegger gave to "Being."

Although Shiga has been seen as a prototypical writer of "I-novels" or *watakushi-shōsetsu*, we cannot find this phenomenon in other *watakushi-shōsetsu*. For these writers the psychological ego is the subject matter of the *watakushi-shōsetsu*. However, for Shiga, the subject exists only in terms of "being subject to It," or, conversely, we might say that there appears to be no subjectivity in Shiga's writings. But it is important to note that this represents an inversion of Uchimura's thought and could only have emerged through Shiga's struggle against Uchimura. It is for this reason that Shiga was held in awe by those like Akutagawa Ryūnosuke and Kobayashi Hideo, who had rejected the *watakushi-shōsetsu*, and even by Marxist writers.

4 Sickness As Meaning

1

The white peak of Fuji, the green isle of Enoshima
Gazing upon them we now shed tears
To the brave souls of the boys who died at twelve
We will dedicate our hearts and minds

This song is known to everyone. When we hear it, we all envision the moving and pitiful story of the Shichirigahama Incident upon which the song is based. The incident involved six students from Zushi Junior High School who were drowned in a boat accident at Shichirigahama in January 1908 (Meiji 4). I had never given second thought to what had really happened in this incident until I read the novel *Shichirigahama: One Man's Fate* by Miyauchi Kan'ya.

At the time of the drownings, a Mr. Ishizuka, a teacher who had been the dormitory supervisor, resigned from his job to take responsibility for the incident. He eventually drifted to Okayama, married, and took on his wife's family name. The novel was written by this teacher's son, now an elderly, little-known writer, as an attempt to elucidate the real nature of the events. According to Miyauchi, one day when his father had been absent from the dormitory six unruly junior high school students had taken a boat out to sea, without permission, in order to hunt sea birds and enjoy a feast, and had drowned in an accident. As dormitory supervisor, Ishizuka was naturally held responsible. Since resignation of a supervisor to take responsibility for an accident is common enough even today, one can only suspect there was another reason why this incident became mythologized almost overnight. It is not unusual for the death of a student in a protest march, for example, to become mythologized overnight as a revolutionary martyrdom. In the mythologizing of the Shichirigahama Incident, however, there seems to lurk some kind of ambiguous inversion.

To be more specific, it was the above-mentioned song, written by a teacher named Misumi Suzuko at the Kamakura Women's

Academy and sung at the funeral by female students (to the melody of the Protestant hymn "When We Go Home") that suddenly transformed the nature of the incident and transferred it to a different level of meaning. What kind of social process was this, that mythologized and thoroughly aestheticized this instance of adolescent impetuosity and foolishness that might have occurred anywhere? One might say first of all that the mythologizing process was based on Christian song, its lyrics and melody. One might also say that what constituted this incident from beginning to end—with the exception of the "fact" of the fatal accident—was "literature."

Without necessarily intending to do so, Miyauchi Kan'ya's interpretation uncovered a scandalous perversion that underlay the mythologizing of the incident. In his view, it was the puritanism and self-deception of Misumi Suzuko, who composed the lyrics of "The white peak of Fuji," that lay at the root of this incident. Thirty-nine-year-old Suzuko had moved to Kamakura to be treated for tuberculosis and was working there as a teacher. In the interests of "improved health" Suzuko hoped to marry. According to Miyauchi, she was obviously unaware of the extent of her self-deception in giving this rationale. The accident happened while the superintendent of the school, who was trying to arrange Suzuko's marriage to the dormitory supervisor Ishizuka, detained the latter in Kamakura to discuss the matter. Although Ishizuka, ten years younger than Suzuko, had accepted the match, he was shunned by Suzuko after the incident. He resigned from his position and withdrew from public life, not only to take responsibility for the accident, but because he was overwhelmed by Suzuko's rejection. Although I do not wish to deny that the popular song was a product of Misumi's puritanism and repressed sexuality, in her case as well as Ishizuka's, we can also observe something about the functioning of Meiji "literature."

Ishizuka, who later took a position at a junior high school in Sakhalin, gave strict orders to his son not to read novels until after he married. When the son disobeyed him and secretly bought an anthology of world fiction, his father burned the books in the garden. The son's reaction was to aspire to a literary career, and he has spent his life as a little-known writer, now in his old age.

On the basis of his father's abnormal fear of fiction, Miyauchi speculates that Ishizuka had been strongly influenced by Tokutomi Roka's extremely popular novel, *The Cuckoo* (*Hototogisu*, 1900) around the time of the incident: under the sway of romantic fantasies stimulated by the novel, Ishizuka resided in Zushi and agreed to marry a teacher, ten years his senior, who was afflicted with consumption. In studying the novel carefully, Miyauchi discovered a web of relationships linking the novel to the Shichirigahama Incident: for example, that the boat used by the six junior high school students had once belonged to the warship "Matsushima," which was later mysteriously lost at sea while bearing as a passenger the youngest brother of General Ōyama Iwao's oldest daughter, the model for the heroine Namiko in *The Cuckoo*. Hatanaka, the obscure, aging writer who represents Miyauchi in *Shichirigahama: One Man's Fate*, finally reaches the following conclusion:

> In any case, the reason he had been born in this world, and had spent his life aspiring, almost against his own best interests, to become a writer, could be attributed to the influence of the novel *The Cuckoo*. Hatanaka started to believe this. And in believing thus, he felt the fire of rancor toward his dead father and the Shichirigahama Incident— which had burned secretly in his breast ever since he had realized that his life had been a failure—being extinguished rapidly.[1]

Such a resolution may be sufficient for this protagonist, and the problems of the "Shichirigahama Incident" may end here. Yet I could not help feeling frustrated upon reading that the protagonist's burning rancor had been extinguished as a result of his belief that everything had its source in the novel *The Cuckoo*. The writer finds consolation in the belief that *his* literature originated in "literature." While demythologizing the incident, he fails to objectify the mythologizing function of "literature" that was at work in this incident. He finds relief in discovering that his own life had been enveloped in the myth of "literature" from beginning to end. Of course, Miyauchi is not alone: most writers ensconce themselves comfortably within the confines of literature without being aware of it. "In the beginning, there was literature." The myth of literature is that it appears to us as a beginning, even though the beginning of "literature" is derivative.

True, the "Shichirigahama Incident" was mythologized by a female teacher and her students, and by the society of the time which was all too willing to accept this. I would prefer to problematize, however, neither the people involved nor the society of the time, but *The Cuckoo* itself. *The Cuckoo* was one of the most widely read novels at the end of the Meiji period, along with *A Woman's Pedigree* (*Onna Keizu*), written in 1907 by Izumi Kyōka. The popularity of this novel was due, not merely to its depiction of Meiji mores, but to a "contagious" inversion condensed within it.

2

As is widely known, the heroine of Tokutomi Roka's *The Cuckoo* (*Hototogisu*, 1898–1900, Meiji 31 to Meiji 33)[2] is Namiko, a woman dying of tuberculosis. She has lost her mother to the same illness and is raised by a strong-willed stepmother who treats her badly. The novel thus follows a traditional Japanese narrative pattern of the "mistreated step-child" (*mamako ijime*). Namiko's mother-in-law is also cruel to her, this too following the traditional pattern. As Yanagita Kunio has pointed out, we should not link the pervasiveness of this narrative pattern to the actual existence of children mistreated by their stepmothers. These tales are beloved even by those who have never experienced such mistreatment. The pattern is thought to have emerged around the time when the patrilineal household system was established. The unnaturalness of the system (which is not to say that the matrilineal system is more natural) produced a need for this kind of narrative. *The Cuckoo*, moreover, rather than undermining the system which sustained the mistreated stepchild narratives, is completely dependent on it. As modern literature, *The Cuckoo* displays none of the sharp inversion found in the works of Futabatei Shimei, Kitamura Tōkoku, and Kunikida Doppo. It is a work perfectly suited to the *shimpa** stage.

We should note, however, that it is neither her stepmother nor her mother-in-law nor any other villain that causes Namiko's death, but tuberculosis itself. It is tuberculosis that places her beyond the reach of her husband Takeo. It is neither interpersonal conflict nor "interiority" that causes Namiko's isolation, but invisible tubercle bacilli that bring about the distance between her and the world. In other words tuberculosis functions as a metaphor in this novel. And the chief interest of the work lies in the fact that Namiko wastes away *beautifully* because of tuberculosis.

*Shimpa, literally "new wave" drama, flourished in the late nineteenth and early twentieth centuries. Characterized by the combination of *kabuki*-style acting techniques and narratives dealing with contemporary subject matter, this form of theater was originally developed to diffuse the political ideology of the People's Rights movement. Such explicitly political narratives were gradually supplanted by highly charged plots dealing with domestic conflict and other popular themes. The term "shimpa" is often synonymous with melodrama.

She was of a fair and clear complexion, and though her eyebrows were a little too close together and her cheeks were somewhat thin, she seemed to be as gentle in nature as she was slender and graceful in figure. She was not like the plum-blossom, daring to bloom in the bleak north wind, nor like the cherry-flower, whose petals are blown hither and thither like butterflies in the spring morn. She was, indeed, like the shy daisy dimly discovering itself in the dusk of a summer eve. . . .

But his feeling toward her could never be changed. It was sunk deep in his breast, and night after night he saw, through his dream over the destruction of the Peiyang Squadron and his death in the battle, the face of the sick girl wrapped in a snow-white shawl.

Three months passed with no news about her. Was she still living? No? Yes, she was. As never a day passed without thinking of her, so it must be with her, too. Did they not pledge to live and die together?

Takeo thought this. And he thought again of the time he had seen her last. Ah, where was she who, on that dim evening at Zushi, cried after him to come back soon, as she stood at the gate to see him off? Pensively he looked up when he felt as if a slender form in a white shawl were about to step out of the clear moon.[3]

This description of Namiko's appearance is typical of romantic writing. Although the connection between romanticism and tuberculosis has been often pointed out, according to Susan Sontag's *Illness as Metaphor*, tuberculosis had already acquired romantic associations in the West by the middle of the eighteenth century. As the myth of tuberculosis spread, the illness became an index of gentility, delicacy, and sensitivity among those with social pretensions. Shelley, suffering from tuberculosis, wrote to Keats, who had the same illness, that tuberculosis was especially fond of those endowed with great poetic sensibility. The visage of the consumptive became the new model for the aristocratic visage at a time when the aristocracy, having lost its power, had to rely on its image.[4]

According to René Dubos, the mood of illness was so widespread in Europe at this time, that good health was almost considered a sign of vulgarity.[5] Those who liked to think of themselves as sensitive actually aspired to becoming consumptive. Byron, for example, said that he wished to die of consumption, and Alexander Dumas, although sturdy and active, tried to appear feeble and sick, as though he were suffering from consumption.

The tuberculosis that was widespread in eighteenth-century

European society was a tragic reality. The image of tuberculosis, however, was far removed from that reality, existing as a "meaning" which inverted the real. In Japan, tuberculosis, or even illness in general, had never existed as a "meaning" capable of producing such an inversion of values. As I will explain later, this could only happen within the Judeo-Christian context. Thus, although the mythologizing of tuberculosis in the West occurred only in the modern era, its roots were very deep. As Sontag says,

> With the new mobility (social and geographical) made possible in the eighteenth century, worth and station are not given; they must be asserted. They were asserted through new notions about clothes ("fashion") and new attitudes toward illness. Both clothes (the outer garment of the body) and illness (a kind of interior décor of the body) became tropes for new attitudes toward the self.[6]

One might say that it was this kind of mode or décor that was disseminated by *The Cuckoo*. Two of its characters—Namiko, the eldest daughter of an army general-viscount, and Kawashima Takeo, a navy lieutenant-baron—are endowed with an aristocratic image. Zushi, their residence, corresponded to places in the West that became famous as sanatoriums. What fascinated the teacher Ishizuka, who had been forced to resign in the Shichirigahama Incident, were precisely these images. Later, Hori Tatsuo was to similarly transform Karuizawa into a fashionable resort. Tuberculosis was mythologized, not because of the existence of large number of invalids, but as an effect of modern literature. Quite apart from the spread of tuberculosis itself, it was the "meaning" of tuberculosis that was contagious.

As Sontag maintains, what one asserted through the garment of tuberculosis were "new attitudes toward the self." There has been an embarrassing degree of collusion between Japanese modern literature and tuberculosis that has extended right up to the emergence of the Third New Wave writers (*Daisan no Shinjin*) in the 1950s. What is embarrassing is not tuberculosis itself, of course, but the meaning of tuberculosis. This can be traced to *The Cuckoo*.

When Sontag came to Japan recently, she claimed that there had been no romanticism in Japan in the nineteenth century—an impression she had probably picked up in conversation. This is perfectly true in the sense that, during the greater part of the nineteenth century, Japan was still in the Edo period. We might of course criticize Sontag's uninformed preconception by pointing to the existence of the Japanese romantic movement in literature at the end of the nineteenth century. Yet to do that would be to essentialize romanticism and to perceive it in a linear historical order. Regardless of whether or not we label *The Cuckoo* a "romantic" novel, it is certain that by the time it was written in 1898 a fundamental inversion had already taken place. To try to dispense with this issue by using the label "romanticism" is to lose sight of the problem. For what we find in condensed form in late-nineteenth-century Japan is an inversion typical of Western culture, of which romanticism is only one part.

As mentioned repeatedly before, what I have sought to examine in this argument is not "literary history" but the origin of "literature." To understand the kind of perversion involved in the meaning tuberculosis (and even life and death) attained in *The Cuckoo*, one need only compare it with *A Sixfoot Sickbed* ("*Byōshō Rokushaku*"), written almost contemporaneously by Masaoka Shiki.

> A six-foot sickbed—this is my entire world. And yet this six-foot sickbed is too wide for me. If I stretch my hand a little, I can touch the tatami mat, but I can't stretch my legs beyond the end of the futon to make my body comfortable. There are times I can't move my body at all because of extreme pain. Pain, agony, crying, anesthesia, . . . how futile my efforts to obtain a little comfort, to find a path to life within the path to death! And yet as long as I am alive, I want to say what I have to say. These days I can only read newspapers and magazines, and sometimes I can't even read these because of the pain, but even so I find matters that anger me, matters that irritate me, and sometimes even matters that make me happy enough to forget the pain. Such is the life of an invalid who has been bedridden for six years and knows nothing about the world.[7]

A romantic image of tuberculosis is not to be found in this work. Shiki also claims that traditionally most of the famous and successful writers and artists in Japan had been blessed with long life and that it must be no different for their counterparts in other countries.[8] In short, he finds nothing valuable in the notion of the genius who dies young. Of course, the reform of tanka and haiku by Shiki was not unrelated to the reality and the physical conditions imposed upon him by tuberculosis. He nonetheless remained untouched by tuberculosis as "meaning."

I mentioned before that the "landscape" discovered by Kunikida Doppo was of a different order from Shiki's "sketches" and that the former was based on a certain internal inversion. The same can be said of tuberculosis. The above sentences by Shiki are a "sketch" of tuberculosis. They recognize pain as pain, ugliness as ugliness, and maintain a practical attitude toward life rather than a "longing for death." In comparison, *The Cuckoo*, written almost contemporaneously, renders tuberculosis a metaphor.

3

I have already talked about what was hidden by the establishment of the systems of knowledge in the third decade of the Meiji period. A system and what it conceals are mutually related. The two define each other and are implicated in each other in such a way as to render any discussion of the phenomenon of inversion during this period problematic. It is a phenomenon impossible to grasp simply from one angle. For example, the aestheticization of tuberculosis, far from being antithetical to knowledge, virtually came into existence along with it.

In *The Cuckoo*, for example, Takeo's mother says the following:

> "I think this is the most dreadful of all diseases. You know, Take, the Governor Togo's family. The mother of that boy whom you used to quarrel with died of consumption about two years ago. And Togo-san himself died of the same disease only six months ago. You know that, don't you? And then his son . . . also died of it lately. They all got it from one person. I can tell you many more cases like this. So, Take, we have to look out very sharply; if not, it will have serious results." [9]

Here, the clinical knowledge that tuberculosis is a contagious disease resulting from the tubercle bacilli is already presupposed. Koch's discovery of the tubercle bacillus was in 1882, or Meiji 17. It was this knowledge which was the cause of the divorce and estrangement of Namiko and Takeo. The two were separated, that is, not by tuberculosis itself, but by the understanding of tuberculosis at that time. What Nietzsche would call the "subject function" was carried out in this novel by the tubercle bacillus. But was this sort of knowledge really scientific? Feyerabend, in *Anti-Method*, goes so far as to say that throughout the history of science it has always been propaganda that created the belief that a particular theory was the truth. Feyerabend's research centered on Galileo but perhaps the circumstances brought about by the discovery of the tubercle bacillus illustrate his thesis even more plainly.

Until Koch discovered the tubercle bacillus, tuberculosis was believed in the West to be hereditary. However, not only did the prevention of the disease become possible when a vaccine was perfected in 1921, but the discovery of streptomycin caused the death rate of those stricken with tuberculosis to fall remarkably. So much is common knowledge. But what I would like to call attention to is the fact that the discovery that tuberculosis resulted from microorganisms created a new paradigm which changed medical thought as it had existed until then. This was the victory of the doctrine of specific etiology advanced by Pasteur and Koch.

> The germ theory, and more generally the doctrine of specific etiology of disease, broke for almost a century the spell of the Hippocratic tradition. The core of the new doctrine was that each disease had a well-defined cause and that its control could best be achieved by attacking the causative agent, or, if this was not possible, by focusing treatment on the affected part of the body. This was a far cry from the emphasis placed by ancient medicine on the patient as a whole, and on his total environment. The contrast between the two points of view manifested itself in a dramatic manner during the controversies stimulated by Pasteur's communications before the Paris Academy of Medicine.[10]

The discovery of the "pathogen" created a mirage which made it seem as though all contagious diseases could now be cured through medical science. However, the contagious diseases of the middle ages and modern times in the West had virtually disappeared by the time the "pathogen" was discovered. The reorganization of many European cities, beginning with the construction of sewer systems, was largely responsible for this, although those who advocated urban reconstruction knew nothing about bacteria or hygiene. The same can be said about tuberculosis.

> During a widespread epidemic of tuberculosis, for example, the most susceptible are likely to die young, leaving no progeny. In contrast, many of those who survive are genetically endowed with a high level of natural resistance which they pass on to their descendants. The low tuberculosis mortality prevailing in the Western world at the present time is in part the result of the selective process brought about by the great epidemic of the nineteenth century which weeded out the susceptible stock.[11]

Thus the tubercle bacillus is not the "cause" of tuberculosis. Almost all human beings are infected with either the tuberculosis bacillus or some other pathogen. We coexist with microorganisms, and indeed without them we cannot even digest food to nourish ourselves. Having a pathogen within the body and becoming ill are entirely different matters.

The spread of tuberculosis in the West from the sixteenth to the nineteenth century was not at all caused by the tubercle bacillus, nor was its decrease necessarily attributable to the development of medical science. Yet it will not do to ask what the ultimate cause was. The very thought of fixing a single, original cause is theological and metaphysical. As Dubos says, the image of a "battle between humans and microorganisms" is a thoroughly theological notion. Germs are, so to speak, a form of invisible, ubiquitous "evil." For example, tooth decay is often illustrated as being the work of small devils. But this creates an illusion. In fact, brushing one's teeth is an insignificant factor compared to the role of heredity in determining an individual's susceptibility to tooth decay. It is simply that toothbrushing has acquired a cultural value, of a different order entirely.

To be sure, Koch discovered something we call the tubercle bacillus. Identifying this as the cause of tuberculosis, however, is propaganda. Moreover, the reason this theory gained widespread acceptance was because it was a form of theological ideology. It was during precisely the same period we have been examining— the third decade of the Meiji period—that this theory was widely diffused. What permeates *The Cuckoo* is the ideological dimension of this theory. Tuberculosis exists in *The Cuckoo* as a sort of original sin. This is why Namiko is fascinated by Christianity. The novel was an ingenious form of propaganda and possessed an infectiousness far exceeding that of the tubercle bacillus.

4

Tuberculosis has been cloaked in a literary image ever since the publication of *The Cuckoo*. The problem I wish to consider now, however, has to do with the imagery of modern medicine itself. The two are interrelated and have a common source.

Susan Sontag came to realize through her experience as a cancer patient the degree to which illness is used as a metaphor, and she medical treatment resides is altogether theological. Conversely, the medical schema is the source of the theological schema.

According to Hippocrates' view of medicine, illness is not traced back to either a specific or local cause, but is regarded as disturbance in the state of equilibrium among various internal factors which regulates the working of the body and mind. Furthermore, what heals the disease is not the doctor but the natural healing powers of the patient. This is, in one sense, a principle of Eastern medicine. Something similar to the repression of Hippocratic medicine by theological and metaphysical thinking in the West took place in an extremely short time span during the Meiji period.

For example, in dealing with the very same disease of tuberculosis, *The Cuckoo* adopts a theological schema, while Masaoka Shiki's *A Sixfoot Sickbed* merely states bluntly that illness is painful. This brings to mind the following words of Nietzsche:

> Buddhism, to repeat once more, is a hundred times colder, sincere, and more objective. It no longer needs to make its suffering, its capacity for pain, decent by the interpretation of sin,—it says simply what it thinks, "I suffer." For the barbarian, on the contrary, suffering in itself is no decent thing: he needs first an explanation in order to confess to himself that he suffers (his instinct points him rather to the denial of suffering, to silent endurance). Here the word "devil" was a God-send: people had an overpowerful and terrible enemy,—they did not need to be ashamed of suffering from such an enemy.[14]

Of course, whether or not Masaoka Shiki was a Buddhist is irrelevant here. Similarly, the fact that Tokutomi Roka was a Christian is of no concern. What is important is that the structure of *The Cuckoo* viewed in relation to *Six-Foot Sickbed* appears thoroughly twisted and that as a consequence the novel was contagious.

5

As is widely known, after the Meiji period Eastern medicine was systematically eliminated. Western medical science became the only form of medicine, and forms of medical treatment which were not sanctioned by the state were thereafter regarded as folk remedies or superstition. There was no other domain in which knowledge and nonknowledge were so blatantly segregated.

Naturally, Meiji medicine as system may appear to us to be

just one part of the Meiji legal system. But when one considers the fact that the only form of Western learning that was sanctioned by the Edo government was Dutch medicine, and that the ideology which rendered the Meiji Restoration a form of bourgeois revolution was created entirely by scholars of Dutch learning, one can see that the acquisition of power by the Meiji proponents of Western medicine science, far from being partial, was in fact most symbolic. More than in any other area, it has been in modern medicine that "knowledge" has effectively constituted power. We are not conscious of this because we have become thoroughly acclimatized to the form of medical practice that has been institutionalized by the modern state. But Hattori Toshirō has described Japanese medicine as it appeared to Dutch doctors who visited Japan during the Edo period:

> The system of medicine in our country in those days differed from that of other countries in that anyone could freely choose to become a doctor and practice medicine. As a result, in the eyes of foreigners, this system appeared strange. Louis Frois had already pointed this out in the Muromachi period, and Charlevoix remarked that the Japanese doctor was a surgeon, a druggist, a pharmacist, and found it curious that a Japanese doctor could freely prescribe *and* administer medicine directly to the patient.
>
> Thumberg remarked that, in Japan, besides internal physicians and surgeons, there were moxa specialists who used herbs, acupuncture specialists who used needles, masseurs and masseuses who specialized in massage; even the common masseur who mingled in the street crowds and summoned customers with special yells was regarded as a doctor. Among these, the internal physician had the highest status and was the most learned.[15]

The reason the Dutch doctors found these things so strange was that by that time, Western medicine had already been centralized. In the case of France, Michel Foucault sees the origins of this in the establishment of the Royal Medical Society [Société Royale de Médecine] in 1776 by the government: the outbreak of epidemics and their research in the eighteenth century had necessitated medical information gathering, management, and control at the national level. Around this time, two myths were formed. One was the idea of nationalized medical care, which gave doctors the aura of priesthood. The other was the belief that illness would completely disappear once a healthy society was built.

of Suzuki Daisetsu, had already been mediated by Western philosophy. It is merely an effect of the inversion produced by linear
perspective that has produced our sense that Buddhism has existed
as a continuous tradition since ancient times or that it is something
completely other than Western modernity.

1

Historians of children's literature seem to agree that the birth of "truly modern children's literature" in Japan was marked by the emergence of Ogawa Mimei, who published "Akai Fune" (The red ship) in 1911. The advent of this "literature of the child's mind" has been regarded as representing the neo-romantic escape of writers from what poet Ishikawa Takuboku described as "our present state of confinement by the times" and also as the result of the influence of Western fin de siècle literature. This has become an accepted view among our writers of literary history. Among scholars of children's literature, however, the very fact that children's literature was derived from the poems, dreams, and regressive fantasies of adult writers remains the object of criticism. In other words children described in such literature are accused of not being "real children," but children as imagined by adults. For instance, Ogawa Mimei has been criticized by the scholar Inokuma Yōko as follows:

> In 1926, the world of Mimei's work changed dramatically. This was because the writer resolved the difficulties that had arisen from dividing his writing attention between novels and children's stories by announcing that he would from then on concentrate exclusively on children's stories. After this point, the imaginary world which had characterized Mimei's children's stories disappeared gradually, and was replaced by realistic portraits of children. At the same time, a strong flavor of moralism started to become apparent in his work.
>
> During the period when he saw children's tales as "my unique form of poetry," Mimei was able to celebrate children. This was because he felt children possessed special qualities which could, in turn, sustain his own imaginary world.
>
> When Mimei finally decided to write stories specifically designed for children, however, he could not avoid facing real children. He began to feel the necessity of "giving advice" to children so they would be able to live in harmony with their surroundings. In the face of real children, he could not help but notice that there were no children in

reality who possessed the qualities of naiv⟍   ⟋, gentleness,
and honesty possessed by the idealized⟋   ⟍us mind.

 We might say that neither in w⟍   ⟍s fantastic nor his moral-
istic children's stories did Mimei   ⟍e his ideas by putting himself
on the side of children: as we   ⟍ seen already, Mimei needed the
imaginary world of children' ⟍ories in order to describe his own inner
world, and once he gav⟍ ⟋ "my unique form of poetry" in order to
try writing "for the ⟍ ⟍e of" children, he instructed them, from the
viewpoint of adult⟍ on how to live harmoniously in the real world. In
both cases, Mir⟍ ⟍ failed to see the world through children's eyes.

 Even th⟍ ⟍gh Mimei's "children's stories" were fundamentally
marked by "children's absence," many others have followed in this
⟍writer's footsteps. This has been partly due to the original and unprecedented beauty of some of the works produced as "children's stories" by
Mimei, but most importantly, because many adults in modern Japan,
like Mimei, have failed to discover real children.[1]

In this passage Inokuma asserts that the child in Ogawa Mimei's
stories is no more than an inversion when considered from the
viewpoint of "real children." Yet while it may be perfectly true that
the children in Mimei's stories were produced through a certain
internal inversion, what we call "the child" was itself discovered
through such an inversion, and it was only after this that "real children" or "realistic children" could be seen. To critique the inversion
in Mimei's children when compared with "real children" serves
merely to obscure the nature of this inversion rather than to elucidate it. Despite the exhaustive attempts of historians of children's
literature to document the origin of children's literature in the Meiji
period, the nature of this "origin" itself has not been addressed.

 Although the objective existence of children seems self-evident,
the "child" we see today was discovered and constituted only recently. Landscapes, too, which seem to exist before our very eyes
were only discovered as "landscapes" in the third decade of the
Meiji period by writers whose "interiority" rejected what up until
then had been the external world. Since this time, landscape has
been perceived as what exists objectively, while realism has been
seen, either as the tracing of that objective existence or as the cap-
turing of a landscape which is even more "real." Yet there was a time
when "landscape" did not exist, and its discovery was predicated
on an inversion.

 As with "landscape," so with "the child." The two had similar "beginnings" and persist in a similar manner. In this sense it was neither unusual nor inappropriate that it should have been writers of the romantic school, such as Ogawa Mimei, who discovered "the child." What is perverse, rather, is the idea that "real children" exist. Moreover, to assert as Inokuma does that "the chief characteristic of Japanese children's literature is that, since the Meiji period, a majority of writers have conceived of their stories from the standpoint of the adult rather than the child," is clearly mistaken.[2] For one thing this is hardly a quality unique to Japanese children's literature: "the child" was originally discovered in the same manner in the West. Second and more importantly, we must bear in mind that the appearance of Japanese children's literature was premised upon the prior discovery of "literature," and thus, if it appeared later than in the West, it was simply because the establishment of "literature" itself took place later. Yet what I have chosen to focus on in the series of essays in this book has been neither the delayed development of modern Japanese literature nor its difference from Western literature, but rather the issue of literature as a system, whose growth was obscured because of the gradual nature of its evolution in the West, but which may be the object of concentrated investigation in Japan of the 1890s.

It is not surprising that the children's literature established by writers such as Ogawa Mimei and Suzuki Miekichi lagged behind "literature" by over ten years. For to look for some kind of historical continuity in "children's literature," in and of itself, is misguided. Furthermore, to base comparisons on the fact that children's literature was already well-established in the West by this time is absurd. We may say with certainty that no matter how much Japanese writers had read of this literature, no matter how much they were influenced by it, children's literature in Japan could never have been directly produced by this "influence." This has been demonstrated by the process through which literature itself was formed. Futabatei Shimei, for example, although he had been profoundly shaken by his reading of Russian literature, could not hold back the flow of Bakin and the *ninjōbon* style when he wrote *The Drifting Clouds*. No matter how inwardly oriented he might have been as a person, his writing *hand* went against him. His interiority or "self," that is to say, rather than existing a priori as something to be expressed, appeared as self-evident only with the establishment of that material form known as *genbun itchi*. As I have already noted, *genbun itchi* was not merely the transcription of speech to writing, but the creation of a new literary language. Therefore, the early experiments in which Yamada Bimyō and Futabatei Shimei simply wrote in the colloquial style were doomed to fade out once Mori Ōgai's "The Dancing Girl" appeared. Nor should we let ourselves forget that for readers of the time—even schoolchildren—*genbun itchi* was difficult to read. For example, Iwaya Sazanami, a writer affiliated with the *Kenyūsha* group and author of the highly acclaimed "Kogane-maru" (Meiji 24, 1891), defended his use of the *bungo* style in the work as follows:

> *Genbun itchi* is fundamentally quite unlike scribbling down the words of *rakugo* and *kōdan* story-tellers: it is one type of writing style, and therefore it is not sufficient to merely string together colloquial words. There must be variation in speed, density and pitch, and not a single one of the customary rhetorical elements may be lacking. Although an abundant use of new and colloquial words may make it appear easier to understand than other written styles, depending on how it is written, *genbun itchi* may be far more difficult to understand than a style in which literary and colloquial language are mixed (the *gazoku setchū* style). It is for this reason that, although I started with an attempt at *genbun-itchi* in writing *Kogane-maru*, I was led by certain considerations to change to a different style.[3]

Kan Tadamichi speculates that since "the creation of literature for children did not bring recognition either from the *bundan* or in society" at the time, Sazanami "might have been consciously assuming a literary pose in using such an elaborate style."[4] Yet this observation may more accurately describe contemporary writers of children's literature. At that time, regardless of whether or not he used *genbun itchi*, Iwaya Sazanami had discovered neither "literature" nor "the child." The fact that it was largely writers like Iwaya, affiliated with the *Kenyūsha* school, who wrote children's literature prior to Ogawa Mimei, suggests that we should regard the birth of "children's literature" in Japan not in terms of historical continuity but as a rupture or inversion and as the consolidation of a material form or system. The discovery of the child took place within the context of the discovery of landscape and interiority and cannot be confined to a matter of children's literature alone.

2

It is because the child seems to exist as fact before their very eyes that scholars of children's literature not only fail to question the concept of the child but try to find "the real child" in literature. The child, like landscape, is considered to have an objective existence that can be observed and studied, and this fact itself has become difficult to question. The further "objective" psychological studies concerning the child progress, the more we lose sight of the historicity of "the child" itself. Of course, children have existed since ancient times, yet "the child" as we conceive of it and objectify it did not exist prior to a particular period. The question is not what is elucidated by psychological research about children, but what is obscured by the very concept of "the child."

We may point to Van den Berg and Michel Foucault as psychologists who were the first to problematize "children," though from different angles. Both took the position that psychology itself must be seen as a historical phenomenon, and in so doing raised the question of the historicity of "the child." Van den Berg, in *The Changing Nature of Man*, claimed that "the child" did not exist before Rousseau and that it was Rousseau who was "the first to view the child as a child, to stop treating the child as an adult."[5] Rousseau wrote, in *Émile*, that "people do not know what children are. Since they hold mistaken notions about children, as arguments progress, they find themselves lost in a maze." Rousseau's discovery of the child may be compared to his discovery of the Alps, previously considered merely an obstruction, as an example of the beauty of nature, in the *Confessions*. In this sense, too, "the child" has been similar to a "landscape."

Van den Berg writes that Pascal's father began to educate the boy at an unusually early age by contemporary standards. A later example was Goethe, who was taught to write German, French, Greek, and Latin by the age of eight. In this sense the two were not treated as children. Needless to say, although the fame of these two men has survived to this day, they were not really exceptional in the way they were educated. Neither was this kind of education unique to the West. In Japan, too, among scholars of the Chinese classics training from early childhood was considered routine: one Confucian scholar in the Edo period gave lectures at the Shōheikō school while he was still in his teens. Whether or not the child was regarded as having the natural talent that would come to play a crucial role in the long term, that child was educated as a small adult. Although this type of education was obviously possible only in the families of scholars, the same could be said of other families. Even today, children of kabuki actors begin their training for the stage as children.

We should not regard the example of someone like Pascal as a "genius," no matter how precocious he may have been. It was only with the romantic movement in Europe that the concept of "genius" appeared. Eric Hoffer has pointed out that the so-called "geniuses" who flourished in Florence during the early Renaissance spent years as youthful apprentices to artisans and craftsmen. They did not have a childhood as we know it, nor were they treated as children. Despite later embellished accounts to the contrary, we should note that in the lives of these geniuses we cannot see the problem of youth and consequent maturation that would afflict the romantic genius. In this sense it was the appearance of "youth" that created the division between the child and the adult and conversely, the division guaranteed that a period of "youth" would inevitably appear. Psychologists who assume "development" and "matura-tion" to be self-evident fail to perceive that this division between childhood and adulthood is itself a historical product. It was not until "the child" came to exist that literature and amusements "for children" appeared. Yanagita Kunio was one of the first to notice this. He wrote:

> It seems that parents in the old days did not create playthings to give to their children. Some may wonder if this did not make the children feel sad, and why they still grew up playing cheerfully and vigorously. Yet the so-called children's culture of the past was very different from that of today. First, in contrast to the current system of dividing chil-dren by age group in elementary schools, elder children often took care of the younger ones. Not only did the older children take on the responsibility with enthusiasm since they became aware of their own growth through this process, but the younger ones also looked forward eagerly to joining the ranks of older children. Although this attitude has nearly died out, it was one force which made the games of old Japan easy to pass on and difficult to forget, and those of us who are now young adults are also grateful that various interesting games were handed down to us because of this.
>
> Another point of difference was that children had autonomy: by themselves they invented games, names for things, song lyrics, and

customs that were indescribably fascinating, the enjoyment of which could make one forget all one's cares, and which I will describe in more detail later.

Third, and not much appreciated these days, was children's imitation of adult behavior. With the exuberance of growing beings, children were particularly fond of imitation. In the old days adults, too, were simpler in their approach to life and had less to hide: by standing near adults and watching them intently, children naturally developed an understanding of what adults were doing. Moreover, since children would have to learn these activities anyway in the near future, adults may have intentionally allowed them to watch. Among the communal tasks there were originally many designed for youths, and the youths were especially close to children. When children reached the age of twelve or thirteen, they would prepare to enter the ranks of youths. Youths, for their part, would also try to hand over certain tasks to the younger children as soon as possible. The annual tug-of-war that is performed in rural Kyushu and Tohoku borders on being a children's game even today. The tug-of-war was originally a serious event that constituted part of the divinations held once each year, whose result was of great consequence. Although even the old men in the village come out to participate later in the night, before dark the event is left entirely to the children. Even the twelve and thirteen year old youths (with the exception of some particularly impulsive ones) will not involve themselves in it. Events like local sumo-wrestling tournaments or the *bon*-dance at village shrines have the same character: children considered these to be games for themselves, and thus in later years adults gradually retired from them.[6]

In these passages by Yanagita we glimpse the child "who was not treated as a child." As I have already noted, what Yanagita describes can be applied to children of the intellectual class as well as to children in rural communities. While differences in occupation and status may have existed among them, in the sense that they were not treated as children, they were all alike. Once Yanagita Kunio had come to recognize the child in the guise he described above, he also came to conceive of adults differently from adults as we think of them today. In other words he tried to perceive what had existed before children and adults were separated from each other.

Although it is only recently that we have started dealing with children as "children," the concept has become so self-evident that it is difficult to overcome the habit of applying this way of thinking to the past. Lévi-Strauss, for example, who struggled mightily to free himself from Eurocentrism and rejected the mythicized analogy between children, the primitive, and the mad, was nevertheless unable to free himself from the prejudices we find in the following statement: "Games are unknown to Nambikwara children. Sometimes they make objects from rolled or plaited straw, but their only form of amusement consists in wrestling matches, or playing tricks on each other, and their life is an imitation of adult behavior."[7]

In his book *Han hattatsu-ron* (Against development theory, 1977), Yamashita Tsuneo points out that in this passage Lévi-Strauss merely applies his own concept of "games" to the activities of Nambikwara children when he proclaims that games are "unknown" to them.[8] The other side of the coin is that adults in the Nabikawara tribe do not perform "labor" as we define it. There is no precise division between labor and play. This was also true of the way craftspeople in industrial societies performed their "labor" until a decade ago. Eric Hoffer, writing in *The Temper of Our Time* of his experiences as a laborer on the San Francisco waterfront, noticed that experienced workers took to their jobs as if playing games and that it was the introduction of automation that transformed their work into "labor."

The division between play and labor bears a profound relationship to the division between child and adult. Although in contemporary thought much has been made of the concept of *homo ludens* developed by Huizinga, we are able to represent play only as already divided from labor—just as we can only think of children as "children." The "discovery of the child," then, is a matter that cannot be considered in isolation but must be placed in the context of the capitalistic reorganization of contemporary society. I do not, however, wish to refer to capitalism deterministically, for the discovery of the child is a matter that must be analyzed in its own specificity.

3

As Yanagita Kunio observed, Japanese folktales were not meant for children and generally games purely for children were unknown. Yanagita not only had a keen awareness of this aspect of pre-Meiji life, but bore a strong aversion to the notion of children's literature. This was because he truly disliked "literature." He correctly perceived that literature written for the sake of children could not have existed prior to the establishment of "literature." Yanagita's indifference to "the child" when he had written so extensively about children may be compared to his disaffiliation from the concept of the "masses" developed by self-conscious modern Japanese intellectuals, despite the fact that he spoke constantly about the *jōmin* or common people. Yanagita, however, did not start out in this vein. His attitude was the result of a decisive about-face. Note, for example, this early poem published in an issue of *Bungakkai* (The world of literature) in February 1897, together with works by Kunikida Doppo, Tayama Katai, and others.

> It is in the land of twilight
> That the ones I long for live.
> Since this world seems all too gloomy
> Lead me onward, evening star.
> To the weak and lonely orphan
> A mother's kind words offer ease.
> Hither through the sky so peaceful
> Send them to me, evening breeze.

This poem conveys the impression of having been based on Yanagita's experience. Upon the successive deaths of both of his parents, with whom he had never been close, he wrote in his book *Kokyō Shichijūnen* (Home seventy years), he had "lost the motivation to do anything, and indulged in romantic fantasies about studying forestry and living in the mountains." Moreover, the "land of twilight" in the poem seems *as if* it alludes to some place which is the object of inner longing, perhaps linked to that *Road Across the Sea* (of his book by the same title, *Kaijō no michi*) that Yanagita emphasized in his later years, dispensing with his characteristically positivistic methodology.

Yet elsewhere Yanagita reminisces as follows:

> I once published poetry written in the new style in *Bungakkai*. Maybe Tōson encouraged me. But the poetry of these fellows was of Western lineage—for them the purpose of poetry was the spontaneous expression of whatever burned in one's heart. Since I had started out practicing with *daiei* (given themes), composing *waka*, I was utterly lost. For *daiei* was the distinctive feature of *waka* poetry: the theme was assigned, and even if a well-bred young lady were assigned the topic of "jealous love," she would have to write about it. However awkward the topic made her, there were always the manuals like *Waka yaegaki* (The Eight-fold Fence of *Waka*) and *Kotoba no yachigusa* (Eight Thousand Leaves of Words), from which she could pick out suitable phrases to

use in composition. The manuals offer from thirty to forty examples of appropriate words, so she would have no problem in combining some of them into a poem. This was what the traditional *daiei* was all about, and the important thing was to do this often enough to become adept at it, so that when someone addressed a poem to you you could reply immediately.

I thought of it as a kind of perfunctory social skill. In later years we explained to people that, without considerable practice in *daiei*, we would not have been be able to compose a poem on the spot when the occasion seemed to demand it, and so forth and so on, but, come to think of it, the distance between *waka* and the lyrical poetry of Tōson was immense.[9]

Reading this kind of reminiscence makes it difficult to see Yanagita's life work as an extension of his early lyrical poetry. However, Yanagita certainly experienced ambivalence over these issues and at the very least emerged as an intellectual against the same horizon as Doppo and Tōson did. Although there was surely a certain discomfort that existed between them, it appears to be one that Yanagita only became aware of during his later conflict with Katai and Tōson and exaggerated in the reminiscence above.

Japanese literary historians are apt to claim baldly that Katai and Tōson proceeded from romanticism to naturalism, but this betrays their superficial understanding of romanticism. The transition from writing poetry to writing novels may have signified the maturation of these two authors, but it was romanticism itself that made "maturation" an inevitable trajectory for them. However much naturalism may be seen as antagonistic to self-consciousness, the two are in fact indivisible, as Geoffrey Hartmann has pointed out, and to this day we remain confined by the problematic of "maturation." Hartmann wrote that "the idea of a return, via knowledge, to naivete—a second naivete—is commonplace among the German Romantics."[10] In this sense even Kobayashi Hideo or Yoshimoto Takaaki's work *Saigō no Shinran* (The last Shinran), must be placed within the realm of romantic thought.

The problem of maturation has been taken up from another angle, inaugurated by Nakamura Mitsuo's *Sakka no seishun* (The youth of the writer) and Etō Jun's *Seijuku to sōshitsu* (Maturation and loss). Since these works do not have the paradoxical quality of Kobayashi's and Yoshimoto's writings, they have become more widely accepted. Erik Erikson's concepts of identity and moratorium are also widely used in literary criticism these days, but we can no longer call these "critical" concepts. This is because the writers do not perceive the historicity of the problematic of maturation itself, but rather treat it as if it were inherently human.

We should also note that the "rites of passage" (initiation rites, such as the Japanese ceremony of *genpuku*) widely found in human societies have nothing to do with "maturation." It would be mistaken for us, for example, to try to find the problem of adolescence in the autobiographical *Oritaku shiba no ki* (Told round a brushwood fire, trans. 1979) of Arai Hakuseki (1657–1725). When a child becomes an adult by means of a rite of passage, it is like a changing of masks: depending on the culture, this may involve a change in hairstyle, dress, or name, or it may involve circumcision or the application of make-up or a tattoo. But we should not conclude that a substantive "self" is concealed behind these masks.

In rites of passage, a clear distinction is drawn between child and adult. The "division" that we know is of a different order. If we examine it from a fresh perspective, we can see that this "division" creates a continuity between child and adult. Instead of the transformation that occurs in rites of passage, we have a "self" that develops and matures gradually. Paradoxically, it is our "division" of children from adults that removes the absolute distinction between the two.

Let me also point out in passing that what Yanagita calls *daiei* (composition about a given theme) can also be called *daiei* (composition by proxy), and that understanding this practice is crucial to our understanding of writing before the establishment of "literature." Where there is no substantive self, composing poetry on assigned themes or writing by proxy seems an obvious thing to do: self-expression does not exist at all. In Western literature, as well, it was only with the German romantics that the idea of Shakespeare's "self-expression" emerged. Prior to this there was no notion of originality, and collaborative authorship, citation, allusion, and imitation were freely practiced.

Of course, it is not impossible to claim that even this writing was already a kind of romanticism, in the sense that Hegel spoke of West European art in general as of the "romantic form." Nietzsche suggested that if the ancient Greeks were to read Shakespeare they would consider it nothing but the rantings of a madman. In other words at the source of all that is romantic is Christianity. The attitude of "becoming like newborn babes" (1 Peter 2:2) is an inversion born of excessive self-consciousness, which was broadly diffused

enabling him to critique "consciousness," which he saw as a present based on accumulated illusions, as well as the obviousness of systems which were, in fact, historical formations. He describes this as "the only means left to us to remove the many obstacles that make us blind to knowledge about the actual basis of human society." The child, for him, then was not a substantive entity but a methodological concept. On the other hand it was as the object of this methodological gaze that the child became observable for the first time. More precisely, as an object of observation, the child became a being that was abstracted and isolated from a traditional *lebenswelt*. Child psychology as it had developed up to and including Piaget's work dealt with the child in this sense.

Piaget, of course, refuted the Lockian postulate of the *tabula rasa*, the empiricist hypothesis that human beings are formed through experience and interaction with the environment. Piaget found "structure" at the origin, and considered this an a priori phenomenon "given" through evolution. Chomsky's Cartesian linguistics reached a similar conclusion, while the zoologist Konrad Lorenz criticized empiricist cultural theory from a different perspective.

Freud, on the contrary, on the basis of his study of neurosis, discovered attachment and regression to childhood and developed the concept of childhood as belonging to "small adults." While Freud thereby dismantled the myth of "the childlike" that was particularly dominant in the nineteenth century, we cannot call his formulations universal. This is because neurosis itself is a product of the division between "child" and adult. Foucault, for example, maintains:

> If regression to childhood is manifested in neuroses, it is so merely as an effect. In order for infantile behavior to be a refuge for the patient, for its reappearance to be regarded as an irreducible pathological fact, a society must establish a margin between the individual's present and past that cannot and must not be crossed; a culture must integrate the past only by forcing it to disappear. And this is certainly a feature of our own culture. When, with Rousseau and Pestallozzi, the eighteenth century concerned itself with constituting for the child, with educational rules that followed his own development, a world that would be adapted to him, it made it possible to form around children an unreal, abstract, archaic environment that had no relation to the adult world. The whole development of contemporary education, with its irreproachable aim of preserving the child from adult conflicts, accentuates the distance that separates, for a man, his life as a child and his life as an adult. That is to say, by sparing the child conflicts, it

exposes him to a major conflict, to the contradiction between his childhood and his real life. If one adds that, in its educational institutions, a culture does not project its reality directly, with all its conflicts and contradictions, but that it reflects it indirectly through the myths that excuse it, justify it, and idealize it in a chimerical coherence; if one adds that in its education a society dreams of its golden age (one has only to remember those of Plato and Rousseau, Durkheim's republican institution, the educational naturalism of the Weimar Republic), one understands that fixations and pathological regressions are possible only in a given culture, that they multiply to the extent that social forms do not permit the assimilation of the past into the present content of experience. Neuroses of regression do not reveal the neurotic character of childhood, but they denounce the archaizing character of the institutions concerned with childhood. What serves as a background to those pathological forms is the conflict, within a society, between the forms of education of the child, in which the society hides its dreams, and the conditions it creates for adults, in which its real present, with all its miseries, can be read.[14]

Foucault's observation that neurosis is the product of an isolated and protected "childhood" and is only generated in such a culture is significant. For it suggests that in a society where adolescence does not "divide" children and adults, this illness does not exist as "illness." Foucault has also declared that, since psychology only came into existence after the mad had been isolated as mad in the latter half of the seventeenth century, psychology does not possess a key to the understanding of lunacy. It is rather the madman who can unlock the secrets of psychology. To use a similar rhetoric, we might say that it is not child psychology and children's literature that reveal "the true child" to us, but rather the separating off of "the child" that holds the key to them.

Many modern writers look back on childhood, as if there they could find their true origins. The only result of this is the construction of a narrative of the "self." At times such stories take the form of psychoanalytic narratives. Yet it is not the case that there is a truth hidden in childhood. What has been hidden from us is the system that produces psychoanalysis itself.

Thus the problematic of "maturation" holds us in thrall. It is a problem that we cannot confront directly, however. For our problem is not that the isolation of childhood makes it impossible for us to mature—it is that our desire to mature makes us immature.

Rousseau, by the way, was not necessarily a pedagogue in the sense that Foucault describes. Rousseau saw *Émile* as a "philosophical work," whose project was to work back through accumulated layers of inversions. It is those who read Rousseau's book as pedagogy who have a problem. The same can be said of Freud. His thesis was not that neurosis will develop if one has had a traumatic experience in childhood. On the contrary, he argued that when there is neurosis, there will always have been a problem in childhood. In other words he merely found "childhood" a posteriori as a structural causality. Nevertheless, when Freud's theories are converted into theories of education and child development, as they have been in American psychoanalysis, they lead to intensified efforts to remove conflict and contradiction from childhood, in order to protect children. As a result, the possibility of neurosis is increased. In this case it is indeed psychoanalysis which has produced illness, something Freud would never have dreamed of. In America, in particular, where the disappearance of traditional norms coexists with the pervasive norm of "being mature," psychoanalysis itself may be seen as generating illness on a broad scale.

Yet we should bear in mind that when psychology or child psychology as sciences undergo this type of transformation, it is not because they have been incorrectly interpreted. Such developments are in the nature of modern science itself. As Husserl lucidly argued in his *Crisis of European Sciences and Transcendental Phenomenology*, "pure science" as it has been conceived of from Galileo onward can be harnessed to any goal whatsoever, precisely because it is fundamentally without goal. Modern science is applied science. Molecular biology, for example, which at one time was purely theoretical research, can always be converted into genetic engineering. The child that is the object of research for the psychologist, whether behaviorist or structuralist, is an existence which has been uprooted from what Husserl called its *lebenswelt*—and the knowledge gained thereby can be applied toward any end. The "crisis" that Husserl was cognizant of grew out of the obliviousness of science to its historicity. Before we deliberate over our knowledge of "the child," we should be aware of its historicity.

5

I have written up to this point about the origins of "the child," that is, about the "child" as an invisible system. In concluding I must comment on the visible sytem. What I will attempt to explore, however, is not what this system aims or intends—in other words, its content—but rather, the way in which it functions as a signifier.

No matter how much the content of education in modern Japan is put into question, the system of compulsory education itself remains unquestioned. In fact our problem does not lie in the what and how of teaching, but in the school system itself—yet all pedagogical theories take this system for granted. Even when historical research is undertaken concerning forms of education which preceded our present system, it deals only with arbitrarily selected phenomena, such as the Edo temple schools (*terakoya*) or private schools run by Confucian scholars (*shijuku*), as if the modern school system simply represented a generalization and expansion of these phenomena.

Once again, it was Yanagita Kunio who doubted the obviousness of this kind of educational concept. What Yanagita called "teaching Japanese" (*kokugo kyōiku*) was quite different from the training given to people by Japanese instructors (*kokugo kyōshi*) and literati of the time. As I mentioned earlier, Yanagita observed that "by contrast to the current system of dividing children by age group in elementary schools, elder children often took care of younger ones. Not only did the older children take on the responsibility with enthusiasm since they became aware of their own growth through this process, but the younger ones also looked eagerly forward to joining the ranks of the older children." Yanagita, too, felt this exposure to different age groups was an important part of education. From this viewpoint, it becomes clear that the grouping of children by age in the compulsory education system of modern Japan signified the uprooting of children, as abstract and homogeneous entities, from the productive relations, social classes, and communities that had previously been their concrete contexts.

It was in the third year of Meiji that attendance at elementary school, as well as a period of military service, became mandatory. Three years later, regulations providing for the establishment of schools throughout the country (*Gakusei Hanpu*) had been issued, contemporaneously with the promulgation of the draft laws (*chōheirei*). It is interesting that the new Meiji government put these two policies into effect before all others. For most of the population at that time, the concepts of the draft and compulsory education must have been difficult to comprehend. There was, in fact, at least one example of a riot against mandatory military service, which arose from misunderstanding of it as a "blood tax" (as some called it). Even though "blood" was not literally wrung from Japanese villagers, however, the draft laws drained traditional societal life of its strata of young men. The school system, too, was passively resisted by the people.[15] For farmers, craftsmen, and merchants, having their children "taken away" to go to elementary schools was the equivalent of having the existing mode of production destroyed.

Although one may find negative references to the conscription system, surprisingly enough, the school system is never questioned. The significance of the fact that the two appeared simultaneously has never been considered. Of course, both were implemented as the basis for achieving the Meiji government's goal of a "wealthy nation and strong army" (*fukoku kyōhei*), but the simultaneous establishment of the two systems has another meaning. For example, it is said that the military was formed for the purpose of defense and resistance against the Western powers. Its actual effect, however, was to cultivate in human beings that had hitherto belonged to diverse classes and modes of production a certain group discipline and functional mode of existence. The military was an organ of "education."

Even today, Eric Hoffer notes:

> It is significant that the transition of blacks in the United States from inferiority to equality has nowhere been more advanced than in the military. At present, the military is the only place where a black is considered to be first of all a human being, and blackness is only a secondary issue. Similarly, in Israel the military is becoming the one and only organ that transforms multilingual immigrants into self-respecting Israelis.[16]

Of course, education is not the overt purpose of the military. But, regardless of the reactionary nature of its content in Japan, the military molded "human beings" who were independent of traditional modes of production and social status. "Human beings," in a word, were produced by both the school system and the military. Nor did it matter much what ideology was instilled by these systems, for they themselves had a more powerful function than did the discourse of the ideologues of democracy. Those, moreover, who hold that, since the Meiji school system was based on the ideology of the emperor system, Japanese education can be made more progressive by replacing this with a democratic or socialist ideology, fail to see the historicity of "education" itself.

Lenin's analysis of the Russian factory also has some bearing on this discussion:

> For instance, this same "Practical Worker" of the new *Iskra* with whose profundity we are already familiar denounces me for visualising the Party "as an immense factory" headed by a director in the shape of the Central Committee. . . . [The] "Practical Worker" never guesses that this dreadful word of his immediately betrays the mentality of the bourgeois intellectual unfamiliar with either the practice or the theory of proletarian organization. For the factory, which seems only a bogey to some, represents the highest form of capitalist cooperation which has united and disciplined the proletariat, taught it to organize, and placed it at the head of all the other sections of the toiling and exploited population. And Marxism, the ideology of the proletariat trained by capitalism, has been and is teaching unstable intellectuals to distinguish between the factory as a means of exploitation (discipline based on fear of starvation) and the factory as a means of organization (discipline based on collective work united by the conditions of a technically highly developed form of production). The discipline and organization which come so hard to the bourgeois intellectual are very easily acquired by the proletariat just because of this factory "schooling."[17]

If the factory is a school and the military a school, the modern school system itself may be seen as a factory. Thus, revolutionary governments in nations that lack factories or what Marx called an industrial proletariat tend to establish school systems and military draft systems before anything else (since building factories is impossible), thus reorganizing the state as a de facto factory through its schools and its armies. It does not matter what the specific ideology of these states is. The modern nation state itself is an educational apparatus that produces "the human being."

The children's magazine first appeared in Japan in the 1890s as a supplement to education in the schools, or "for the sake of schoolchildren." Again, any critique of the content of these magazines must be preceded by an awareness that the school system had already created the new "human being" or "schoolchild" for whom these magazines were produced. Of course, at this time, the philosophy of education implemented in both the new schools and the magazines was Confucian. But, since the Confucian philosophy which in China had been the ideology of the bureaucratic class had been introduced to Edo Japan as that of the samurai class, it had little meaning for farmers and townsmen, except those of the highest strata. By the Meiji period the Confucian ideology propagated through the public schools was already an abstraction. The ideal of *chūkō* (loyalty and filial piety) had become merely a concept imparted in the abstract, conflict-free world of the school, and it became caught up in contradictions as soon as it was taken out into society. Adolescence is this very state of conflicted consciousness. By contrast, the *chūkō* with which the children of Edo samurai were thoroughly inculcated was quite concrete.

So far the critiques of the Meiji educational system have always overlooked the significance of the school system itself, and "education" has not been subject to question. While the content of Japanese education since the Meiji period has been criticized in good conscience by humanistic educators and those involved with children's literature, all in the name of the "true human being" and "the true child," their efforts are in fact a product of the modern nation-state as system. If, as Hannah Arendt remarked, the one who conceives of utopia may become its dictator, those educators and writers devoted to the "true child" must also be this kind of "dictator." They remain, moreover, completely unaware of this.

That modern literature became a generalized phenomenon after 1900, rather than existing in the form of isolated, sporadic protrusions, may be linked to the implementation and consolidation of the school system. It was on this basis that the discovery of the child by Ogawa Mimei and others was possible. The writers of the *Kenyūsha* school, who continued to cling to the apprentice system of the Edo period, could not locate this kind of child. On the periphery of this group we can find outstanding works written not *for* children but about them among the writings of Higuchi Ichiyō. One might say that what Higuchi described was not the "adolescence" critics so often noted, but the appearance of a fissure in a world where children had been "small adults," not adolescence itself, but the symptoms of that transitional period which would be called adolescence, and which was just beginning to become visible. Higuchi Ichiyō was, in fact, the sole writer of the time who could write about the childhood years and yet avoid the inversions of "childhood" and "the child's mind."

Afternote to Chapter 5

When I wrote this chapter I was not aware of the book *L'Enfant et la vie familiale sous l'ancien régime*, written by Phillipe Aries of the French Annales School. My ideas in this essay derived solely from my reading of Yanagita Kunio. It has now occurred to me that Yanagita, rather than being an ethnologist or anthropologist, was a historian in the broad sense of the term and that his methodology as an ethnologist was that of the historian. Yanagita's work bore some resemblance to that of the Annales School. Yanagita sought for events in what was not seen to constitute an event and looked for "history" in areas not covered by written documents. Yanagita's project, as he himself was aware, extended concerns of the National Learning scholars of the Edo period. Yet, as I have emphasized elsewhere in this book, no matter how strongly Yanagita may have reacted against modernity later in his career, his point of departure was one which involved him directly in the "origins" of modern Japanese literature.

In chapter 2, for example, I cite a passage written by Kunikida Doppo in the Hokkaido wilderness: "Where was society, where was the 'history' that humankind transmitted so triumphantly?" I note that Doppo cites the words of a Russian poet, "when the last human being vanishes from the earth it will not cause a single tree leaf to tremble." Kunikida Doppo's writings, however, ignore the prior existence of the Ainu people in Hokkaido, as well as the Meiji government's colonial policy which entailed forcible expulsion and assimilation of the Ainu. The radical imagination that envisioned the extinction of the human race was not extended, by Doppo as a colonial settler, to the Ainu minority who were literally being driven into extinction at the time. Doppo, that inward man, was oblivious to the relative otherness that existed before his very eyes. Similarly, the fact that Yanagita Kunio's scholarship as a bureaucrat with the Ministry of Agriculture was deeply linked to Japan's colonial administration of Korea and Taiwan is usually obscured. Yet Yanagita's complicity is no different from that of Western anthropologists whose "knowledge" cannot be divorced from the "original sin" of colonialism. In Yanagita's writing the relationship with the colonized other overseas is internalized and projected onto the Japanese homeland, especially onto Okinawa, which was, in fact, another Japanese colony. Yanagita called his ethnology "New

Nativism" (*shin kokugaku*). But Yanagita's methodology was characterized by a kind of romanticism that was not manifested in nativist scholarship in the eighteenth century.

As modernity brought a separation between child and adult, so did it sever the link between artisan and artist. A writer like Higuchi Ichiyō (1872–96), for example, was an artisan who did not have an awareness of herself as a modern artist. This does not mean Higuchi's writings did not attain an artistic excellence of the same type achieved by the great artisans of the Italian Renaissance. Nor is there anything surprising about the fact that a female writer like Higuchi Ichiyō appeared before the emergence of feminism in the late Meiji period. Although writing by women reached its zenith in the Heian period and then declined, women continued to be active literarily. Even in the Edo period, the writing of *waka* poetry was considered a social grace necessary for daughters of the warrior and merchant classes, as well as for courtesans. Along with poetry composition, a reading of classics such as the *Tale of Genji* was common among these young women. Ichiyō was not the isolated product of a particularly exceptional background.

It is noteworthy that Ichiyō did not write in the *genbun-itchi* style and that she died before *genbun-itchi* had been firmly established. The writings of feminists in the *Seitōha* (Bluestocking Society, founded in 1911), which was formed after Ichiyō's death, relied on the monotonous and impoverished *genbun-itchi* style. Despite their assertions to the contrary, Taishō feminists in their writings employed the dominant mode of realism established by the masculinist White Birch Society writers.

6 On the Power to Construct

Part I: The "Submerged Ideals" Debate

1

When we read so-called premodern literature, we often have the feeling that it is lacking in depth. Since people of the Edo period lived under routine exposure to a wide variety of terrors, epidemics, and famines, however, it is unlikely that they were not feeling things deeply. If, in spite of this, we say there is no depth to their literature, what can this mean? It seems best not to try to attribute this feature to Edo reality or interiority, nor should we strain to read depth into Edo literature. On the contrary, the questions we must ask concern what "depth" is and by what means it was produced.

The question is perhaps more comprehensible if we transpose it to the area of painting. Japanese premodern painting also appears to lack something like depth; to wit, it lacks linear perspective. But the linear perspective we now see as natural because we have long been accustomed to it was originally not a natural thing. European paintings, too, could be said to have lacked depth before linear perspective was established. The depth that we see in them is based on the system of drafting by vanishing point, consolidated over several centuries of effort, largely in the area of mathematics rather than art. Their depth, that is, is not a matter of perception but arises out of techniques of drafting. As Erwin Panofsky has observed, according to the techniques of drafting (or engineering drawing), "the values of breadth, depth, and height are altered in a fixed ratio. In so doing, the apparent size of the several objects under consideration is unmistakably determined in proportion to their actual size and their position with respect to the eye of the observer."[1] The viewer accustomed to this perspectival space has become oblivious to its nature as a product of drafting and is apt to think that objective reality simply isn't to be seen in earlier paintings. Paintings from the Edo period, for example, though they were certainly realistic in their own way, do not exhibit what we think of as realism. This is because people of the Edo period did not know "reality" as we know it and, conversely, because what we know as "reality" has been produced through a specific perspectival configuration.

Returning to literature, the same could be said. The depth we sense in modern literature is not something found in reality, perception, or consciousness, but in a single type of perspectival configuration prevalent in this literature. We see it as a result of the deepening of "life" or "interiority" in modern times because we are not aware that modern literature represents a mutation of this configuration. When we say premodern literature lacks depth, then, we are not so much saying that people of the time had no conception of depth as that they lacked the configuration that makes us feel "depth."

Similarly, when we turn to premodern literature, we have the feeling we cannot simply slip casually into its world. This is not necessarily because the historical context is unfamiliar to us or because the characters are not lifelike. In Chikamatsu's domestic plays (*sewamono*), for example, people of ordinary stature are transformed into tragic heroes and heroines in a way which is quite exceptional among world literatures. Still, facing these plays we feel as if we are separated by a kind of membrane, not as if "it could have been written about me." Why is this?

In this point too, we can refer to the case of painting. As we look at a painting done according to the laws of linear perspective, the scene extends unbroken in our direction. In such a picture, whatever the subject matter, we have the feeling that we can enter into the scene. When perspective is inconsistently applied, we lose that feeling. In the case of literature, too, it is not to consciousness that we should turn for a sense of emotional identification and the feeling that "it could have been written about me." Nor should we think that this way of responding to literature is a uniquely human impulse. It is a response made possible by a specific configuration based on the linear perspective system. Although we hear repeatedly of scholars whose "rich imaginative power" has enabled them to penetrate the membrane that separates us and "enter deeply into" premodern literature, for the time being it is more important to stay with the sense of discomfort it evokes in us.

Two points emerge from the foregoing discussion. First, that it is for want of a configuration producing such a sense that premodern literature lacks "depth," and secondly, that the presence or absence of such a configuration can in no way be used to determine literary merit. Modern Japanese literary history has been dominated by the notion that a deepened interiority and its expression are the criteria of literary merit. Literature, however, isn't even slightly possessed of such a necessity.

As I have already noted, the establishment of the linear perspective system in Western European painting required several centuries of effort in the mathematical field of drafting. However as Erwin Panofsky has observed, these techniques of drafting are "strictly a matter of mathematical interest, not of artistic interest," and they "bear no relation to questions of artistic merit."[2] By describing linear perspective as a "mathematical problem," Panofsky implies that the application of the perspective system to art not only represented its imposition on a question of form that was originally unrelated to art, but also that linear perspective came mistakenly to constitute a criterion of artistic merit. The same may be said of literature. It is in no way essential for literature to be the "literature" that we take to be the self-evident axis of critical evaluation. Yet asserting this is not enough to overturn our assumptions. Again from Panofsky: "However, even though we don't take the laws of perspective to be of moment for artistic merit, it is of moment for style, which is all the more important."[3] Consequently, we must subject these laws of perspective to a new examination.

2

What is the origin of the laws of perspective that we take to be self-evident? In answering this question, we must set aside the biased notion, itself a product of the type of perspective that developed in modern Western Europe, that the arts of premodern Greece, Japan, and East Asia did not utilize perspective. Forms of perspective existed in classical Greece and Rome, as well as in the painting of premodern East Asia, but my concern here is to locate the appearance of a specific perspective rather than of perspective in general.

Panofsky claims that modern linear perspective did not represent, as has often been asserted, an extension or renaissance of classical perspective. It could only have arisen from a complete rejection of that perspective, which is what we find in medieval fine art. In the perspective of classical antiquity, the homogeneous space we find in medieval art did not exist. "Classical art was a purely solid art. Here, it was not enough that you could see something, to be recognized as artistic reality, it had to be something you could grasp in your hands. Here, we did not have separate elements occupying three dimensions, fixed as solid bodies in function and proportion, personified by some means so that they would cohere pictorially into a spatial unity, rather, the separate elements were assembled into an architectural or plastic group structure."[4]

In classical fine art each individual object occupied a heterogeneous space quite different from our concept of a uniform space. Once medieval fine art had dissolved the independence of these individual objects, it recombined them in the coherent space of the level plane. Here the world was reconstructed in a "homogeneous continuum." It was only from this "immeasurable," "non-dimensional fluidity,"[5] that modern, measurable, systematic space (that of Galileo and Descartes) could arise.[6] "For art to acquire this systematic space, which was not only infinite and 'homogeneous' but also 'isotropic' (even if Late Hellenistic and Roman painting had to some extent the appearance of modernism) we can say clearly to what extent these medieval developments were a prerequisite. So, in the medieval 'mass style' is created the first expressive basis of homogeneity. Without this homogeneity, it's not likely that the infinite aspect of space, and further its indifference to direction, could be conceived."[7]

Panofsky's observations suggest that, paradoxically, the depth we find in modern perspective couldn't have emerged without a rejection of classical perspective. In the classical period Plato had rejected a linear perspective because it distorted the "true size" of things and in the place of actual existence and the *nomos* (law) brought out arbitrary and fleeting subjective images.[8] In this sense medieval space, with its rejection of laws of perspective, can be seen as having been constituted within Christian and Neo-Platonist metaphysical systems which also denied perceptual space. If this was true, than the Renaissance notion of depth, as that of a measurable, homogeneous space, as well as the epistemological perspective that generates the dichotomy between subject and object, exists in a relation of dependence on, rather than opposition to, Christian and Neo-Platonist metaphysics.

It was an awareness of a discrepancy between the "homogeneous space" of linear perspective (as an effect of the techniques of drafting) and what is given in "perception" that constituted the starting point for the reaction, in modern painting (from late impressionism on) against the laws of perspective. For these artists "perception" included, for example, the activity of "grasping with one's hands" and could not be limited simply to vision. Nor, they maintained, did perception consist of isolated, disparate sensations. Perception, like the body, has the structure of an intricate network. The revolt of cubism and expressionism against the laws of perspective corresponded to phenomenology's intense scrutiny of perception and the body. As Panofsky noted:

> The precise construction of linear perspective, whose fundamental structure is lacking this type of psycho-physiological space, misses the fact that we don't see with a single fixed eye, that we see with two constantly moving eyes, and that for this reason our "field of vision" is spherical. This perspective doesn't carefully take into account the important distinction between the psychologically constituted "apparent image," which the visual world gives to our consciousness, and the mechanically constituted "retinal image" which is formed in our physical eyeball.[9]

The space in modern linear perspective is a Cartesian space. It was in this space that Descartes's *cogito* emerged. Thus, the critique of perspective, that in the fine arts arose out of awareness of the slippage between this kind of perspective and perceptual space, paralleled the movement whereby phenomenology, beginning with Husserl, criticized the perspective that generated the subject-object dichotomy in modern epistemology and then attempted (as in Heidegger's work) to move on to ontology and the analysis of *Dasein* or (as with Merleau-Ponty) to analysis of the body and perception. In Heidegger's case, particularly, the critique of the subject-object dichotomy takes the form of something like a history of philosophy. But what Heidegger refers to as the post-Platonic "loss of being" or "age of the world view" is nothing other than the concealment of the space of perception. It was indeed this space of perception, rather than any direct confrontation with antiquity, that he sought to grasp through the analysis of *Dasein*.

We find similarities in the case of Japan. This is because, as I shall argue later on, we find in those Japanese writings which have been called *shishōsetsu* (I-novels) something resembling the methods of phenomenology. These writings, moreover, grasp a perceptual space quite different from that of modern linear perspective. We should be careful, however, not to equate in any fundamental sense these European and Japanese phenomena. What Panofsky calls the perspective of classical antiquity is quite distinct from anything that emerged in Japan or Asia, despite the fact that both differ from modern perspective. Yet perhaps it was these similarities that Akutagawa Ryūnosuke correctly sensed when he observed that, "What calls to me from the 'West' always comes from the plastic arts." As he wrote,

> . . . it is the vastness of India which will probably allow our Orient and the West to come face to face. But this will happen in the future. At the present time the East, and that most Western of traditions, Greece, are not in contact with each other. Heine wrote in his *Exiled Gods*, that the Greek gods driven out by the Cross dwelled in the out-of-the-way places of the West. But it was nevertheless the West, no matter how out-of-the-way. Surely these gods could not have lived for even a single moment in our East. For the West, despite its Hebraic baptism, is somehow of a different bloodline from our Orient. Perhaps their pornography offers the most vivid example. Their sensuality itself is of a different nature from ours.
>
> Certain people find their West in the German Expressionism, that died out in 1914 or 1915. Many others find their West in Rembrandt or Balzac. Hata Toyokichi, at the moment, finds his in the art of the Rococo Period. I do not hold that all these Wests are not the West. But what I fear is the mysterious Greece, hidden in the shadows of their Wests like an eternally wakeful, immortal phoenix. Did I say fear? No, it is probably not fear. But I cannot help feeling, even while I strangely resist it, a kind of animal magnetism inexorably drawing me in.[10]

3

At this point I must take up a completely different kind of conceptualization of "depth," as a base, substratum, or infrastructure. It goes without saying that the concept of a base or substratum is premised on a notion of stratification. But this would not be the kind of stratification envisaged in Aristotelian, Scholastic, or Neo-Confucian philosophy. In these systems of thought the identification of strata of material objects corresponds to the identification of human strata on the basis of social position. The notion of substratum to which I wish to call attention, however, is premised on a concept of stratification that presupposes the existence of homogeneous space.

Lévi-Strauss has observed that if not for the development of the Linnaean system of classification, Darwin's theory of evolution probably could not have come about. We may wonder how this was possible, since Linnaeus believed that species were created by God, while the contribution of Darwin was to historicize the genealogical categories that had previously been represented in spatial terms. Could not this transformation have arisen from Aristotle's classification table? Considered in this way, the distinction between Aristotle and Linnaeus emerges as more salient than that between Linnaeus and Darwin. For Aristotle, each individual object was affiliated with a heterogeneous topos, while the Linnaean system presupposes a homogeneous space. In the end, for Linnaeus, the species classification system became a study in comparative anatomy, and differing species were no longer heterogeneous. The possibility of the transformation represented by Darwin's thinking arises from precisely that point.

The concept of spatial stratification is convertible into one of temporal stratification and in this case produced demands for an explanation of the evolution of strata, whether in the form of Hegel's dialectic or Darwinian evolution. But in this case what should concern us is not so much the nature of these explanations themselves as the question of what it is was that made such space-time conversions possible. In the contemporary natural sciences, for example, while biology, chemistry, physics, and nuclear physics are seen as constituting discrete stratified levels which are researched in their own right, each of these levels may always be transposed according to a temporal schema of evolutionary development. Recent discoveries of the structure of subatomic particles, for example, have been immediately absorbed into theories of the origins of the universe. Not only that, but the evidence for the existence of these subatomic particles is in such historical data as cosmic rays. What sustains contemporary natural science, then, appears to be a kind of horizon that makes the conversion of space to time possible or, more precisely, a certain perspectival configuration. As Husserl has said, this perspective first appeared in the coordinate space of Galileo's analytical geometry. The basis of the time-space transformation in the natural sciences is thus not given scientifically, but is merely a projection based on techniques of drafting.

Just as the impression of depth in post-Renaissance painting emerged from the arrangement of objects in reference to a single, central vanishing point in homogeneous space, the conception of depth as substratum exists neither in reality nor perception but represents a projection based on a specific perspectival configuration. A substratum must be a subordinate structure. That is to say, it is the perspectival configuration of high vis-à-vis low that makes this conception possible. Eighteenth-century knowledge (Kant, Linnaeus) was still affiliated with the conception of "depth" produced by the one-point perspective system. They could not envision history, for example, in terms of *strata*. Even Rousseau's vision was based on a notion of discontinuous succession rather than stratification, as when he spoke of a "natural state" that "has never existed and will never exist." What occurred in the nineteenth century was the transformation of a perspectival configuration emphasizing the horizon (parallel lines extending to an infinitely distant vanishing point)[11] to one that emphasized vertical depth. It was the latter perspectival configuration which made nineteenth-century history possible.

Of course, this view of history now appears self-evident to us and as if it were objective. We are not aware that it is simply one specific way of ordering things. While the theories of Marx or Freud, for example, are often described as discoveries of a kind of substratum or base, what they actually accomplished was a dismantling of precisely that teleological and transcendental perspectival configuration that produces the concepts of substratum and stratification: it was the surface level, rather, that commanded their attention. That they are known as thinkers who discovered a substratum, conversely, demonstrates just how tenacious the perspectival configurations of knowledge are. However, before we discuss Freud's apparent discovery of a substratum which made it look as if he had dissolved the "boundary" between reason and madness, we have to examine the following point. As Foucault has said, the boundaries of the eighteenth century arose, literally, as spatial exclusion and confinement. But what must be closely noted in the establishment of these boundaries is the fact that madness, as well as the mad, were no longer considered to have a "saintly dimension" and that consequently that very boundary between reason and madness was made possible by homogeneity. A distinction had been made, of course, between reason and insanity even in the Middle Ages. In order for this to become a spatial boundary, however, a notion of homogeneous space was necessary. Before the mad could be isolated within a heterogeneous *space,* it had to be recognized that they no longer belonged to an entirely heterogeneous *dimension* but were "human." This boundary between reason and madness is thus based on the one-point perspective system of modernity.

How did Freud deal with this boundary? According to psychoanalytic theory, madness is caused by a failure of integration at a certain level of development, arresting the patient at an earlier stage (regression). Such a conception, however, was not original with Freud but had already been established in Hegel. Rather than excluding madness as a heterogeneous state, Hegel had seen it as a kind of autonomy, as adherence to a lower level of stratification. Illness in general, in his system of stratification, was apprehended as autonomy, as an arrest at a lower form of development. In this sense, not only could madness itself for Hegel be apprehended as a normal stage or juncture in development but reason too (as Hegel analyzed it in the "enlightenment" of Kant and Robespierre) could be seen as illness when it attempted to establish autonomy at a higher level. Thus Hegel was able to establish a viewpoint according to which reason and unreason were no longer seen as antinomies—reason could in and of itself evolve into unreason. Of course, this view was predicated on the notion of a transcendental "highest rank."

It was thus on the premise of the existence of the transcendental that Hegel could view illness as autonomy. It was out of this view that the notion of a "cure" developed, prior to the discoveries of Freud. Freudianism, or the notion of psychoanalysis as cure, was in this sense a return to Hegel. Similarly, the schema of Erik Erikson, who sought to liberate Freudianism from its preoccupation with the Oedipus complex and sexuality-based interpretations by developing a notion of life stages (emphasizing identity crisis and its resolution), was thoroughly Hegelian. But by this time Hegel had been forgotten, and the fact that it was a certain kind of metaphysics which made the stratified perspective itself possible had become obscured.

Insofar as psychoanalysis is a cure, it entails the doctor reorienting the patient, whose development has been arrested, in the direction of integration. We should note that it is unclear whether or not Freud himself regarded psychoanalysis as a cure. But insofar as psychoanalytic therapy grows out of the application to madness of a concept of stratification, according to which madness is seen as a kind of "lower stratum" (rather than as belonging to a different dimension or as something to be spatially confined and excluded) Freud cannot be seen as a pioneer, nor should he be credited with discovering a substratum. What Freud did, rather, was to reject that stratified perspective. We can see this in Freud's rejection of Breuer's method of hypnotism and espousal of the technique of free association. For in so doing Freud called attention to the paradigmatic and syntagmatic structure of information as manifested on the "surface" in dreams and free association. What Freud called the unconscious was the configuration, on the surface, of all that had been expelled as meaningless and irrational from the perspectival configuration (linear, integrative) of "consciousness." It is ironic that Freud, whose fundamental innovation was his denial of the existence of a substratum, should be regarded as one who discovered it.

It was Marx who pointed out that, whereas Hegel found the cause of stratified development in conflict and contradiction, it is only from the perspective of a telos (the end understood as the goal) that conflict and contradiction can be identified. Conflict and contradiction are thus, as it were, posited through techniques of drafting (projection), as is causality. By contrast, what Marx discovered was a concept of becoming as natural growth, or what he envisioned as a kind of rhizomorphous structure undergoing transformations in the process of natural extension. In contradistinction to conceptions of history produced by the perspectival configuration of vertical depth, Marx's discovery was like that of the body by phenomenology. Marx's discovery was certainly not of a substratum, but rather was made possible by dissolving the oppositions between upper and lower, near and far, depth and surface which were effects of perspective. The so-called "death of Man" in Marx or "death of God" in Nietzsche did not mean that Man or God had ceased existing but rather were proclamations that it was nothing other than drafting's vanishing point that had made the transparency of words and objects possible. But, in the final analysis, even this insight will be absorbed by a perspective, historicized. For the metaphysics which credits Marx and Freud with discovering substrata is not perceived by us as a specific conceptual framework but rather as natural and self-evident.

4

We can find a dramatic outcropping of the perspectival shift that occurred in Western Europe from the eighteenth to the nineteenth centuries in the debate which took place between writers Tsubouchi Shōyō and Mori Ōgai during the third decade of Meiji over whether literature contained, or should contain, what Shōyō called "submerged ideals."[12] That this outcropping has remained undetected by experts in Japanese literature (*kokubungaku*) and literary history is not because it has been suppressed, but because the one-point perspective system has impeded our vision. For the notion of an evolution, deepening, or progress that took place from antiquity through the middle ages to modernity is a basic schema of Japanese literature and literary history from the time of their founding in the third decade of the Meiji period. My aim here is not to counter this perspective with another one (such as antimodernism), but simply to call attention to the schema that makes this perspective possible and gives it the status of common sense.

In examining a debate like this one it is misleading to try to identify the problem that was at stake. Since a problem usually has the structure of an opposition or contradiction, it is the debate itself as a form which provides the problem with its conditions of possibility. Even though it may be the case that any kind of reality must appear in our consciousness in the form of oppositions or dualism, we should at least bear in mind that every problem is in some sense a construction. The same applies, for example, to the more recent debates over "politics and literature," "postwar literature," and so forth. What the opposition in each case conceals is diversity as difference. In interpreting the "submerged ideals" debate, we have to see if we can pry loose the site which produced meaning, or a problem, out of the opposition between Shōyō and Ōgai.

Let me first cite Tsubouchi Shōyō, who wrote in introducing his commentary on *Macbeth*:

> There are two methods of textual commentary. The first is to explain the meaning of words and grammatical constructions just as they appear in the text, and this includes commenting on rhetorical strategies. The other form consists of exposing the writer's true intentions, or the *ideals* that can be seen in the work. When I first wrote about *Macbeth*, I thought I would chiefly employ the second type of commentary, but then I reconsidered and decided to use the first type. This is because the second form of commentary, that is to say, interpretation,[13] when it is carried out by a highly discerning critic, may be beneficial and deeply moving for the reader. But there is the danger that someone of lesser discernment may, for example, take a cat and carelessly (frivolously) interpret it as a tiger, conveying a misconception to the unwary reader.[14]

basis of the specific, the eclectic, and the human." Ōgai already possessed a linear historical perspective, expressed, for example, in his statement that, "to conclude that the entry of humanism into the world of the novel is distinctive to the nineteenth century would not necessarily be amiss." Of course, Shōyō's thinking was not altogether free from a certain kind of linear historicism. But where Shōyō excelled was in daring not to accept a Western view of "literary history," making him similar to Sōseki, who conceived of his own theory of literature while in London. Thus Shōyō juxtaposed the Japanese fiction (going back to the Edo period) he had loved as a child with Western fiction and tried to evaluate them both in terms of their "submerged ideals." Although he attempted to reform Japanese fiction, he never "cut it off."

Ōgai, by contrast, wrote:

> Shōyō bases his three schools on the concepts of the specific, the eclectic, and the human. Eduard von Hartmann differentiated between the three categories of *Gattungsidee*, *Individualidee*, and *Mikrokosmus* in establishing classes of beauty. The thought of having to choose one man's system over the other's is enough to make me weep.
>
> Hartmann's distinction between his three categories as three classes of beauty may be linked to his basic aesthetic philosophy, according to which he rejected the aesthetics of abstract idealism and attempted to promote an aesthetics of concrete idealism. In his eyes, the road from a kind of unconscious formal beauty (pleasing only to the senses) to that secret and sublime realm of art which is the *Mikrokosmus* is the road from the abstract to the concrete. The Gattungsidee and Individualidee are merely mileposts on the way to that sublime capital which is the Mikrokosmus.[17]

What Ōgai asserts, to recapitulate, is that the three schools Shōyō set up as parallels are classes or strata, in fact, developmental stages. He uses Hartmann as a basis for his assertion, but, as he himself admits, there was really no necessity for him to rely on Hartmann.

Hartmann's notion of "unconscious philosophy" may be seen as a fusion of Hegel's "Idea" and Schopenhauer's "Will." Where Hartmann differs from Hegel is in his conception of the Absolute as consisting of this "Unconsciousness" or "Irrational Will" rather than as "Idea." In a different sense we can see in Hartmann's unconscious a fusion of Hegel's theory of dialectical evolution and Darwinian evolution, in that for Hartmann the world is a stratified unfolding brought about by the self-dissolution of the unconscious. But it should be noted that the substratum Hartmann called the unconscious could only have been discovered within a transcendentalist, teleological structure. Hartmann is thus ultimately Hegelian and does not break out of the Hegelian framework.

But the precise nature of Hartmann's philosophy is not at issue here. What is significant is that Ōgai, without adopting the positivism and linear sense of history dominant in his own time, took up an extremely one-dimensional idealism. We can recognize this, not in the philosophical content of Ōgai's writings, but in their perspectival configuration. For what Ōgai sought to achieve by emphasizing ideals was a rearrangement of Shōyō's juxtaposed categories into a temporalized, stratified schema. That he happened to find such a schema, in the context of German thought, in Hartmann's writings, is more or less irrelevant. For before Hartmann, there was Hegel. But there was nothing for Ōgai to go back to—only Shōyō's writings existed as a systematic theory. It was for this reason that Shōyō consistently took the offensive in the debate over "submerged ideals."

Certainly Shōyō and Ōgai used the term "ideal" with utterly different meanings. Ōgai's espousal of "ideals" was born out of his search for new configurations, which by means of a vanishing point would make texts transparent. The concept of the spirit of an age or *Zeitgeist*, according to which discourses of a single era are arranged around a single center (vanishing point), is one such configuration. Idealism, conversely, on the same basis regards texts as externalizations, or expressions, of the spirit of the age. A critique of such idealism, therefore, would consist not of replacing the notion of the spirit of the age with the concept of an economic base, or some other idea, but in critiquing the techniques of drafting by vanishing point themselves. As I have already suggested, Marx's project was of this nature. For Ōgai, on the other hand, the one-point perspective system was a necessity. When he talked about "ideals," it was not in the sense of simply reforming Edo-style literature, as Shōyō had hoped to do, but of a thoroughly reconstituted perspectival configuration, centralized around a vanishing point. In a very strict sense, it was only out of such a perspective that Japanese modern literature could emerge. By this I do not mean to credit Ōgai's theory with producing modern Japanese literature. What I want to point out is that it was Ōgai who took a position of opposition in this debate and who formulated the problem. He took all that coexisted as difference and diversity in the second decade of Meiji—all that Shōyō had affirmed in his conception of submerged ideals—and out of it structured an opposition. He situated the stream of Edo-style literature as a substratum and made this stratification appear inevitable.

5

It is interesting to note that once the Taisho period began, Ōgai rather abruptly started resisting this kind of configuration.

Though I have pointed this out in the essay "History and Nature: Ōgai's History Novels" in my book *Imi to iu Yamai* (The illness called meaning), I would like to reiterate my argument here. It is said that Ōgai wrote "Okitsu Yagoemon no Isho" (The last will and testament of Okitsu Yagoemon, 1912) in a single stretch, after General Nogi's ritual suicide following the death of the Meiji emperor, and that this work marked Ōgai's entry into the genre of history novels. What is significant, however, is not the first version that Ōgai wrote in a single stretch, but the fact that he subjected it to a major revision eight months later.

In the first version, the will ends with the following passage:

> There is no longer anything whatsoever that troubles my mind, except that I should die from old age or illness. This very day of this month of this year, on the thirteenth anniversary of the death of Lord Shōkōji to whom I owe the greatest gratitude, I would like to follow him to the realm of shadows. Though I am certainly aware of the fact that ritual suicide is forbidden by national law, I have been but a living corpse ever since I failed to die in battle in the peak of manhood; therefore I trust that there will be no reprimand. . . .
>
> I have been writing this last will and testament under the light of a candle, which has now burned down. It is no longer necessary to light a new candle: in the snow-reflected light from the window, I should be able to slit my wrinkled stomach.[18]

In the first version the ritual suicide "forbidden by national law" is to be performed in "the snow-reflected light from the window." According to the revised version, however, Yagoemon is given his master's permission and commits *seppuku*, or ritual disembowelment, in a "suitably ceremonious" place. Moreover, it is added that "the temporary shelter was surrounded by the populace of Kyoto, old and young, men and women, who gathered like a wall to watch the proceedings."[19] What does this difference signify?

The first version certainly reminds the reader of General Nogi. Indeed, this work was first published in *Chūō Kōron* magazine, with the note "This is a work modelled on the last will of someone who committed ritual suicide in the first year of Manji following the death of the previous emperor."[20] The work was published together with various commentaries on Nogi's suicide, leaving no doubt that Ōgai wrote the first version as an interpretation of Nogi's suicide. The first version therefore has a clear "theme" and a feeling of concentrated suspense. In the revised version, however, no such suspense is present, and the "theme" has also become ambiguous. It is not that the theme differs between the first and the revised versions; rather, in the revised version Ōgai tries to deny theme itself.

To be precise, it is from the time of composition of this revised version that Ōgai's writing of historical novels began. Whereas the works of Ōgai up to that point had been expressions of meaning, whether "great" or "lesser," works after this revised version refuse a concept of transcendental "meaning." This is an effect of the decentering of the work's configuration. Various fragments, even those that contradict each other, are merely juxtaposed as signifiers, and there is no vanishing point which would allow them to be seen through.

For example, in *"Abe Ichizoku"* (The Abe family, 1913), Tsukamoto Matashichirō, the neighbor whose entire family had close ties to the clan, is described as follows after he has killed off the clan: "The corpses of the Abe clan were brought out to the Ide no kuchi to be examined. When the wound of each person was cleansed in the Shirakawa River, the wound of Yagohei, whose breastplate had been pierced by Tsukamoto Matashichirō's spear, was more impressive than all the others, thus contributing even further to Matashichirō's honor."[21]

At this point the expectations of one who has been reading the work as a tragic tale are dashed. We are given no glimpse at all into the "interior" of the man called Tsukamoto Matashichirō. This is not simply because Ōgai confines himself to "external" description. Nor is it because he is using a style that attempts to allude to depth from the surface. The man called Tsukamoto has no "interior" to begin with, no "interior" in the sense that we know it; by juxtaposing such fragments, Ōgai rebuffs the reader who attempts to approach "depth."

Ōgai employs various strategies in order to prevent his historical novels from being read as simply another kind of fictional narrative. In Ōgai's case, notes and appendices are added not in order to help the reader's understanding of the work, but in order to intentionally prevent the work from focusing in on one point. This is even more thoroughly carried out in the *shiden*, or chronicles. These are works that refuse to be "works" at all. Nevertheless, there is no dearth of scholars who base their interpretations and criticism of Ōgai's novels on psychological or historical grounds.

Instead of repeating further what I have written before concerning this about-face by Ōgai, I would like to reconsider the problem from the viewpoint of the "submerged ideals" debate. Ōgai described his historical novels as follows:

> The kind of works I have mentioned before are different from novels written by anyone else. Whereas it is customary for novels to bear traces of the way the author picked freely among facts and tied the strands together, this is not the case with these works. I myself have used such strategies. For example, when writing the play-script *"Nichiren Shōnin Tsūji Zeppō"* [The street sermon of Nichiren Shōnin], I folded into it an earlier street sermon given at Kamakura, the *"Risshō Ankoku-ron"* (On a just and peaceful nation), which came much later. It is this kind of strategy that I have recently rejected entirely in writing novels.
>
> If you ask me why I do this, the answer is simple. While examining historical documents, I came to respect the "nature" found therein. And I became weary of altering it recklessly. This was one motivation. I also saw contemporary people writing about their daily lives undisguisedly, and thought that if one can write of the present undisguisedly, one should be able to write of the past in that manner, too. This is the second motivation.
>
> Although there may be a number of other ways in which my [historical] writings differ from others' works, setting aside the question of skill, I believe the main points to be those that I have explained above.[22]

Though Ōgai may no longer have remembered this fact, this was almost exactly what Shōyō had written about Shakespeare's text. It looks as if Ōgai has come full circle, arriving at the position where his adversary stood in the second decade of the Meiji period. It is this circular pattern that seems to me most significant about

Ōgai's role in the debate. Having taken the lead by establishing the perspectival configuration of modern literature, Ōgai himself attempted to decenter it.

It is problematic that Ōgai's about-face was accomplished in the form of an atavistic return, rather than of a new opening. As he put it, he had simply "gotten tired" of writing modern novels. For a Western writer, the kind of about-face executed by Ōgai would probably have required, and would still require, an extraordinary degree of intellectual tension. In Ōgai's case, however, this took place as a kind of natural process. Nor was this a problem unique to Ōgai. The aversion to "tying the strands together," which some writers have called an aversion to "construction," or *kōsei*, was to become a dominant trend embodied in the *shishōsetsu*, parallel-ing Ōgai's increasing inclination toward the historical novel. If one considers perspectival configuration rather than meaning and con-tent, Ōgai's historical novels and the *shishōsetsu* shared a common movement.

For example, the *shishōsetsu* deals with the space of concrete family ties rather than with society as a homogeneous space and depicts a precognitive realm of feelings and perceptions rather than the "I" as defined in relation to such a society. Consequently, the *shishōsetsu* form is fundamentally antagonistic to "construction," in such a manner that even nineteenth-century Western novels could appear "impure" or "vulgar." What is paradoxical is that in Japan this movement which was so contrary to "literature" should have come to constitute "pure literature" or *junbungaku*.[23] Yet where does this aversion come from? It is obviously from an aversion to the con-figuration of linear perspective, to the conception of transcendental meaning or vanishing point. Novelists, of course, were not clearly aware of this, nor did they have to be. It was only Akutagawa Ryūnosuke, in his later years, who became actuely conscious of it and who came to feel an aversion to what he called "constructed" works. We may observe this in his "novel without plots" debate with Tanizaki Junichiro.

sufficient to promote Western literature as a counterpoint. No matter how strongly the critics argued for the need for fiction, it was to no avail.

Yoshimoto Takaaki argued against these "modernist critics," who cite of all people Akutagawa:

> In so far as the ability for formal construction can be seen as a function of the social basis of the writer's consciousness, it was an effortless and natural matter for Shiga to accomplish both what Inoue Yoshio calls "Goethean perfection of character" and the meticulous formal perfection of the works themselves. On the other hand, for Akutagawa, who found his zone of stability, in terms of day-to-day consciousness, in the lower middle class, it was inevitable that even the formal construction of works were to be the results of intense intellectual perseverance. It is no wonder that those critics who misconstrued the ability for formal construction to be determined by intellectual ability alone, misconstrued Akutagawa's sculpted fictional narratives to show the author at his best.[29]

The claim that "constructional ability" is determined by the writer's "zone of social stability the self" requires reservation, since "meticulous formal perfection" was not "an effortless and natural matter" for Shiga: it was in Shiga's work that Akutagawa saw "the novel without plot." The mere fact that it took Shiga over ten years to write his only full-length novel clearly shows that he lacked "the ability for formal construction." What is important in Yoshimoto's observation, however, is that the ability for construction is not a problem that can simply be resolved through intellectual ability or will. Indeed, it is not a problem of consciousness at all. The Japanese psychologist Kawai Hayao has said, on the basis of clinical experience, that in contrast to the dreams of Westerners, which have "structure," "those of the Japanese are rather rambling; most of them can be cut off anywhere, finished off anytime, rather like *shishōsetsu*."[30]

It was the emergence of an irresistibly forceful idea, like Christianity in the second decade of the Meiji period, that made it possible to transform the configuration of the *shishōsetsu*. Marxism in Japan functioned as just such an idea. Kobayashi Hideo accurately grasped this point:

> There is, however, one thing that must not be forgotten. Though it may sound paradoxical, I believe this to be the case: that what made these writers live was none other than the formulism that they them-

selves were later to attack. Theory is fundamentally formulaic. Ideas cannot attain force in society without having a universal character. They lived because they believed in this universality. What they attained by taking sole responsibility for an imported philosophy of this nature, unheard of in the *bundan* before that time, was truly valuable. It was not a matter of some trivial problem like formulism.

It may be true that they left no masterpieces for future generations. It may also be true that what they depicted in their novels were merely assemblages of highly schematized personalities. But this was because their philosophy resulted in distortions, and their theory in exaggerations in their work, which can in no way be seen as failing or succeeding on the basis of the writers' personal predelictions.

The naturalist (*shizenshugi*) novels of this country should be seen as feudalistic rather than bourgeois literature, and while we could say that the masterpieces of naturalist literature in the West found their boundaries in the age itself (in which they were written), the masterpieces of *shishōsetsu* in this country show the clear visage of the individual. What the proletarian writers obliterated was this visage. Who can deny that purification through the power of ideology is evident in all works of Marxist literature? In comparison to that feat of subjugating the so-called literary disposition through the power of ideology, their inability to provide vibrant descriptions of the tastes and habits of the characters in their works is insignificant.[31]

In this essay, which evoked numerous inquiries concerning Kobayashi's use of the concept "the socialized I" (*shakaikashita watakushi*), Kobayashi Hideo is not really claiming something profound. He is merely saying that the "I" is not a matter of psychology (consciousness) but a matter of configuration. Formulaic Marxism destroyed the author's "visage," that is, the heterogeneous and personalized space of *shishōsetsu*. It was in the same manner that the ferocious puritanism of the Uchimura Kanzō type constituted "interiority" in the third decade of the Meiji period. Of course, these did not completely destroy what Kobayashi called "feudalistic literature." Indeed, Kobayashi Hideo was writing after Marxist literature itself had been destroyed.

Paradoxically enough, whereas Marxism in the West had the effect of relativizing the I as cogito, in Japan it functioned to give birth to an existential "I" that was different from the "I" of the *shishōsetsu*. The existentialist concern and will to construct that were to be inherited by Japan's postwar writers after the Pacific War were products of the powerful transformation of configuration achieved by formulist Marxism.

3

Marxism, too, seeks to realize a "plot," which is one reason why the debate between Akutagawa and Tanizaki (in the second year of the Shōwa period) seemed to fade away under the force of Marxism. Yet what Tanizaki meant by "plot" was altogether different from this kind of plot. He criticized Akutagawa as follows:

> Beauty of construction can also be called architectural beauty. The realization of this kind of beauty, therefore, must entail a process of unfolding, and requires a fair amount of space. Mr. Akutagawa, who finds the beauty of construction even in haiku, would no doubt find it in a tea-room but the tea-room does not convey a sense of accumulation, of layered building. To quote Mr. Akutagawa himself, the tea-room shows no evidence of what, in a different context, he has referred to as "the physical stamina to go on writing full-length novels." I believe this lack of physical stamina is the most glaring weakness of Japanese literature.
>
> If I may be so bold as to be personal, the difference between Mr. Shiga and Mr. Akutagawa although both write short fiction, has to do with the presence or absence of signs of physical stamina in their works. Powerful breathing, muscular arms, robust loins—such attributes are found even in short stories if they are superior pieces. In the case of full-length novels, it is the anemic ones that run out of breath in the middle, while the great novel has the beauty of an unfolding of event upon event, the magnificence of a mountain range rolling on and on. This is what I mean by ability to construct.[32]

Though Tanizaki is being sarcastic, this difference in the ability to construct is of course not literally a difference in "physical stamina," but in what might be called "conceptual capability." It was this conceptual ability that made it possible for Tanizaki himself, unlike Akutagawa or Shiga, to keep on writing full-length novels even in his old age. Tanizaki relied on a conceptual framework that was different from Marxism, but almost equally formulaic. (In this sense it might be possible to make a connection between Tanizaki's "physical stamina" and the masochism which did not allow him to perceive the body [sexuality] as something natural.)

However, even if Tanizaki possessed a magnificent "ability to construct" and criticized *shishōsetsu* from that perspective, he, too, was alien to the configuration of modern literature. Let me suggest that what Tanizaki called plot can be equated with the Japanese word *monogatari* (tale or narrative) and that *monogatari* may be seen as a space that was excluded, becoming visible in the process of being excluded, by what was established as system in the third decade of the Meiji period and by the homogeneous space of one-point perspective. In this sense *monogatari* had certain aspects in common with the "space" of *shishōsetsu*. Both emerged from within, and as reactions against, the configuration of modern literature as system and therefore actually shared a common foundation. One might even say that they branched off from a common root. This is what is symbolized by the "opposition" between Yanagita Kunio and Tayama Katai. There was a striking resemblance between Yanagita's vehement critique of Katai's *shishōsetsu* and Tanizaki's aggressive attack on Akutagawa. The vehemence revealed how closely the "opponents" were related.

But at this point, in order to consider what the *monogatari*-like is, we must again focus our attention on questions of configuration. Yamaguchi Masao, for example, has analyzed the structures of the myths of Susano-o and Yamato Takeru described in the *Kojiki* and *Nihon Shoki*, of *monogatari* such as the *Tale of Genji*, and of Noh plays such as Semimaru and has extrapolated a structure of *monogatari* common to all:

> To bring our discussion back to the level of Susano-o Yamato Takeru, we can say that the function of these two was as medium whereby kingship confronts chaos and disorder. Whereas the king, by consolidating the order of the center, gives latent birth to a chaos which is constituted by being excluded from that order, the role of the prince is to mediate between chaos and order by developing techniques of confronting chaos at the margins.
>
> . . . Within the hierarchical order perfected under the *ritsuryō*, the movement of the common person in the political world was a centripetal movement disguised as "promotion," while the movement of the prince was in a mythologically centrifugal direction, expanding the spiritual realm of the kingdom by going out from the center. The situation of Hikaru Genji as a protagonist of *monogatari* also reflects this fact.[33]

Yamaguchi Masao argues that when the early Japanese states established order through a legal system imported from China (*ritsuryōsei*), "the various powers (especially the violent powers) which could not be assimilated into the order of the center found a compensatory function in the myth of the Emperor system. Thus, folkloric logic came to pervade even the universe of the Emperor system as it represented a public world."

This analysis can probably be applied to the third decade of the Meiji period when the legal system imported from the West became established. Moreover, I believe that *minzokugaku* (ethnology) itself emerged in Japan in this manner. The story of Japanese ethnology is like the "nobleman's exile" tales of early Japan—Yanagita Kunio was a prince of the literary world as well as a bureaucrat who founded agricultural administration studies for the Meiji state.[34] This is why it is impossible to talk about the study of folklore in Japan without referring to Yanagita's presence. Moreover, Yanagita's study of folklore can not simply be described as anti-establishment. If, as Yamaguchi Masao puts it, "kingship is not only the establishment of order but entails an apparatus which domesticates disorder/chaos on the mythologic and symbolic level," then we must say that Yanagita's study of folklore itself existed within such an "apparatus." In this sense one might say that neither what is *shishōsetsu*-like nor what is *monogatari*-like ever served to subvert the institution of modern literature, but on the contrary, existed within an apparatus which supplemented and revitalized that institution.

Tanizaki's novels fundamentally reproduce the configuration of *monogatari*, even if the setting is modernized. To take *Chijin no Ai* (A fool's love, 1925, translated as *Naomi*, 1985) or *Manji* (1928) as examples, the everyday order, in which the protagonist is hierarchically superior to the woman, gradually begins to stagnate and degenerate. What is required in order to revitalize this mundane time is a carnival in which the woman, subordinate in daily life, is made "noble" by inversion and in which the protagonist submits and submerges himself in the woman's wantonness and chaos. Described in this way, it should be obvious that Tanizaki's novels constitute a series of repetitive rituals. This is more important than the fact that he was a devotee of Japanese *monogatari* literature. He is a *monogatari* writer in a more fundamental sense.

Now we can say that Akutagawa was also a *monogatari* writer, but not in the sense that Saeki Shōichi uses the term. This is evident in Akutagawa's works from "Rashōmon" onward and also in his interest in Izumi Kyōka and Yanagita Kunio. Though Sōseki praised Akutagawa's earlier works, it might be misleading to regard Akutagawa as of the same genealogy as a writer like Sōseki. For one might say that, up until the very end, Akutagawa never wrote a "novel" in Sōseki's sense of the term, that he never wrote anything but *monogatari*. Akutagawa's *monogatari*, however, did not have the structure of festive rituals like those of Tanizaki. For example, in "Rashōmon" there is a descent to "chaos," while "The Nose" describes the discomfort of advancing socially. This is usually read as an expression of Akutagawa's "complex over his class origins" (Yoshimoto Takaaki) but the *monogatari* was a matter of "class" to begin with. We might say instead that what Akutagawa's *monogatari* lacks is the kind of configuration in which the upper class and the lower class are inverted, allowing oppositions to be harmonized, as was the case in Tanizaki's fiction.

Seen from this perspective, the debate between Akutagawa and Tanizaki concerning "plot" presents a radically different mien. Tanizaki not only saw the *monogatari* in Akutagawa's works, but must have read Shiga's *Anya Kōro* (A dark night's passing, 1921–37) as *monogatari* too. As a matter of fact, *Anya Kōro* has a configuration resembling the *monogatari* more than the *shishōsetsu* and contains a mythological-ritualistic space. Tanizaki missed the point when he tried to locate Akutagawa's intellectuality in his "will to sculpt." What Akutagawa's "intellectuality" did was to repress the *monogatari*-like, and it is small wonder that Tanizaki should look upon it with contempt.

4

The term *monogatari* cannot be equated with either "story" or "fiction." To write *monogatari* has nothing to do with an ability to construct. *Monogatari* is pattern, nothing more, nothing less. Paradoxically this fits well with what is *shishōsetsu*-like. Whereas the *shishōsetsu* lacks structure, the *monogatari* is nothing but a structure. What Akutagawa and Tanizaki each advocate when they draw examples from Western literature actually has no connection to Western literature. On the contrary, what is notable is the fact that Akutagawa and Tanizaki quote Western literature without the unease felt by Sōseki and Ōgai, or, to put it differently, that it was in the cosmopolitan atmosphere of the Taisho period that the *shishōsetsu*-like and the *monogatari*-like became visible.

Ability to construct has nothing to do with the structure of *monogatari*. Yamaguchi Masao's structural analysis, for example, considers myth, *monogatari,* and drama in the same terms.

In analyzing literature, however, one is concerned not with construction as a pattern, but with qualitative and quantitative differences in construction. In this sense we can only speak of an ability to construct once *monogatari* is no longer narrated orally but written down in script. In other words, in Japanese *monogatari* we no longer have myths, but something whose existence was predicated on a certain ability to construct. The writing down of the myths of the *Kojiki*, for example, occurred only *after* the chronicles in the *Nihon Shoki* had been recorded in writing.

Tanizaki Jun'ichirō wrote:

> To disregard the interest of plot is to cast away the privilege of the novelistic form. And I think that what the Japanese novel lacks most is this ability to construct, the talent to geometrically assemble various intricately intertwining story lines. This is why I have brought up this problem here, and it seems to me that the Japanese are generally deficient in this kind of ability, not only in literature, but in all matters. Of course, one could argue that being deficient in that kind of ability does not matter, that in the East we have Eastern-style literature, but then it makes no sense for us to choose to work with the novelistic form. Moreover, even among Easterners, the Chinese seem to have a rather high degree of constructional ability in comparison to the Japanese (at least in literature). Anyone who has read Chinese novels and fictional narratives would feel the same way. Novels with interesting plots have not been unheard of in Japan, but the longer and even slightly extraordinary ones are usually imitations from the Chinese, and when compared to the originals they seem distorted and misshapen because the foundations are so uncertain.[35]

It is to Tanizaki's credit that he does not consider the lack of ability to construct in Japanese literature to be a characteristic of the East in general. This becomes evident not only when Japan is compared with China and India, but even in the comparison with Korea, which, like Japan, was a marginal culture of China. For example, whereas Confucianism was thoroughly incorporated into Korean culture, this was not the case in Japan. Moreover, in the case of both Buddhism and Chu Hsi philosophy (a form of Confucianism which had assimilated the impact of Buddhism), although the Japanese may at first have welcomed these systematic theories, they eventually lost sustained interest and developed them into such "practical" philosophies as those of Shinran or Itō Jinsai. Marxism underwent a similar process.

What is the significance of this? I can only give the commonplace answer that because Japan is an island nation in the Far East, its geographical condition has prevented it from assimilating foreign culture in any form other than as "cultural artifact." This is a cliché, but it has been and continues to be a peculiar condition that we have been unable to eliminate. That the ability to construct is lacking in Japan means that it is not seen as important and also that this constructional element has always been introduced from the "outside." Expatiating on Yamaguchi Masao's argument, one could assert that Japanese "public power," when not confronting pressure from the outside, reduces itself to the level of the village community and rejects whatever is alien. However, what Yamaguchi Masao calls "the Emperor system as a deep structure" is not something that can be dismantled by the general principles of semiotic analysis, for what has allowed the continued existence of that system as a symbolic form has been Japan's geographical peculiarity. It was, in fact, only in the Taisho period, after the end of the Russo-Japanese War and Japan's release from the international pressures it had faced since the last years of the Tokugawa shogunate, that the emperor system, in the sense that Yamaguchi has defined it, began to function in modernity. Indeed, the emergence of the *shishōsetsu*-like and the *monogatari*-like was symptomatic of the situation. For let me stress again that it was only in an atmosphere of cosmopolitanism, not exclusionism, that they could appear.

Yet to extrapolate effects of geography and treat them as Japanese thought (*Nihon no shisō*) is to install absence of theory as theory. What Motoori Norinaga accomplished was just such an inversion. Discussing the *Tale of Genji*, he argued:

> Although from of old there have been various theories about the purport of this *monogatari*, all of them discuss the tale in terms of Confucian and Buddhist texts rather than inquiring as to what the meaning of a *monogatari* is; this is not what the author would have wanted. Although there are ways in which the *monogatari* quite spontaneously manifests similarities and correspondences with such Confucian and Buddhist writings, one should not make generalizations on this basis.

The tone of most *monogatari* is very different from that of those kinds of writings, and all *monogatari* share one specific feature that I have discussed before. Of many different types of ancient *monogatari* this one concerning Genji was written with an especially profound awareness of this feature, and this must be discussed elsewhere in greater detail.[36]

Norinaga argues that the *Tale of Genji* is different from Confucian and Buddhist writing although it resembles them in certain respects and that it is not only *Genji* but all ancient *monogatari* that share "a certain feature," of which the author of the *Tale of Genji* was clearly aware. From this perspective Norinaga's ideas appear to have been inherited by Tsubouchi Shōyō, who in *The Essence of the Novel*, rejected Kyokutei Bakin and attempted to establish what it was that the novel's particular "feature" or raison d'être was. Tsubouchi simply substituted "ninjō" or "human pathos," for what Norinaga had called *mono no aware* or the "pathos of things."

I would like to point out, however, that even though the *Tale of Genji* bears only a superficial resemblance to Confucian and Buddhist writings and differs from Chinese literature as well, it demonstrates an "ability to construct" that would not even have come into existence without the latter. The construction of the *Tale of Genji* has its basis in Chinese literature and the philosophy of esoteric Buddhism. It is a basis that cannot be dissolved away through the application of ethnological or semiotic analysis.

> Though the *Tale of Genji* does not display physical stamina overtly, it has stored within it an abundance of elegant and poignant Japanese sensibilities, and it contains a beginning, an ending, and internal correspondences—it is indeed a peerless work of Japanese literature, displaying beauty of construction to an unparalleled degree. When we come to Bakin's *Tale of Eight Dogs*, however, we find not only that it is an imitation from the Chinese but that its foundations are rather rickety.[37]

What Tanizaki calls the "beauty of construction" or "physical stamina" of the *Tale of Genji* would not have been possible without Chinese literature. Motoori has the tendency to refer to the "ability to construct" in general as if it were a characteristic of Chinese culture (*karagokoro*). But without that "ability to construct" that it derived from Buddhism and Confucianism, the *Tale of Genji* would never have come into existence, regardless of the fact that *Genji* itself rejects Buddhist and Confucian ideas. Moreover, one might even say that the solid logical structure of Motoori's Japanese prose was based on the very Chinese learning that he attacked. For in order to become a theory, the aversion to construction itself is in need of the "ability to construct." The particularity of the *Tale of Genji* derives not only from the fact that it contains within it the pattern of *monogatari*, but that it made use of the constructive force of the Chinese literature which was the official literature of the time, while inverting it from within. Thus the *Tale of Genji* is *monogatari*-like in a double sense.

If one reads the "novel without plot" debate as symptomatic, what emerges is not the *shishōsetsu*'s "global contemporaneity" (*sekaiteki dōjisei*), a term used by Akutagawa as well as those currently reevaluating the *shishōsetsu*, but a similar *monogatari*-like pattern. For the "Submerged Ideals" debate and the "novel without plot" debate formed a single circle. Whereas the former attempted to establish "literature" as an institution, the latter was an inevitable reaction against it. Yet the *shishōsetsu*-like and the *monogatari*-like do not only oppose that institution, they revitalize it. Indeed, it is because of its ambivalent nature that such literature continues to thrive.

Kobayashi Hideo asked, "The *shishōsetsu* (I-novel) is dead, but have we overcome the 'I'? The *shishōsetsu* will doubtless reappear in new forms, as long as Flaubert's celebrated formula, 'Madame Bovary—c'est moi,' lives on."[38] Yet this manner of speaking makes no sense. We should rather ask: the ancient tales have died, but have we overcome *monogatari*?

Afternote to Chapter 6

The second half of this chapter, unlike other chapters in the book, deals with literature written after the Taisho period. Although the discursive space of this period may appear quite cosmopolitan at first glance, it was actually complacent and insular. This is because, with its victory in the Russo-Japanese War, Japan lost both its sense of tension vis-à-vis the West and its sense of solidarity with Asia—it had lost its "other." Symbolic of this situation is the writing of Akutagawa Ryūnosuke, who was conversant with contemporary Western literature as well as the Chinese and Japanese classics. In the absence of "history" or "otherness" within Japan, Akutagawa succeeded in utilizing these diverse texts to produce finely wrought short fiction. He remarked that "life was not equal to a single line of Baudelaire." Borges's admiration for Akutagawa is understandable in this sense. But Akutagawa, plagued by anxieties and a sense of crisis, began to turn to the *shishōsetsu* and even to defend it. It was against this background that he engaged in the debate I have mentioned with Tanizaki. When the Taisho period came to an end and Marxism was gaining ascendancy, Akutagawa committed suicide.

Many critics have explained the *shishōsetsu* as a retreat into premodern forms and away from the novel which is essentially modern. But Akutagawa saw the *shishōsetsu* as what we might call postmodern. This is because it could be seen as a kind of deconstruction of the late nineteenth-century Western novel. While there is some truth to these different positions, they miss the point. Yet they continue to appear in different form even today—for example, in the debate over whether the Japanese social formation or capitalism is premodern or postmodern. My own opinion at present is that these questions are profoundly related to the fact that until very recently Japanese society maintained a matrilineal structure (although strictly speaking we should call it bilinear, in the sense that matrilineal and patrilineal structures coexisted). In this sense Japanese society differed not only from European society but from India and China as well. Indian and Chinese society had been patriarchal from ancient times. It is no exaggeration to say that this feature of the Japanese social structure has left its mark, not only on Japanese structures of power such as the emperor system but on the modern literary modes represented by the *shishōsetsu*.

In this chapter I point out certain parallels between seventh- and eighth-century Japan, during the period when Buddhism, Confucianism, and the legal system were being extensively introduced from China, and the Meiji period with its massive importation of Western systems. From some perspectives, the "Sinicization" undertaken in the premodern period was ill-suited to Japanese society, particularly Chinese patrilineal marriage customs and the power structure based on them. In terms of Chinese values, Japanese were uncivilized and lacking a sense of morality. Because continental philosophy and customs, be they Confucian or Buddhist, were rooted in a patriarchal society, they were not suited to Japan.

The Japanese emperor system itself has roots in a matrilineal system. The dominance of the Fujiwara clan during the Heian period hinged on the position of the emperor's matrilineal grandfather. It should be noted that, unlike the Chinese emperor, in whose person all authority was concentrated, the Japanese emperor always existed as a "symbol" or null sign. When warrior families took over control from the Fujiwara, this structure remained unchanged. Even the Tokugawa shoguns legitimated their own control by formally subordinating themselves to the emperor. This is the structure of what should really be denoted as the emperor system in Japan. To use the English term "emperor" is misleading unless one is referring to one period in the ninth century, when an attempt was made to model the Japanese emperor after the emperor of China, or to post-Meiji Japan, when the German emperor was used as a model.

Japanese achieved forms of self-expression as a reaction against Chinese philosophy during the ninth and tenth centuries when relations with China were cut off. The works of many female writers—for example, Murasaki Shikubu, author of the *Tale of Genji*—who wrote in a phonetic syllabary known as *onnamoji* (women's script) represent these new forms. It was, of course, the matrilineal system which made possible these various writings by women. Yet after this was finished, these matrilineal arrangements continued to prevail among the middle and lower classes in Japan. This was the case even after the fourteenth century, when a certain shift to patrilocal marriage arrangements is said to have occurred. We can see evidence of this in the writings of the Jesuit missionary Luis Frois in the late sixteenth century. Frois wrote that, "In Europe wealth is usually jointly possessed by husband and wife. In Japan, each person owns his or her own share. Sometimes wives lend husbands money at high interest." Also, "In Europe, husbands usually leave their wives. In Japan, the wives leave their husbands." Finally, "A virgin's chastity is not at all valued by Japanese women. It is no dishonor to lose it, and they still marry."[39] This situation probably prevailed throughout the Tokugawa period, except in samurai families.

Furthermore, the literary tradition which centered on the composition of *waka* poetry was maintained even during long periods of rule by the warrior families, together with a certain cultural and political authority of the Imperial family and the aristocracy. In the latter part of the eighteenth century, the nativist scholar Motoori Norinaga, who attached great importance to classical narratives and histories written in the phonetic syllabary, declared that the quality of *taoyameburi* (femininity) was the essence of literature. Motoori criticized the then dominant Chinese philosophical and literary writings, including those of Lao-tzu and Chuang-tzu whom he saw as excessively theoretical and artificial precisely in their desire to overcome the theoretical and artificial nature of Confucian philosophy. In a more general sense Motoori rejected the theorizing attitude itself as *karagokoro* or the Chinese spirit. But Norinaga was not simply an idealist who was preaching a return to ancient ways. For in his time the matrilineal customs still survived in diverse forms in different regions and among the different social classes. It was only during the Meiji period that a Confucian system and morality were promulgated among the population at large through the schools. It was, specifically, the Civil Code enacted by the Meiji government in 1898 that established patriarchy in Japan. It was for this reason that the feminist movement, with its "antifeudal" stance, emerged in the late Meiji period. "Feudalism" was, if anything, strengthened by Japan's modernization.

In this sense Japan's modernization entailed a certain "Sinicization," as well as Westernization, for in it premodern patriarchy and the form of patriarchy imposed by modern industrial capitalism were fused. Modernization as carried out by those in power entailed the creation of a modern subject who was *subjected* to the authority of the emperor and the state. This subject was created out of those who, up until that time, had held differing social ranks, each with its discrete ethos. Confucian thought was used to effectuate this process from above. However, if this Confucian thought can be characterized as patriarchal, the same is true of those who opposed the authority of the Meiji state. I have already described the process through which Protestant Christianity produced subjectivity. If, as Deleuze and Guattari maintain, modern subjectivity is produced through a process of Oedipalization whereby patriarchal norms are internalized, patriarchal thought first attained a stable form in Japan during this period.

After the Russo-Japanese war there was a reaction against patriarchal thought. Although on its verbal surface this reaction took the form of humanism and cosmopolitanism, it contained within it a kind of "return to Japan." This was comparable to the reaction against Chinese and Indian culture in the late Heian period, when writing by women using the *kana* syllabary reached its zenith. In the Taisho period a comparable phenomenon was the appearance of the *shishōsetsu* as a reaction against the structure of the modern novel. The "I" of the *shishōsetsu* was no longer a subject—on the contrary, for that "I," subjectivity was a fabrication. The *shishō-setsu* was fundamentally antithetical to structure, to logic, and to intellectuality.

Akutagawa, as a supporter of the *shishōsetsu*, wrote the following passage in a short story about a seventeenth-century Jesuit missionary. The European missionary hallucinates the appearance of a "spirit" of Japan, who informs him that every thought system that has been brought into Japan from outside, including Buddhism and Confucianism, has been "remade." "It is possible that Deus himself could turn into a native of our country. China and India were transformed. Now the West, too, must change. We inhabit the woods. We are in the shallow streams. We are in the breeze that wafts over the rose. We are in the evening light that lingers on the temple wall. We are everywhere, always. You must be very careful, very careful."[40]

It is probable that Akutagawa was here alluding, not to Japanese Christians of the seventeenth century, but to Uchimura Kanzō's type of Christianity. At the same time Akutagawa's remarks presage the conversions which were to take place a few years later among those Japanese Marxists who declared that Akutagawa's suicide represented the "defeat" of Japan's petit bourgeois intelligentsia. With these conversions, patriarchal thought in Japan was undermined. From another perspective, what Akutagawa called "Deus" was the Western novel, which was "remade" into the *shishōsetsu*.

Materials Added to

the English Edition

7 The Extinction of Genres (1991)

1

In 1905, at the age of thirty-eight, Sōseki began writing *I Am a Cat* (*Wagahai wa neko dearu*, 1905–6). Two years later he resigned from his teaching position at Tokyo Imperial University, joined the staff of the *Asahi* newspaper, and became a professional writer. His entire literary output was produced over the following ten years. This has usually been interpreted as a shift, on Sōseki's part, from the role of the theorist to that of creative writer. Sōseki's maturation and development as a writer has been examined in terms of this output, from his first works of fiction to his final *Light and Darkness* (*Meian*, 1916). But the notion that Sōseki's view of literature changed fundamentally during the brief period of his engagement with creative writing is erroneous. Sōseki's literature cannot be dissociated from his "theory."

Between the production of his early writing (*I Am a Cat*, and his first collection of short stories) and the composition of his last novel, Sōseki produced works in diverse genres. If one were to classify them according to categories set forth in Northrop Frye's *Anatomy of Criticism*, Sōseki's writings include examples of all four genres: novel, romance, confession, anatomy. *I Am a Cat*, with its pedantic dialogues and display of encyclopedic knowledge, could be seen as anatomy. Many other works of short fiction written by Sōseki during this period may be considered romances. Those which recreate Arthurian legends or tales of the Knights of the Round Table, or deal with the mystical and otherworldly, are romances in the most literal sense. But even a work like *Poppies* (*Gubijinsō*, 1907), which at first glance might not appear to be so, is a romance. This is because its characters have an archetypal quality, making the work rather allegorical. Even the seemingly fictional *Kokoro* is based on what Frye calls the confessional mode. According to Frye, "Nearly always some theoretical and intellectual interest in religion, politics, or art plays a leading role in the confession."[1] Thus, Frye's confession is a genre entirely different from the Japanese *shishōsetsu*.

It was not until his second-from-last novel, *Grass on the Way-*

side (*Michikusa*, 1915), that Sōseki attempted to write something like a nineteenth-century novel. This was, indeed, the reason Sōseki's writings were so popular among the mass of readers who had not yet developed a taste for the modern novel. Yet, Sōseki's writings had been held in low esteem by literati, among whom naturalism was the dominant trend. They did not grant him recognition until the publication of the autobiographical *Grass on the Wayside*. For a writer to experiment with a number of different genres over a short period of time is, of course, not a phenomenon seen only in Japan. That Sōseki did so was not merely a sign of cleverness and versatility. Rather, we might see here the manifestation of a positive will: Sōseki was either unable or boldly refused to accommodate the modern novel. Sōseki questioned modern literature from within and sought other possibilities. This has gone largely unnoticed until the present time. If Sōseki was isolated as a theorist, he was isolated as a creative writer—in both cases for the same reason. Yet even today Sōseki scholarship is dominated by the view that his work developed away from the style of the early works, culminating in the production of *Light and Darkness*. This view assumed as standard something called "the nineteenth-century Western novel," a form into which all the other genres Sōseki wrote could ultimately be dissolved.

Yet Frye's formalistic categorization of genres might be seen as intended to counter precisely this type of chronological developmental schema. From Frye's perspective the nineteenth-century Western novel must be seen as merely an ideal propounded by naturalists at the end of that century. Even a writer like Flaubert, who was taken to be the epitome of pure literature, produced satirical writings such as *Bouvard and Pécuchet*, *The Dictionary of Trite Phrases*, and so forth. In *Madame Bovary*, as with *Don Quixote*, we see the novel emerging as a parody of romance. Naturalists celebrated Flaubert as the founder of the realist novel by emphasizing only one aspect of his writing. In American fiction Hawthorne's *Scarlet Letter* may be seen as an example of Frye's romance, while *Moby Dick*, with its detailed factual accounts of whaling, is both romance and anatomy. Even if we grant that a "pure" Western novel at some point existed, it is not among the works we read today.

The Japanese novel cannot be judged on the basis of such a standard. Although Masao Miyoshi has proposed that the term *shōsetsu* be used to differentiate the Japanese genre from the Western novel, this method implicitly assumes the Western novel as the standard. Rather, the novelistic form in both the West and non-West is one which accommodates the most diverse types of writings. In this sense it may be seen as the form which deconstructs genres as they had existed previously. For example, the first two volumes of Sterne's *Tristam Shandy* were published in 1760, just two decades after the appearance of Richardson's *Pamela* and Fielding's *Joseph Andrews*. Sterne's novel, a thorough dismantling of the modern European novel, appeared in the very era when that novel was being established. But this is characteristic of the novel form. The significance of Sōseki's commencing his career as a fiction writer with *I Am a Cat* lies in this. His was not a process of "maturation" toward the so-called modern novel, *Light and Darkness*. Had Sōseki lived longer, he would surely have written another work like *I Am a Cat*.

It should be noted that in the Japanese context, the problem of genre was taken up by Tsubouchi Shōyō's *Essence of the Novel*. Sōseki examined various formal aspects of what he termed *tsuku-rimono* (Shōyō's translation of the English "fiction"). The *Essence of the Novel* contains a "Rough Sketch of Different Types of Fiction," which may be said to represent Shōyō's own theory of genre (see chart on p. 178).

As I discussed in the preceding chapter, Ōgai opposed this kind of synchronic schematization of genres and insisted that genres be seen as developing in successive historical stages. He was able to maintain ascendancy in this debate because the nineteenth-century Western novel did indeed so develop, constituting itself out of the ruins of other genres. This dominance of the Western novel was interchangeable with a certain temporal, developmental order. It was on this basis that Ōgai, in the debate, argued that the "extinction of genres" was inevitable.

This clarifies Sōseki's position. Needless to say, he questioned this notion of historical inevitability. This position is also manifest in Sōseki's scholarly writing on English literature, in which he gave the highest evaluation to the writings of Swift and Stern. Late-nineteenth-century British scholars saw these works as representing a stage of immaturity and germination of the novel. As a critic, Sōseki could only stand apart from British scholarship. At the same time, Sōseki could not fully endorse Shōyō's type of formalism. Shōyō had attempted to ascribe to Japanese fiction since the Edo period a significance equal to that of Western literature. He had failed, however, to come to terms with a certain inevitability of

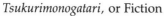

Tsukurimonogatari, or Fiction

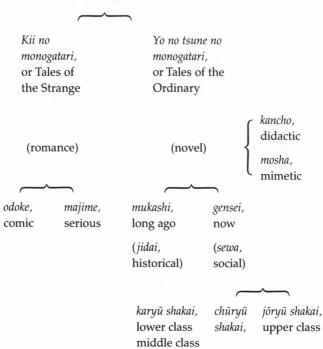

Kii no monogatari, or Tales of the Strange	*Yo no tsune no monogatari,* or Tales of the Ordinary	
(romance)	(novel)	*kancho,* didactic *mosha,* mimetic

odoke, comic	*majime,* serious	*mukashi,* long ago (*jidai,* historical)	*gensei,* now (*sewa,* social)

		karyū shakai, lower class middle class	*chūryū shakai,*	*jōryū shakai,* upper class

modernity, with the fact that Edo literature had to be temporarily rejected. It was, in fact, Sōseki, and not Shōyō, who carried on the legacy of Edo fiction, with its diversity of genres, in his writings. Although it is true that, without Swift, there might never have been an *I Am a Cat,* the novel is also an extension of that genre of Edo humorous fiction known as *kokkeibon. Poppies* extends the tradition of *yomihon.*[2] *Poppies* was actually denounced by naturalist critics as a "modernized Bakin." Since Sōseki wrote these works in a period when naturalism had already been established as the dominant trend in Japanese literature, however, his work can in no way be regarded as a replication of Edo fiction pure and simple. We should note that Ōgai, as well, resuscitated the Edo genre of *shiden,* or biography, in his declining years.

2

Although Sōseki may appear to have suddenly turned to creative writing at the age of thirty-eight, he had practiced haiku composition with Masaoka Shiki since his student days and had become deeply involved in Shiki's "sketching" or *shaseibun* movement. When Sōseki began the writing of *I Am a Cat*, it was not as a novel, but as "sketching" to be featured in the haiku journal *The Cuckoo* (*Hototogisu*), edited by Takahama Kyoshi. In this sense we might even say that it was "sketching," rather than the novel, that Sōseki was engaged with writing through the composition of *Grass by the Wayside*.

For Masaoka Shiki, *shaseibun* did not connote "sketching" in the sense of copying or writing realistically—it was an attempt to revitalize language in all its diversity. It was Sōseki rather than Shiki's disciples who carried on this mission. For Sōseki "sketching" meant the liberation of writing, the liberation of diverse genres. Accordingly, *I Am a Cat* is written in a number of different styles. It uses the *sōrōbun* of epistolary writing, the style of scientific debate, the language of the upper-middle-class Yamanote area in Tokyo, Edo dialects, and so forth. The stylistic virtuosity demonstrated by Sōseki in works ranging from *The Phantom Shield* (*Genei no tate*) and *Grass Pillow* (*Kusa makura*, 1906) to *Botchan* (The young master, 1906) is well known. This type of versatility is generally lacking in the monotonous style of sketching that came to prevail among the naturalist writers.

One characteristic feature of "sketching" is that it is written in the present tense. In narratives written after the emergence of modern literature, in fact, sentences are concluded with the *ta*, or past, suffix. The use of *ta* in Japanese corresponds to the use of the preterite which Roland Barthes saw as a condition of possibility for the modern novel. This mode of narration had been fully consolidated by the time Sōseki began writing. For Sōseki to use present or present progressive, rejecting the use of *ta*, was a deliberate resistance to this new style. Barthes proposed that, by adopting the indicative mood in *L'Étranger*, Camus achieved a kind of neutral or "zero degree" of writing, which went beyond the regulatory *passé simple* which dominated the modern novel. Although the two writers are different, Sōseki's choice of the present tense may be compared to Camus's use of the indicative.

If the suffix *ta* may be defined as marking a point from which one reconstructs the past, Sōseki's rejection of *ta* was a refusal of this kind of synthesizing, totalizing viewpoint. It was also a rejection of the apparent actuality of the "self" (*watakushi*). Sōseki felt similarly about plot: "What is plot? Life has no plots. Is it not pointless to construct a plot from what has none?" Sōseki also wrote that, "If this position of the writer of *shaseibun* is taken to the extreme, it is completely incompatible with the views of novelists. Plot is the foremost necessity for the novel."

The rejection of *ta* in *shaseibun* may be linked to its retention of a narrator that the modern novel did away with. In the first volume of *The Drifting Clouds* (1888), for example, Futabatei attempted to carry on the literary style of Shikitei Samba's comic fiction (*kokkeibon*) but could not do so without the use of a narrator (author).

> His lips twisted into a distorted smile as he bid his companion a curt goodbye and went on alone toward Ogawamachi. Bit by bit the smile left his face and his steps grew slower until he barely crawled along. He went a few more blocks, his head hanging forlornly. Suddenly he stopped, looked around, then retreated two or three steps and went down a side street. He entered the third house from the corner, a two-story building with a lattice door. Shall we go in too?[3]

We should note that Futabatei uses present, or progressive, suffixes in this passage. But in the second volume we find this "author" (narrator) has been neutralized. The narrator appears to have entered deeply into the "interiority" of the protagonist. It is at this point that something like "objective description in the third person" is achieved, earning *The Drifting Clouds* the reputation of being Japan's first modern novel. But what makes this kind of narration possible is the use of the sentence-ending *ta*.

In rejecting *ta*, "sketching" revives the narrator. Sōseki's works consistently feature narrators. It is not until the final *Grass by the Wayside* and *Light and Darkness* that this narrator disappears and the synthesizing *ta* appears at sentence endings. But Sōseki's narrators bear only an apparent likeness to those of Edo parodic fiction. They are thoroughly imbued with the characteristics of "sketching." Sōseki writes, for example:

> In narrating human affairs, the attitude of the writer of *shaseibun* is not like that of a nobleman surveying the lowly. It is not that of the wise man regarding fools. Nor is it that of a man regarding a woman or

a woman regarding a man. The writer of *shaseibun*, that is to say, is not an adult looking at children. It is that of a parent toward a child. Readers apparently do not understand this. *Shaseibun* writers themselves do not understand it. But anyone who thoroughly analyzes this writing will reach this conclusion.

Accordingly, *shaseibun* writers use the self-same style even when describing the movements of their own feelings. Surely, they too quarrel. They experience mental torment. They weep . . . yet as soon as they take pen in hand, they describe that quarreling, tormented, weeping self from the position of an adult regarding a child.[4]

Sōseki sought the basis of "sketching" in a certain disposition toward the world. It was an attitude of detachment toward "human affairs" (including those of the self), but it was neither cold nor lacking in compassion. In the novel *Grass Pillow*, Sōseki uses the term *hininjō*, or "asympathetic." Since *ninjō* (feeling) refers in this text to Japanese romanticism and *funinjō* to the naturalists, writing which fell in neither category was seen to be "asympathetic," or *hininjō*. An "a-sympathetic" perspective could be called humor. But this is not a quality to be found in narrators who are ambiguously fused with the author. Or, to state the converse, insofar as *shaseibun* writing maintains this distance, it will have a narrator.

This is the kind of narrator we find in *I Am a Cat* and in *Botchan*. Needless to say, even in writings that appear to be "objective third person description," we find this kind of narrator. This is true of all of Sōseki's novels except the final *Grass by the Wayside* and *Meian*. When Sōseki did not write in the third person, he used the epistolatory style (as in *Until After the Equinox* or *Higansugi Made*, 1912) or narrator agents (the *hanashi* style we find in *The Wayfarer* and *Kokoro*).

Sōseki's two final novels are only mildly humorous. Without a narrator, without what Sōseki called the "disposition of the writer," humor does not emerge. If some kind of comic spirit still seems to make itself felt in these works, it is because the narrator has not yet been completely erased.

Sōseki's "sketching," then, does not represent a nascent form of later novelist writing, but a deliberate and positive resistance to the novel. This kind of awareness, of course, was not present in other *shaseibun* writers. Moreover, Sōseki conceived of "sketching" within a field of vision that included Western literature. For example, he linked it to haiku in the following manner: "This mental disposition is in every way that of haiku, transposed. It is not a Western import which arrived in Yokohama after drifting across the seas. Within the limits of my own, rather shallow knowledge, there appears to be nothing written with this kind of mental disposition among the works which have been hailed as Western masterpieces throughout the world."[5] This does not mean, however, that Sōseki asserted that "sketching" was unique in the world nor that he wished to construct an opposition between the literature of the West and "Eastern literature." For he went on to cite Dickens's *Pickwick Papers*, Fielding's *Tom Jones*, and Cervantes's *Don Quixote* as examples of "works in which this attitude is evident to a certain degree." It is in this sense that "sketching" is fundamentally implicated in the question of genre.

3

The work of Mikhail Bakhtin, a theorist who called attention to the significance of genre, should not be overlooked in this relation. Unlike Frye, whose taxonomy is ahistorical and formalist, Bakhtin asserted that modern literature, historically, had led to the extinction of diverse genres and that these genres must be revived as a way of transcending modern literature.

> A literary genre, by its very nature, reflects the most stable, "eternal" tendencies in literature's development. Always preserved in a genre are undying elements of the archaic. True, these archaic elements are preserved in it only thanks to their constant renewal, which is to say, their contemporization. A genre is always the same and yet not the same, always old and new simultaneously. Genre is reborn and renewed at every new stage in the development and in every individual work of a given genre.—For the correct understanding of a genre, therefore, it is necessary to return to its sources.[6]

Bakhtin found Dostoevsky's "sources" in Menippean satire and a carnival sense of the world. "We can now say that the clamping principle that bound all these heterogeneous elements into the organic whole of a genre, a principle of extraordinary strength and tenacity, was carnival and a carnival sense of the world." This could also be said of Sōseki's "sketching." Sōseki saw "sketching" as a transposition of haiku, but the source of haiku was linked verse. In this sense "sketching" could be said to have a "linked verse sense of the world." If we can speak, as Bakhtin did, of the "memory of genre," then the *haikai*-esque spirit of ribaldry and satire that existed in linked verse can be traced to an even more archaic form, that of the premodern carnivalesque ritual called *utagaki*.[7]

Yet there are two senses in which Bakhtin's inquiry cannot be applied to Sōseki. First, for Bakhtin, genre is that which has already been repressed and exists as creative memory. But Sōseki, unlike Bakhtin, lived at a time when different genres and writing styles which had existed since the Edo period were being eradicated through the consolidation of the new style called *genbun-itchi*. Although for the next generation these genres may have been a "memory," for Sōseki they were not. Secondly, Bakhtin's theory of genres is psychoanalytic, despite his negative comments on Freud. What was important for Bakhtin about the carnival had nothing to do with the forms in which it had survived into his own day, but rather with carnival as a literary tradition, that which had been repressed from consciousness and remained only as a trace. Bakhtin's theory is indeed based on the model of neurosis. According to this scheme, the repressed Id, that is, the polyphonic, free-floating desires that are regulated by the everyday order, are liberated by carnival. If Bakhtin had read Freud's comments on wit, he would have certainly remarked that carnivalesque laughter was incomparable to the shriveled "wit" of modern bourgeois society. But the theoretical schemes used by the two men are similar.

Freud dealt with the subject of humor as a matter quite different from jokes and the comic. "If we turn to the situation in which one person adopts a humorous attitude towards others, a view which I have already put forward tentatively in my books on jokes will at once suggest itself. This is that the subject is behaving towards them as an adult does towards a child when he recognizes and smiles at the triviality of interests and sufferings which seem so great to it."[8] Freud's observations are just like Sōseki's comments about "sketching." The attitude that Sōseki has defined as fundamental to *shaseibun* writing is what Freud calls "humor." On the other hand, humor as a "sense of the world" should be distinguished from Bakhtin's carnivalesque. For Freud the joke, as a "contribution to the comic by the unconscious," is to be differentiated from humor, "the contribution made to the comic through the agency of the super-ego." However, Freud encounters a difficult problem here, for he must explain how it can be possible for the superego to contribute pleasure. He thinks about the problem in the following manner.

It is true that humorous pleasure never reaches the intensity of the pleasure in the comic or in jokes, that it never finds vent in hearty laughter. It is also true that, in bringing about the humorous attitude, the super-ego is actually repudiating reality and serving an illusion. But (without rightly knowing why) we regard this less intense pleasure as having a character of very high value; we feel it to be especially liberating and elevating. Moreover, the jest made by humour is not the essential thing. It has only the value of a preliminary. The main thing is the intention which humour carries out, whether it is acting in relation to the self or other people. It means: "Look! here is the world, which seems so dangerous! It is nothing but a game for children—just worth making a jest about!"

If it is really the super-ego which, in humour, speaks such kindly words of comfort to the intimidated ego, this will teach us that we have still a great deal to learn about the nature of the super-ego. Furthermore, not everyone is capable of the humorous attitude. It is a rare and precious gift, and many people are even without the capacity to enjoy humorous pleasure that is presented to them. And finally, if the super-ego tries, by means of humour, to console the ego and protect it from suffering, this does not contradict its origin the parental agency.[9]

Here, we can see Freud attempting to use the "neurotic model" to explicate a matter that cannot be conceptualized in terms of that model. Nevertheless, Freud modestly acknowledges that humor has its distinctive nature and value. This value has to do, not so much with psychology, as with one's "psychological disposition"— that attitude which would enable even a person who has lost all goals and ideals to confront reality without falling into despair or nihilism. In my view humor may bear some relation to psychosis, and Sōseki's *shaseibun* may be linked to a kind of suffering that cannot be easily healed by jokes or tragic catharsis. It is not the suffering of neurosis, but of psychosis. It is the suffering of the modern person, yet it cannot be fully narrated in the style of the modern novel. By the standards of modern literature, all of Sōseki's long novels are failures. T. S. Eliot, for example, remarked that Shakespeare's *Hamlet* was a failure as tragedy because it lacked an objective correlative. In Sōseki's works, too, slippages appear which cannot be resolved into a synthesis, because the subject matter is a psychotic suffering for which there is no objective correlative. Still, there is no reason for us to see Sōseki's novels as failures. They constituted instead Sōseki's struggle against that fictionality through which modern literature sought to resolve and synthesize such slippages.

Afterword to the Japanese Paperback Edition

The ideas in this book were formulated, for the most part, while I was teaching Japanese literature at Yale University between 1975 and 1977. My point of entry was a seminar on Meiji literature that I taught in the fall of 1975. This was my first experience of teaching Japanese literature to foreigners. In fact, I had never taught a course in Japanese literature before. I chose Meiji literature because I wanted to use the opportunity to examine modern literature in a fundamental way and moreover to reassess the course my own critical writing had taken up to that point. My critical writing at the time had not been solely concerned with literary matters. It was a period when I was also concerned with more abstract questions of "language, number, money," as articulated in texts by Saussure, Gödel, and Marx. This is a line of inquiry I have pursued to the present day, which I see as being separate from my work in literary criticism. (See my *Architecture as Metaphor: Language, Number, Money*, Any Press, 1992.)

Up until that point in time, however, I had not felt it a necessity to be a "theorist." But the process of questioning the self-evidence of my own sensibilities compelled me to become a "theorist." I can remember experiencing a kind of quiet excitement when I discovered that I was the same age (thirty-four) Sōseki had been when he conceived his "On Literature" in London. I felt I could well understand why Sōseki had been compelled to write that book. This was one reason that I chose to write about Sōseki in the opening pages of the book.

The anthropologist Yamaguchi Masao provided a comment for the first edition of the book, in which he described it by saying, "Karatani Kōjin's methodology is that of phenomenological reduction: to subject everything to doubt. The result is an intellectual history of the process through which literature was constituted and became a framework for thought; it also takes on the quality of a semiotics of literary landscape." I was not that conscious of a methodology when I wrote the book. But being in a foreign country, and speaking and thinking in a foreign language, necessitates some kind of phenomenological reduction. One is forced to examine one's preconceptions. The "phenomenology" Yamaguchi notes is not a method I learned by reading Husserl, but refers to my existence as a stranger in the United States.

In this book I attacked notions like "the inner self" and "subjectivity." The "subjectivity" I rejected, however, was none other than that which, refusing to question its own origins in mediation, appears as directly present to itself, and therefore self-sufficient. The Cartesian cogito, for example, which structuralists and poststructuralists invariably take as an object of critique, is in fact neither the psychological self nor the transcendental self, but a process of doubt that the "difference" between diverse systems ineluctably produuces. Descartes's doubt cannot be separated from his existential condition "between" systems, as a traveler and exile from France. Perhaps we may borrow the formulation of Spinoza, who did not belong to any system and who sought to oppose Descartes by being faithful to Descartes; Spinoza rejected the idea that "I think, therefore I am" was a syllogism, insisting instead that "doubting, I am."

A methodology which does clearly inform this book may be said to be the genealogical method of Friedrich Nietzsche and Michel Foucault. This genealogical method attempts to expose the way in which we take what has been historically produced as natural, the contingent as the necessary. But this methodology finds it necessary to exclude from consideration people or texts which demonstrated an awareness of a discursive formation even while they were a part of it. Foucault, in *The Order of Things*, for example, carefully excluded discussion of Marx and Nietzsche. Although they both belonged to the late-nineteenth-century episteme, it was precisely that episteme that they attempted to elucidate critically. They rejected Cartesianism, and yet they were both "cognitos" who found, in Spinoza's phrase, that "doubting, I am." Foucault himself was another cogito—which has nothing to do with his "inner self."

Although I might have written this book consistently according to the genealogical method, I did not do so. In the genealogical method, when proper names appear, they are treated merely as arbitrary signs, denoting the contingency of the event. In this book I frequently discuss Kunikida Doppo, for example. I did not do this because I thought Kunikida was a great writer—it was the reverse. Only Sōseki was an exception. For Sōseki perceived the inversion of modern literature from within modern literature. He resisted modern literature but was unable to escape its inevitability. Privileging

ı   in the first edition of this book I neglected to express
my aɟ   ıtion to Edwin McClellan, who invited me to teach at
Yale, ɪ   ı Fredric Jameson, who has stimulated and encouraged
my wc   ɔm that time until the present. I would like to thank
them hₑ

As with the Japanese paperback edition of *Origins of Modern Japanese Literature*, I have decided to publish this English translation of my book without revision. I have already discussed my own areas of dissatisfaction with the book in the "Afterword" to the Japanese paperback edition. In addition to the points mentioned there, I have been concerned that the book was not written with foreign readers in mind nor as an academic book. If anything, it has historical significance as a project undertaken within the context of Japanese journalistic writing in the late 1970s. Had I intended to address a foreign audience, I would certainly have written the book differently, attempting to make it accessible even to readers with no prior knowledge of Japan. However, writing the book in such a way would have entailed a certain amount of rearrangement and abbreviation, consciously or unconsciously accommodating the foreign reader. As a result, the book might easily have slipped into the vein of broad generalization quite typical of books on Japanese literature. This mode of generalization does not tell us much about how Japanese themselves think about things. Although there may be sections of my book which are meaningful only in relation to the late 1970s context within which they were written, I nevertheless believe that the book is basically "accessible" to foreign readers. It was for this reason that I finally decided not to make any changes in the English version. I have simply added as a final chapter the essay on "Sōseki and Genre." Now the book which opened with a consideration of Sōseki as a theorist ends with a discussion of Sōseki as a creative writer. I have also appended some simple notes at the end of each chapter. They represent something of my thinking about these topics at the present time.

The type of "critique" of modern Japanese literature I undertook in this book was not particularly new, even within the Japanese context. In fact there had been a widespread movement to critically assess the modern in the early 1970s. This was linked both to Japan's rapid economic growth in the 1960s and to the politics of the New Left. Even this critique, however, was not entirely new.

It could be seen as a transposition of the debate over "Overcoming the Modern," an idea which was being advocated in the late 1930s. Three different groups of philosophers and critics—disciples of the philosopher Nishida Kitarō and of literary critics Kobayashi Hideo and Yasuda Yojūrō—participated in the debate, in which it was proposed that Cartesian dualism, historicism, industrial capitalism, and the nation-state all be "overcome." These views, of course, were a manifestation of a Japanese imperialist ideology which aimed at war with the Western powers and establishment of a Greater Asia Co-Prosperity Sphere. But the phenomenon cannot be explained away quite so simply. For the thinkers whose positions were represented in the debate (Nishida, Kobayashi, Yasuda) differed, not only from the fascist ideologues of the time but even from their own disciples, in that they were among the leading philosophical and critical minds of their day. Thus, in this debate we can see in concentrated form the different contradictions which have haunted Japanese discourse since the Meiji period. It is the forerunner of both the critique of modernity carried out in the 1970s and the postmodernism which became visible in the 1980s.

Mishima Yukio, for example, who committed suicide in 1970 after calling for the Self Defense Force to stage a coup d'état, had been one of the Japanese romanticists, and his writings and actions cannot be understood without historical reference to the notion of romantic irony. In the left-wing radicalism of the same era, as was the case with Maoism, pan-Asianism (anti-Westernism) was linked with a critique of modern civilization. The subtle link between the critique of modernity of the 1970s and that of the 1930s, however, is not characteristic of Japan alone, but can also be seen in Europe. For at the intellectual core of the radicalism of the late 1960s (particularly the discourse of poststructuralism, or what has come to be called postmodernism), we may note the impact of the "critique of modernity" developed by certain controversial thinkers. One was Heidegger, who was positively complicitous with Nazism. That this matter was problematized anew as postmodern thought gained influence in the 1980s is well known. In America this problematization took the form of the debate over Paul de Man, which was also fueled by the conservative revival of new versions of modernist and enlightenment thought. But the issues raised by the critique of modernity cannot be simply dismissed on the basis of its relation to fascism. Rather, we must develop new ways of interrogating modernity which take this problem into account.

The concept of the "modern" is an extremely ambiguous one. This is true, not only for Japanese, but for non-Western peoples generally, among whom the "modern" and the "Western" are often conflated. Since, in the West as well as Asia, the modern and premodern are distinct from one another, it stands to reason that modernity must be conceptualized separately from Westernness, but since the "origin" of modernity is Western, the two cannot so easily be separated. This is why in non-Western countries the critique of modernity and the critique of the West tend to be confused. Many misperceptions arise out of this. One, for example, is that Japanese modern literature, because it is not Western, is not fully modern. The flip-side of this idea is that, if a work's materials and themes are non-Western, the work must be antimodern. These two assertions are as common in Japanese literary criticism as they are in Western scholarship on Japanese literature.

However, as long as a work is seen as the "expression" of the "self" of an "author," that work is already located within the apparatus of modern literature, no matter how antimodern and anti-Western it may be. Mishima Yukio and Kawabata Yasunari, for example, are not the slightest bit "traditional," but are clearly modern authors. If we are truly to subject modernity to interrogation, it is the self-evidence of the apparatus of "author," of the "self," and of "expression" that must be interrogated. In the Japanese debate "Overcoming the Modern," this kind of critical inquiry was entirely lacking. If we question the origins of these apparatuses, however, we may fall into another trap, since all of them originated in the West. We would seem to be returned once again to that idle, shallow debate that can be summed up in the word "influence." The concept of influence suggests the relationship of an original to a copy. Needless to say, countless books have been written by both Japanese and Western critics about ways in which Japanese writers received, incorrectly received, or resisted modern Western "originals."

This perspective might be transformed if we look into the "inversion" that exists within the origin itself. Do we, in fact, need to return to the ancient West as Nietzsche did? I tried to turn this question around. Even if we grant that modern literature was the product of an inversion peculiar to the West, might it not be possible to discover this inversion more dramatically revealed in the non-West than in the West itself, where its origins have become concealed? This was why I made the focus of my study the decade of the 1890s.

At the time I sought to locate in *genbun itchi* the basic condition which had made the self-evidence of modern literature ineluctable. Contrary to what its name has been taken to imply, the *genbun itchi* movement resulted in the production of a certain kind of "writing." At the same time, insofar as it was maintained that writing was only a transparent instrument for the transmission of ideas, *genbun itchi* eradicated writing. An internal subject and an objectively existing "object" were thus simultaneously produced. This was the starting point both for the notion of self-expression and for that realistic mode of writing known in Japanese as *shajitsu* (copying). We can perceive the difference quite clearly if we look at writing done by writers in the 1890s shortly before the consolidation of *genbun itchi*. Despite the fact that landscape was thematized pervasively in premodern Japanese literature, this was not landscape as we see it today. What they saw was a preexisting text. We might say that "landscape" was not so much discovered within the epistemological inversion concentrated in *genbun itchi* as it was invented. In this book I used the term "discovery of landscape" to connote the inversion whereby something which had never existed before came to be seen as self-evident, as an existence which in fact preceded the inversion. It is an allegorical representation of the material apparatuses of modernity.

It should be stressed that *genbun itchi* was solely propagated by novelists and not by the state or by various state ideologues. In his *Imagined Communities*, Benedict Anderson states that the development of vernacular languages was indispensable to the formation of the modern nation-state, and suggests in a general manner the role played in effecting this by newspapers and novels. This was also the case in Japan. Despite the progress made toward political and economic modernization within the first two decades following the Restoration (with the establishment of the diet and promulgation of the constitution), something necessary to the formation of a nation was lacking. It is no exaggeration to say that it was novelists who provided this. It is because of this that criticism of the modern in Japan has to begin with criticism of modern literature. Furthermore, it was in this period that the discipline of Japanese literature (*kokubungaku*) was established, involving the production of a reorganized history of "national" literature from the Imperial poetry anthology, the *Manyōshū*, onward. This academic discipline of Japanese literature (*kokubungaku*) should be distinguished from the nativism (*kokugaku*) of the Edo period. It entailed a reconstitution of the literature of the past in terms of a modern perspective.

My book, then, is not a literary history but a critique of that history of Japanese literature which includes classical literature. A critique that returns to the "origins" must also critique the "origins." For the nationalism that seeks the originality of Japanese literature in a source prior to modernity is itself nothing other than the forgetting of origins. In this sense perhaps we could say that *genbun itchi* is something that occurred in every non-Western society and even in the emerging European nation-states. At the very least we can say that this phenomenon certainly appeared in China and Korea. This was effected not so much through Western pressure as through the course of Japan's imperialist aggression. But in the case of any nation, the inquiry into origins contains a trap. The Western equivalent of *genbun itchi*, for example, developed over a very long period of time. In order to trace it precisely, it is necessary to go back to the phonocentrism of Greek thought, as Derrida did.

But my own feeling is that the genealogical "return," that is, the tracing back of origins, should not be taken too far. By contrast to many scholars who sought the origins of anti-Semitism in medieval and ancient times, for example, Hannah Arendt looked to the late-nineteenth-century consolidation of state economies. As she argues in *The Origins of Totalitarianism*, the spread of anti-Semitism accompanied not the strengthening, but the dwindling, of Jewish economic power. The victory of Prussia over France in 1871 symbolized this ascendance of the state. Writing about this victory in "Untimely Meditations," Nietzsche observed that it was not culture, but merely the state, that had triumphed. Nietzsche himself was one who had tried to pursue hidden origins no matter where—or on what level—they were concealed. Yet in the end wasn't the inversion that was proceeding in the "times" Nietzsche himself lived in and confronted the decisive one for him? Despite his intense effort to locate the origins of an inversion in Christianity and Platonism, it was the nation-state and its literature that Nietzsche self-consciously opposed when he insisted on identifying himself as a "European."

In discussing the nearness of origins, we may note the outcome of the tracing of origins undertaken by Heidegger, who had criticized Nietzsche for remaining caught within the confines of Western metaphysics. Heidegger fully endorsed the anti-Semitism and nationalism produced by the "times" that Nietzsche had resisted. And this notion of the nearness of origins has an even deeper significance in terms of the considerations I have undertaken in this book. The period around the year 1870 was one of worldwide upheaval. It was a period in which nation-states appeared in many regions: not only in Germany, but in America, Italy, and postwar France. Over the next ten years these modern states become imperialist powers, and as a reaction to this nationalism developed in every part of the world.

The Meiji Restoration of Japan in 1868 must be seen in this world-historical context. Because of the outcome of the Franco-Prussian War, Japan's revolutionary government made Prussia its model. Then Japan, which had escaped the fate of colonization, became a colonizing power itself, joining the ranks of Western powers through the Sino-Japanese (1894) and Russo-Japanese (1904) wars. This transformation was manifested in a relatively brief period of time between 1868 and 1911, during the Meiji period. Thus, during the decade of the 1890s upon which I focus in this book, we can find not only the concentrated emergence of phenomena which developed over a long period in the West (*genbun itchi*, the discovery of landscape), but developments which are virtually contemporaneous with the West. Foucault has remarked that "literature" was established in the West only in the late nineteenth century. The standardization of literature may have been linked to the establishment of the nation-state. This entailed, for example, suppressing the diverse possibilities that the English novel manifested in the eighteenth century. If this is the case, it is in the latter half of the nineteenth century itself that we should look for the "origins" of modern literature, and not before. While it might appear that a more deep-rooted origin can be traced further back, to do so would be to ignore the inversion that emerged in this time period itself; indeed, it would strengthen that very inversion. For this reason I believe that the problems I have inquired into in this book on the origins of modern Japanese literature do not concern Japan alone.

Finally, I would like to express my thanks to Brett de Bary. More, even, than for the translation itself, I am grateful for her interest in this book, which renewed my concern about and prompted me to reconsider a number of problems I might have forgotten in the Japanese context.

Notes

Introduction

1. The discussions of different modern critical debates interspersed throughout the two volumes of Donald Keene's *Dawn to the West* (New York: Holt, Rinehart, and Winston, 1984) proved invaluable to us in the course of translating *Origins of Modern Japanese Literature*.

2. From the afterword published in the Kōdansha 1980 edition, p. 218.

3. Naoki Sakai, "Modernity and its Critique: The Problem of Universalism and Particularism," in Miyoshi and Harootunian, eds., *Postmodernism and Japan* (Durham: Duke University Press, 1988), p. 112. The parallels between Japanese postmodernism and philosophical tendencies in the 1930s is touched on in several others essays in this volume.

4. Takeuchi Yoshimi, *"Kindai no chōkoku"* (Overcoming the modern), in *Takeuchi Yoshimi zenshū* (Complete works of Takeuchi Yoshimi) (Tokyo: Chikuma Shobō, 1980), vol. 8, p. 17.

5. Ibid., p. 34.

6. Ibid., p. 22.

7. Ibid., p. 21.

8. See Yasuda Yojūrō, "Nihon bunka no dokusōsei" (On the originality of Japanese culture), in *Yasuda Yojūrō zenshū* (Complete works of Yasuda Yojūrō) (Tokyo: Kōdansha, 1986), vol. 11, pp. 269–86.

9. Janine Beichmann, *Masaoka Shiki* (Boston: Twayne, 1982), p. 46.

10. Andrew Feenberg, *Lukacs, Marx, and the Sources of Critical Theory* (New York and Oxford: Oxford University Press, 1986), p. 134.

11. *Origins*, p. 13.

12. Ibid., p. 37.

13. William Haver, "A Preface to Translation," paper delivered at Cornell University, November 30, 1990, p. 4.

14. Although much mischief has been done by citing this term out of context, let me include the following, from the *Archaeology of Knowledge*, because of its scope: "By *episteme* we mean . . . the total set of relations that unite, at a given period, the discursive practices that give rise to epistemological figures, sciences, and possibly formalized systems. . . . The episteme is not a form of knowledge (*connaissance*) or type of rationality which, crossing the boundaries of the most varied sciences, manifests the

sovereign unity of a subject, a spirit, or a period; it is the totality of relations that can be discovered, for a given period, between the sciences when one analyzes them at the level of discursive regularities." *The Archaeology of Knowledge*, tr. A. M. Sheridan Smith (New York: Harper, 1972), p. 191.

1   The Discovery of Landscape

1. Natsume Sōseki, *"Bungakuron"* (A theory of literature) in *Natsume Sōseki zenshū* (The complete works of Natsume Sōseki, hereinafter abbreviated *NSZ*) (Tokyo: Kadokawa Shoten, 1960), vol. 16, pp. 9–10.

2. Natsume Sōseki, *"Tsubouchi hakase to hamuretto"* (Doctor Tsubouchi and Hamlet), *NSZ*, vol. 8, pp. 291–92.

3. Natsume Sōseki, *"Sōsakka no taido"* (The creative mentality), *NSZ*, vol. 5, pp. 334–35.

4. Oka Saburō cites Sōseki's description, in *Bungakuron*, of the moment-by-moment transition of perceptions of a viewer scanning St. Paul's cathedral from its base to its dome and notes its similarity to the following analysis in Morgan's *An Introduction to Comparative Psychology* (London: W. Scott, 1894): "Repeat aloud some familiar lines of poetry, and stop suddenly after any word in the course of your recitation. You will be conscious of the last words you have uttered just falling away, and of new words, not yet uttered, but, as we say, on the tip of the tongue, just coming into consciousness. So too in hearing a familiar piece of music, one feels the coming harmonies before they are played" (p. 12). See Oka Saburō, *Natsume Sōseki kenkyū* (Tokyo: Kokubunsha, 1981), p. 252.

5. Ibid., pp. 334–35.

6. Natsume Sōseki, *"Bungakuron," NSZ*, vol. 16, pp. 8–9.

7. Usami Keiji, *"Sansuiga ni zetsubō o miru"* (The despair of Japanese landscape painting), *Gendai Shisō*, May 1977.

8. Ibid.

9. Kunikida Doppo, *"Wasureenu hitobito"* (Unforgettable people), trans. Jay Rubin, *Monumenta Nipponica*, vol. 27, no. 3 (1972): 298–99.

10. Ibid., pp. 303–4.

11. Ibid., p. 303.

12. Valéry, Paul, *Degas, Danse, Dessin* (Paris: Gallimard), p. 131.

13. Jan Hendrik Van den Berg, trans. H. F. Croes (New York: Norton, 1983), p. 231.

14. Kitamura Tōkoku, *"Jōnetsu"* (Passion) in *Kitamura Tōkokushū, Meiji bungaku zenshū*, vol. 29 (Tokyo: Chikuma Shobō, 1976), p. 156.

15. Etō, Jun, *"Shajitsushugi no genryū"* (Sources of realism), *Shinchō*, October 1971.

16. Kobayashi Hideo, "Samazama naru isho" (Different types of designs), in *Kobayashi Hideo zenshū* (The complete works of Kobayashi Hideo), vol. I (Tokyo: Shinchosha, 1967), p. 17.

17. Langer, Suzanne, *Philosophy in a New Key* (New York: New American Library, 1951), pp. 11–12.

18. Nakamura, Mitsuo, *Meiji bungakushi* (History of Meiji literature), in *Nakamura Mitsuo zenshū* (Tokyo: Chikuma Shobō, 1973), pp. 169–70.

2 The Discovery of Interiority

1. Futabatei Shimei, *"Yoga genbun itchi no yurai"* (How I came to use *Genbun Itchi*), first published in *Bunshō Sekai* (The world of writing) in 1906. This citation may be found in *Futabatei Shimei zenshū* (The complete works of Futabatei Shimei) (Tokyo: Iwanami Shoten, 1964–65), pp. 170–71.

2. Mori Ōgai, "The Dancing Girl" (*Maihime*), trans. Richard Bowring, *"Maihime"* (The Dancing Girl), in *Monumenta Nipponica* 30, no. 2 (1975): 154.

3. The difficulty of translating the opening chapters of Futabatei's *The Drifting Clouds* has often been noted. In these sentences Futabatei draws on a broad range of stylistic conventions, including archaic pillow words (*makura kotoba*), as well those of Edo popular fiction (*gesaku*) and storytelling (*rakugo*). I have used Marleigh Grayer Ryan's translation in *Japan's First Modern Novel: Ukigumo of Futabatei Shimei* (New York: Columbia University Press, 1967), p. 197. The long and elaborate syntactical units of Futabatei's prose have been rearranged and divided into shorter sentences by Ryan in an effort to accommodate English grammar.

4. Yanagita Kunio, *An Anthology of Travel Literature* (*Kikōbunshū*) in *The Collected Works of Yanagita Kunio* (*Teihon Yanagita Kunio Zenshū*) (Tokyo: Chikuma Shobō, 1972), vol. 23, pp. 328–38.

5. Masaoka Shiki, *More Letters to a Tanka Poet* (*Futatabi Utayomi ni atauru sho*), 1899.

6. T. S. Eliot, "Dante" (1929) in *Selected Essays* (London: Faber, 1972), pp. 237–77.

7. Takahama Kyoshi, "The Origins and Significance of the Realist Style" (*Shaseibun no yurai to sono igi*), in *The Complete Works of Takahama Kyoshi* (*Takahama Kyoshi zenshū*) (Tokyo: Mainichi Shimbunsha, 1973).

8. Nakamura Mitsuo, *Japanese Fiction in the Meiji Era* (*Meiji bungakushi*) (Tokyo: Chikuma, 1963).

9. Itō Sei, *A History of the Japanese Bundan* (*Nihon Bundanshi*), vol. I (Tokyo: Kodansha, 1953–73), pp. 131–32.

10. Yanagita Kunio, "Life in the Mountains" (*Yama no jinsei*), in Yanagita, *Collected Works*, vol. 4, p. 60.

11. Masaoka Shiki, *Talks on Haiku from the Otter's Den* (*Dassai shooku haiwa*) in *Complete Works of Masaoka Shiki* (*Shiki zenshū*) (Tokyo: Arusu, 1924–26), vol. 4, pp. 165–66. This passage is translated by Janine Beichman, *Masaoka Shiki* (Boston: Twayne, 1982), pp. 35–36.

12. Yoshimoto Takaaki, *A Theory of Early Poetry* (*Shoki Kayōron*) (Tokyo: Kawade Shobō Shinsha, 1977), pp. 15–16.

13. Yoshimoto Takaaki, *Theory*.

14. Jan Hendrik Van den Berg, *The Changing Nature of Man*, trans. H. F. Croes (New York: Norton, 1983). Van den Berg writes, "The landscape behind her is justly famous; it is the first landscape painted as a landscape, just because it was a landscape. A pure landscape, not just a backdrop for human actions: nature, nature as the middle ages did not know it, an exterior nature closed within itself and self-sufficient, an exterior from which the human element has, in principle, been removed entirely," p. 231.

15. Edmund Husserl, *The Crisis of European Sciences and Transcendental Phenomenology: An Introduction to Phenomenological Philosophy*, trans. David Carr (Evanston: Northwestern University Press, 1970), pp. 48–49.

16. Konrad Lorenz, *Civilized Man's Eight Deadly Sins*, trans. Marjorie Kerr Wilson (New York: Harcourt Brace Jovanovich, 1974), pp. 93–94.

17. Kunikida Doppo, "On the Banks of the Sorachi River" (*Sorachigawa no Kishibe*), in *Complete Works of Kunikida Doppo* (*Teihon Kunikida Doppo zenshū*) (Tokyo: Gakushū Kenkyūsha, 1978), vol. 3, pp. 7–24. The quoted passages occur on p. 9 and p. 23.

18. Kunikida Doppo, "Musashino," in *The Complete Works of Kunikida Doppo* (*Teihon Kunikida Doppo zenshū*) (Tokyo: Gakushu Kenkyusha, 1978), pp. 73–74. This excerpt is cited with some revisions of phrases where the grammatical construction has immediate relevance for Karatani's argument, from David Chibbett, trans., *River Mist and Other Stories* (New York: Unesco, 1983), pp. 104–5.

19. Kunikida, *Complete Works*, p. 75.

20. Chibbett, *River Mist*, pp. 109–110.

21. Kunikida Doppo, "Unfathomable Nature" (*Fukashiginaru daishizen*), in *Complete Works*, vol. 1, pp. 539–40. The article was first published in *Waseda Bungaku* in February 1908.

22. Jean Starobinski, *Jean-Jacques Rousseau: Le transparence et l'obstacle* (Paris, 1954), translated by Arthur Goldhammer, *Jean-Jacques Rousseau: Transparency and Obstruction* (Chicago: University of Chicago Press), p. 125.

23. Ibid., pp. 199–200.

24. Kunikida Doppo, "Death" (*Shi*), in Kunikida, *Complete Works*, vol. 2, pp. 154–55.

25. André Leroi-Ghouran, *Le Geste et la Parole*, 2 vols. (Paris: Albin Michel, 1964, 1965). My English translation is based on the citation in-

cluded in Karatani's text, from the Japanese translation of Leroi-Ghouran by Araki Jun.

26. Tayama Katai, "Doppo as Natural Man" (*Shizen no hito Doppo*), an essay first published in the journal *Shinchō*, July 15, 1908. The comment by Akutagawa Ryūnosuke appears in the short story "Kappa," in *The Complete Works of Akutagawa Ryūnosuke* (*Akutagawa Ryūnosuke zenshū*) (Tokyo: Iwanami Shoten, 1977–78), vol. 8, p. 357.

27. Roland Barthes, *Writing Degree Zero*, trans. Annette Lavers and Colin Smith (New York: Hill and Wang, 1967), p. 32.

28. Masaoka Shiki, *Nanatabi utayomi ni atauru sho*, in vol. 7 of *Complete Works*, p. 39.

29. Ibid., p. 40.

30. Natsume Sōseki, *Chūgaku kairyōsaku*, written in 1891 and cited by Karatani.

31. Masaoka Shiki, *Principles of Haiku* (*Haikai no taiyō*), in vol. 4 of *Shiki zenshū*, p. 342.

3 Confession as a System

1. Tayama Katai, "Thirty Years in Tokyo" (Tokyo no sanjūnen), in *The Complete Works of Tayama Katai* (Tokyo: Bunsendō Shoten, 1974), vol. 15, p. 601.

2. Shimamura Hōgetsu, "A Review of *The Quilt*" (*Futon o hyōsu*), in *The Complete Works of Shimamura Hōgetsu* (*Hōgetsu zenshū*) (Tokyo: Nihon Tosho Center, 1979), vol. 2, p. 49.

3. Michel Foucault, *The History of Sexuality Volume I: An Introduction*, trans. Robert Hurley (New York: Vintage Books, 1980), p. 61.

4. Masamune Hakuchō, "A General Assessment of Meiji Literary Society" (*Meiji Bundan Sōhyō*), in *The Complete Works of Masamune Hakuchō* (*Masamune Hakuchō zenshū*) (Tokyo: Shinchōsha, 1976), vol. 6, pp. 209–10.

5. Kitamura Tōkoku, "A Discussion of *Iki*, Extended to the Aloes-Wood Pillow" (*Iki o ronjite Kyara-makura ni oyobu*), in *The Complete Works of Kitamura Tōkoku* (*Tōkoku Zenshū*) (Tokyo: Iwanami Shoten, 1980–81), vol. 1, p. 269.

6. Karatani refers to the distinction between two words for "love" in contemporary Japanese: *koi* (恋) and *ren'ai* (恋愛). Building on Kitamura's observation, Karatani claims that "love" in Edo literature was exclusively referred to by the term *koi*, which always connotes sexual love. The term *ren'ai* came into use only during the Meiji period, when Kitamura Tōkoku's writings on the subject were particularly influential. *Ren'ai* may refer to platonic, idealized love, as well as to sexual love, but, because of its early associations with Japanese Christianity and literary romanticism, is often

translated into English as "romantic love." In contemporary speech it is used to describe a "love" marriage (*ren'ai kekkon*) as opposed to an arranged marriage (*miai kekkon*).

7. Friedrich Nietzsche, *The Anti-Christ*, trans. Walter Kaufmann, in *The Portable Nietzsche* (New York: Viking, 1954), p. 632.

8. Yamaji Aizan, "A History of the Church in Contemporary Japan" (*Gendai Nihon Kyōkai-shiron*), in *Selected Works of Yamaji Aizan* (*Yamaji Aizan-shū*), vol. 3 of *Minyūsha Shisō Bungaku Sōsho* (Tokyo: Sanichi Shobō, 1985), p. 225.

9. Yamamoto's statement was originally written in English and translated by Uchimura. Our source is the Japanese translation by Matsuzawa Hiroaki in *Uchimura Kanzō*, vol. 38 of *Great Books of Japan* (*Nihon no Meicho*) (Tokyo: Chūōkōronsha, 1971), pp. 192–93.

10. In this passage Karatani plays on the similarity between the words *shujin* (主人), meaning "master" (of a feudal domain, of a household, etc.) and *shutai* (主体), the term used in modern Japanese philosophy for "subject" and "subjectivity." Samurai became modern "autonomous" subjects by giving up their status as masters.

11. Uchimura Kanzō, in Matsuzawa, *Uchimura Kanzō*, p. 83.

12. Ibid., p. 88.

13. Ibid., p. 93.

14. Ibid., p. 171.

15. Shiga Naoya, "An Impure Mind" (*Nigotta Atama*), from *The Complete Works of Shiga Naoya* (*Shiga Naoya zenshū*) (Tokyo: Iwanami Shoten, 1983), vol. 1, pp. 204–6.

16. Nietzsche, *Portable Nietzsche*, p. 590.

17. Shiga Naoya, "Diary of Claudius" (*Kuroodeius no nikki*) in *Shiga Naoya zenshū*, vol. 2, pp. 21–22.

18. Maurice Merleau-Ponty, cited from the Japanese translation, *Me to Seishin*, by Takiura and Kida. I have used William Cobb's translation of "Les relations avec autrui chez l'enfant" (The Child's Relations with Others) in James M. Edie, ed., *The Primacy of Perception: And Other Essays on Phenomenological Psychology, the Philosophy of Art, History, and Politics* (Evanston: Northwestern University Press, 1964), pp. 148–49.

19. Ichikawa Hiroshi, "The World of 'Person' in Language" (*Ninshōteki Sekai no Kōzō*).

20. Friedrich Nietzsche, *The Will to Power*, trans. Walter Kaufmann and R. J. Hollingdale (New York: Vintage Books, 1986), p. 270.

21. Ibid., pp. 271–72.

22. Uchimura Kanzō, in Matsuzawa, *Uchimura Kanzō*, p. 86.

4 Sickness as Meaning

1. We have not been able to locate a copy of this Shinchōsha publication. We have translated the passage from Karatani's text.

2. Tokutomi Roka, *Hototogisu* (translated as *Nami-ko: A Realistic Novel*), trans. Sakae Shioya and E. F. Edgett (Boston: Herbert B. Turner, 1904), p. 2.

3. Ibid., pp. 207–8.

4. Susan Sontag, *Illness as Metaphor* (New York: Farrar, Straus and Giroux, 1977).

5. René Dubos, *Mirage of Health: Utopias, Progress and Biological Change*, vol. 11 of *World Perspectives*, ed. Ruth Nanda Anshen (New York: Harper & Brothers, 1959).

6. Sontag, *Illness*, p. 28.

7. Masaoka Shiki, "Byōshō Rokushaku" (Sixfoot sickbed), vol. 11 of *Shiki zenshū* (Collected works), 22 vols., plus 3 supplements (Tokyo: Kōdansha, 1975–78), p. 231.

8. Masaoka Shiki, "Bashō Zōdan," (Some remarks on Bashō), vol. 4 of *Shiki Zenshū* (Collected works), 22 vols., plus 3 supplements (Tokyo: Kōdansha, 1975–78), pp. 224–71.

9. Tokutomi, ibid., pp. 154–55.

10. Dubos, *Mirage of Health*, p. 65.

11. Dubos, ibid., pp. 127–28.

12. Sontag, *Illness*, p. 3.

13. Friedrich Nietzsche, *The Genealogy of Morals: A Polemic*, trans. Horace B. Samuel (New York: Macmillan, 1911), pp. 45–46.

14. Nietzsche, *Portable Nietzsche*, p. 264.

15. Hattori Toshirō, *Edo jidai igakushi no kenkyū* (A study of medical history in the Edo period) (Tokyo: Yoshikawa Kōbunkan, 1978), p. 350.

16. Michel Foucalt, *The Birth of the Clinic: An Archaeology of Medical Perception*, trans. A. M. Sheridan Smith (1973; New York: Vintage Books, 1975), p. 33.

17. Ibid., p. 34.

5 The Discovery of the Child

1. Inokuma Yōko, "*Nihon jidō bungaku no tokushoku*" (Special characteristics of Japanese children's literature) in *Nihon jidō bungaku gairon* (Survey of Japanese children's literature), ed. Nihon Jidō Bungakkai (Tokyo: Tokyo Shoseki, 1976), pp. 34–35.

2. Inokuma Yōko, pp. 38–39.

3. Iwaya Sazanami, cited in Kan Tadamichi, *Nihon no jidō bungaku* (Japanese children's literature) (Tokyo: Ohtsuki Shoten, 1966), p. 28.

4. Kan Tadamichi, *Nihon no jidō bungaku*, pp. 29–30.

5. Jan Hendrik van den Berg, *The Changing Nature of Man*, trans. H. F. Croes (New York: Norton, 1961), p. 23.

6. Yanagita Kunio, *Kodomo Fūdōki* (Record of children's customs), in *Teihon Yanagita Kunio zenshū* (Definitive complete works of Yanagita Kunio), vol. 21 (Tokyo: Chikuma Shobō, 1972), pp. 23–24.

7. Claude Lévi-Strauss, *Tristes Tropiques*, trans. John and Doreen Weightman (New York: Atheneum, 1974), p. 284.

8. Yamashita Tsuneo, *Han-hattatsuron: Yokuatsu no ningengaku kara no kaihō* (Against development: throwing off the oppression of humanism) (Tokyo: Gendai Shokan, 1977), p. 69.

9. Yanagita Kunio, *Kokyō Shichijūnen Shūi* (Home seventy years: gleanings).

10. Geoffrey Hartmann, *Beyond Formalism: Literary Essays, 1958–1970* (New Haven: Yale University Press, 1970), p. 300.

11. Gaston Bouthoul, *L'Infanticide differe* (Paris: Hachette, 1970).

12. Yanagita Kunio, *Mukashibanashi kaisetsu* (A commentary on folktales).

13. Sakaguchi Ango, "Bungaku no furusato" (The birthplace of literature), in *Teihon Sakaguchi Ango zenshū* (Definitive complete works of Sakaguchi Ango), vol. 7 (Tokyo: Fuyukisha, 1967–71), p. 116.

14. Michel Foucault, *Mental Illness and Psychology*, trans. Alan Sheridan (New York: Harper and Row, 1876), pp. 80 and 81.

15. Concerning the school system established in the Meiji period, Tamiya Yūzō, scholar of children's literature, has pointed out to me the existence, not only of "passive resistance by the people," but of active resistance. For example, one year after the implementation of the school system, there was a riot of *Shinshū* Buddhists in Tsuruga, while in the prefectures of Okayama, Tottori, Kagawa, and Fukuoka, there were riots against both the education and conscription laws, and many schools were burned. Tamiya writes, "The elementary school in the early Meiji period was, together with the town hall and the police station, the bastion of the policies of the new age that were being diffused to the communities, ranging from the conscription system to cultural enlightenment. It is not without reason that the three top officials in the villages in modern Japan were the village master, the police chief, and the school principal." Tamiya Yūzō, "Yamanaka Tsune no sedai: Shokokumin sedai no seishin keisei" (Yamanaka Tsune and his generation: The psychological development of the generation of young patriots), published in *Shiihorun*, vol. 9.

16. Eric Hoffer, *The Temper of Our Time* (New York: Harper and Row, 1964), p. xii.

17. Vladimir Lenin, "One Step Forward, Two Steps Back (The Crisis in

our Party)," in *Collected Works*, trans. Abraham Fineberg and Naomi Jochel, ed. Clemens Duit (Moscow: Foreign Languages Publishing House, 1961), vol. 7, pp. 391–92.

6 On the Power to Construct

1. Erwin Panofsky, "Die Perspektive als symbolische Form," in *Aufsätze zu Grundfragen der Kunstwissenschaft* (Berlin: Wissenschaftsverlag Volker Spiess, 1950), p. 108.

2. Ibid.

3. Ibid., p. 108.

4. Ibid.

5. Ibid., p. 112.

6. Ibid., p. 117.

7. Ibid., p. 125.

8. Ibid.

9. Ibid., pp. 101–2.

10. Akutagawa Ryūnosuke, "Bungeitekina, amari ni bungeitekina" (Literary, all too literary), in *Akutagawa zenshū* (Tokyo: Iwanami Shoten, 1978), vol. 9, pp. 57–61.

11. We have added the parenthetical explanation to clarify Karatani's rather tersely stated contrast between *suihieteki na okuyuki no enkinhō* and *suichokutekina fukasa no enkinhō*, literally, "horizontal depth" and "vertical depth."—Ed.

12. Karatani refers to the debate carried out between Shōyō and Ōgai between 1891 and 1892. Ōgai responded to two articles published by Shōyō which attempted to classify types of Meiji fiction with reference to characterization. Donald Keene has translated a passage from the second article, "*Azusa no miko*" (The medium's divining rod), in which Shōyō asserted: "Criticism must be objective, especially when it deals with objective poetry—that is dramatic poetry; in other words, it must be inductive criticism. The critic, like a botanist describing plants or a zoologist writing about animals, should avoid preconceptions when writing about a work." Although Ōgai sympathized with Shōyō's attempt to establish an inductive criticism, he devoted a number of erudite articles to disputing what he took to be Shōyō's position that literature did not express "ideals." Karatani's observation that Ōgai appeared to have overwhelmed Shōyō is substantiated by Keene's comment that at a certain point "it became apparent that the context was unequal between the two men, certainly when it came to a discussion of philosophical concepts; in fact, they were using the same word, *risō*, in two quite different senses. For Shōyō it meant didactic intent,

a quality in literature he had rejected in *The Essence of the Novel*, but for Ōgai it meant a Platonic or universal ideal that lay behind the composition of a work of art or the appreciation of that work of art by the critic." For Keene's discussion of the debate, see *Dawn to the West: Japanese Literature in the Modern Era*, vol. 2, *Poetry, Drama, Criticism* (New York: Holt, Rinehart, Winston, 1984), pp. 505–12.

13. In Shōyō's text the English word "interpretation" appears in romanization, written in the *katakana* phonetic syllabary.

14. Tsubouchi Shōyō, "Preface to a Commentary on *Macbeth*" (*Makubesu hyōshaku no shogen*), in *Shōyō senshū* (Selected works of Tsubouchi Shōyō) (Tokyo: Shōyō Kyōkai, 1977), supplementary vol. 3, p. 163.

15. Ibid., p. 165.

16. Karatani refers to *Shōsetsu shinzui*, published by Tsubouchi in 1885, a work which has usually been seen as the first Japanese articulation of a theory of the modern psychological novel. Tsubouchi's writings inspired many pioneers of Meiji fiction, including the author of the *Drifting Clouds* (*Ukigumo*), Futabatei Shimei. The work has been translated as *The Essence of the Novel* by Nanette Twine, Brisbane, University of Queensland, Department of Japanese, 1983, Ph.D. dissertation.

17. Mori Ōgai in "*Shigaramizōshi no sanbō ronbun*" (Essays from a mountain villa, written for *The Weir*), in *Ōgai zenshū* (Tokyo: Iwanami Shoten, 1973), vol. 23, pp. 6–7.

18. Mori Ōgai, "Okitsu Yagoemon no Isho" [first version], in *Ōgai zenshū*, 38 vols. (Tokyo: Iwanami Shoten, 1971–75), vol. 38, pp. 497–500.

19. Ibid., pp. 580–81.

20. Ibid., p. 497.

21. Mori Ōgai, "Abe Ichizoku," in *Ōgai zenshū*, vol. 11, pp. 309–51. First published in *Chūōkōron*, vol. 28, no. 1 (1913).

22. Mori Ōgai, "Rekishi sonomama to rekishi-banare" (History as it is and beyond history), pp. 508–9. First published in *Kokoro no Hana*, vol. 19, no. 1 (1915).

23. The belief that the "pure" novel should be more autobiographical than fictional has been advocated and widely discussed in the Japanese literary world since about 1925. It was in this year that novelist Kume Masao wrote, "I cannot believe that art in the true sense of the word is the 'creation' of someone else's life. . . . I see it rather as the recreation of a life that actually took place." Translated and cited by Edward Fowler in *The Rhetoric of Confession* (Berkeley: University of California Press, 1988), p. 46.

24. Karatani refers to the celebrated literary debate between Akutagawa Ryūnosuke (1892–1927) and Tanizaki Junichirō (1886–1965), cut short by the former's suicide in 1927. As Karatani observes, the debate has usually been described as one in which Akutagawa advocated "pure" (autobiographical) writing while Tanizaki upheld the aesthetic value of the fictional.

Major essays are cited below. Discussions of the debate in English can be found in Noriko Mizuta Lippit's *Reality and Fiction in Modern Japanese Literature* (London: Macmillan, 1980) and in Keene's *Dawn to the West*, vol. I, pp. 575–77 and 754–56.

25. Saeki Shōichi, *Monogatari Geijutsuron: Tanizaki, Akutagawa, Mishima* (Essay on narrative art) (Tokyo: Kōdansha, 1979), p. 34.

26. Akutagawa Ryūnosuke, "Bungeitekina, amari ni Bungeitekina" in *Akutagawa Ryūnosuke Zenshū (Complete Works of Akutagawa Ryūnosuke)*, 12 vols. (Tokyo: Iwanami Shoten, 1977–78), vol. 9, pp. 3–80. First published in *Kaizō*, vol. 9, nos. 4–8 (1927).

27. Ibid., p. 6.

28. See "*Watakushishōsetsuron*" ("On the I-novel"), in *Kobayashi Hideo zenshū (Complete Works of Kobayashi Hideo)*, vol. 3 (Tokyo: Shinchōsha, 1975–77), p. 132.

29. Yoshimoto Takaaki, "Akutagawa Ryūnosuke no Shi" in *Yoshimoto Takaaki Zenchosakushū (Complete works of Yoshimoto Takaaki)*, 15 vols. (Tokyo: Keisō Shobō, 1968–75), vol. 7, pp. 154–55. First published in *Kokubungaku Kaishaku to Kanshō*, vol. 23, no. 8 (1958).

30. Cited in Nakamura Yōjirō, "*Seishin no Toposu*" (Topos of the mind).

31. Kobayashi Hideo, "Watakushishōsetsuron" pp. 131–32.

32. Tanizaki Jun'ichirō, "Jōzetsu-roku" in *Tanizaki Jun'ichirō zenshū (Complete Works of Tanizaki Junichirō)*, 28 vols. (Tokyo: Chūōkōronsha, 1972–75), vol. 20, p. 108.

33. Hamaguchi Masao, *Chi no Enkinhō* (The perspective of knowledge) or *Hanenkinhō* (Against perspective).

34. In the expression "*Bungakkai no purinsu*," Karatani alludes both to the Meiji literary world and to the journal *Bungakkai* (The world of literature), with which many of Yanagita's intellectual colleagues were associated.

35. Tanizaki, "Jōzetsu-roku," pp. 76–77.

36. Motoori Noringa, "*Genji monogatari tama no ogushi*," *Motoori Noringa zenshū*, (Tokyo: Chikuma Shobō, 1969), vol. 4, p. 183.

37. Tanizaki Junichirō, "Jōzetsu-roku," p. 108.

38. Kobayashi Hideo, "*Watakushishōsetsuron*," p. 145.

39. Luis Frois, *Europa esta provincia de Japao* (1585).

40. Akutagawa Ryūnosuke, "Smiles of the Gods" (*Kamigami no bishō*), *Akutagawa Ryūnosuke zenshū* (Tokyo: Chikuma Shobō, 1972), p. 10.

7 The Extinction of Genres

1. Northrop Frye, *Anatomy of Criticism* (Princeton: Princeton University Press, 1973), p. 308.

2. *Yomihon,* or "reading book," designated a popular genre of Edo prose fiction associated with Ueda Akinari, Takizawa Bakin, and others. *Yomihon* contained fictional narratives, often characterized by complex plots and fantastic events.

3. Futabatei Shimei, *Ukigumo,* trans. by Marleigh G. Ryan, *Japan's First Modern Novel: Ukigumo of Futabatei Shimei,* p. 199.

4. Natsume Sōseki, "*Shaseibun,*" in *NSZ,* vol. 4, pp. 280–83.

5. Ibid., p. 284.

6. Mikhail Bakhtin, *Problems of Dostoevsky's Poetics,* trans. Caryl Emerson (Manchester: Manchester University Press, 1984), p. 106.

7. An ancient custom whereby men and women gathered together to exchange poems, dance, and revel. A form of courtship ritual.

8. Sigmund Freud, "Humor," in *Collected Papers,* ed. James Strachey (London: Hogarth Press, 1959), p. 218.

9. Ibid., p. 220.

Glossary

Akutagawa Ryūnosuke (1892–1927). Writer. His first published short stories, *"Rashōmon"* (1915) and *"Hana"* ("The Nose," 1916) drew on both grotesque and comical elements from medieval literature, especially the twelfth century collection of tales, *Konjaku Monogatari*, and won him encouragement from Natsume Sōseki shortly before the latter's death. Over the next five years, Akutagawa maintained his distance from naturalism, composing short, often fantastic, stories that reworked elements of earlier Japanese, as well as European, literature. After 1921, as his health declined, Akutagawa turned increasingly to the *shishōsetsu* mode, which he defended in the "Plot Controversy" with Tanizaki Junichirō. Akutagawa's suicide in 1927 shocked the Japanese literary world. Over four hundred of his works have been translated into foreign languages.

Chikamatsu Monzaemon (1653–1724). Author of plays for the puppet and *kabuki* theaters. While his historical plays (*jidaimono*) dealt with military campaigns such as the Battles of Coxinga (*Kokusenya Kassen*, 1715), his most affecting works explored tragic dimensions of the subject matter of popular *sewamono* (gossip) dramas: domestic conflicts, events of the pleasure quarters, love suicides. Meiji critics often described Chikamatsu as a Japanese parallel to Shakespeare.

Edo period (also Tokugawa period) (1600–1868). Period when Japan was ruled by the Tokugawa shoguns, who established their capital in Edo, the site of present-day Tokyo. The term "Edo," by contrast to "Tokugawa," is used particularly with reference to cultural or literary events of the time.

Futabatei Shimei (1864–1909). Author of *Ukigumo* (*Drifting Clouds*, 1887–1889), a prose narrative describing the gradual withdrawal from society of a young man who has lost his position in the Meiji bureaucracy. Futabatei studied and translated modern Russian literature and undertook extensive stylistic experimentation prior to producing *Drifting Clouds*, which was hailed for its innovative subject matter and style. A passionate social critic who was constantly dissatisfied with his own writing and refused to write for money, Futabatei published two other novels (*Sono Omokage*, 1906, and *Heibon*, 1907). He became ill soon after being assigned to Russia as a newspaper correspondent, and died on a ship while returning to Japan.

Genbun Itchi. Term usually translated into English as "unification of spoken and written language." It refers to the gradual emergence, after the Meiji Restoration in 1868, of a new writing style called *kōgo,* which replaced the classical styles of the written language, or *bungo. Kōgo* was adopted in primary school textbooks in 1903 and within several years, paralleling the emergence of naturalism, became the dominant style in literary prose narratives.

Ihara Saikaku (1642–1693). Influential and prolific seventeenth-century writer. Although known primarily as a *haikai* poet, Saikaku turned to prose fiction when, in 1682, he published *Kōshoku Ichidai Otoko (The Life of an Amorous Man).* This marked the emergence of the genre called *ukiyo zōshi,* erotic fiction set in the Tokugawa licensed quarters or in merchant society, and which, in Saikaku's case, included such works as *Kōshoku Gonin Onna (Five Women Who Loved Love,* 1685), *Nanshoku Ōkagami (The Great Mirror of Male Love,* 1687), and many others. Saikaku's brilliantly stylized and satirical works reflected the cultural dynamism of the ascending Tokugawa merchant class of the seventeenth century. Among members of the *Kenyūsha* (Friends of the Inkpot) literary group at the beginning of the third decade of Meiji, there was a renaissance of interest in Saikaku's writing, now admired for its "realistic" qualities as well as for its concern for the lives of commoners.

Kanbungaku. Term for texts written in classical Chinese or in *kanbun,* a writing method widely used in premodern Japan. According to this method, classical Chinese text is accompanied by annotation, permitting a Japanese reader to rearrange the Chinese word order to conform to Japanese grammar. The prestige of classical Chinese as a written language on the eve of the Meiji Restoration made it something akin to Latin in preeighteenth century Europe and (again, as was the case with Latin) this language was shared by Chinese, Japanese, and Korean intelligentsia. *Kanbun* texts—including poetry, philosophical and moral essays, and history—were the basis for the higher education of the Tokugawa elite.

Kitamura Tōkoku (1868–1894). Major theorist of Meiji Romantic movement. Born into a samurai family, Kitamura was active in the People's Rights movement and through it met his future wife, Ishizaka Minako, who was responsible for his conversion to Christianity in 1887. Kitamura's essays, published in *Bungakkai,* represented the first sustained philosophical articulations of modern notions of romantic love and interiority. He committed suicide at the age of twenty-six.

Kobayashi Hideo (1905–1983). Leading literary critic, who established his influence around 1933 after the repression of the Marxist Proletarian Art movement. Kobayashi's essays, especially his *"Watakushi-shōsetsuron"* ("On the I-Novel"), published in 1935, have been seen as establishing a new genre of criticism which interpreted Japanese literature in a broader context. Kobayashi's influence extended well into the postwar period, when his writing included works on the Japanese classics, Japanese and Western painting, modern philosophy, and so forth.

Kunikida Doppo (1871–1908). Writer. A student of English literature, especially English Romantic poetry, Kunikida Doppo was baptized as a Christian in 1891. His early works included the diary *Azamukazaru no ki* (*A Truthful Account*, 1897) and the "new-style" poetry collection *Doppo Gin*, published in the same year. After an unhappy marriage that ended in divorce in 1896, Kunikida gradually withdrew from the community of Christian intellectuals and social reformers. He developed a deep and important friendship with Tayama Katai. Works like *"Gen Oji"* ("Old Gen," 1897) and the collection *Musashino* (1901) established Kunikida's reputation for lyrical evocation of natural scenes, although his writing also manifested the tormented introspectiveness that deeply moved later writers like Akutagawa Ryūnosuke. Doppo died of tuberculosis at the age of thirty-seven.

Kokugaku. "National Learning School" or nativism. The term for the broad-ranging eighteenth century discourse which sought to define the distinctiveness of Japanese cultural forms and practices in the face of pervasive Chinese influence. *Kokugaku* refers inclusively to many different schools and thinkers, the most pertinent, for this study, being Motoori Norinaga.

Masaoka Shiki (1867–1902). Influential teacher, writer, and critic of poetry in the *tanka* and *haiku* forms. Shiki's series of articles published in 1892 (*Dassai Shooku Haiwa*, or *Talks on Haiku from the Otter's Den*) shocked poets by predicting the imminent death of these two forms. As a columnist for the newspaper Nippon in 1893, Shiki continued to urge the reform of haiku. As a writer and teacher, he advocated the compositional technique of "sketching" (see *shasei*). Shiki wrote prolifically until his death from tuberculosis at the age of thirty-three.

Meiji Period (1868–1912). Reign name of Emperor Mutsuhito. Commencing with the overthrow of shogun Tokugawa Keiki by forces loyal to the Emperor, Meiji was the period of Japan's transformation into a modern nation-state.

Mori Ōgai (1862–1922). Author, editor, and medical officer. The oldest child of a samurai physician, Mori Ōgai became a medical officer in the Japanese army after graduating from Tokyo Imperial University, and as such was sent to study public hygiene in Germany for four years. In 1889, he founded the journal *Shigarami-zōshi* (*The Weir*) to introduce the philosophy and literature associated with European romanticism, particularly German romanticism, to Japan. Ōgai's first short story, "Maihime" ("The Dancing Girl," 1890) is set in Berlin and based on his experience there, describing the love affair between a Japanese student and German dancer. Throughout his life-long career as high-ranking army medical officer, Ōgai wrote and translated prolifically, experimenting with different styles but cultivating a "distanced" narratorial technique that contrasted with that of Japanese naturalism. After the death of Emperor Meiji, Ōgai ceased to write about contemporary subject matter and turned exclusively to the composition of scholarly *shiden*, biographies of historical figures.

Motoori Norinaga (1730–1801). Leading nativist scholar. Critical of the "artificial" qualities of Chinese writings which were a pervasive influence in Japanese culture, Motoori wrote extensively on early Japanese poetry and narrative. Motoori's major work was a forty-four volume translation and commentary on Japan's oldest chronicle, the *Kojiki*.

Natsume Sōseki (1867–1916). Writer, still regarded by many as the greatest Meiji novelist. In 1907 Sōseki resigned from his position on the faculty of Tokyo University to edit a literary column at the Asahi newspaper. During the period of his employment at the newspaper he wrote approximately one long novel a year. Although Sōseki's stylistic versatility is stressed by Karatani, most Japanese criticism has located Sōseki's modernity in his detailed psychological depiction of brooding, neurotic characters such as those in *Sore Kara* (1909), *Mon* (1910), *Kokoro* (1912), or his last novel, *Meian* (*Light and Darkness*, 1916).

Naturalism (*shizenshugi*). Literary movement, seen as culminating in the dominance, achieved by the early twentieth century, of the prose narrative over previously privileged poetic literary forms, of the *genbun itchi* over the *bungo* written style, and of conventions of realism. The publication of Shimazaki Tōson's *Hakai* (*Broken Commandment*, 1906) and Tayama Katai's *Futon* (*The Quilt*, 1907) have been seen as marking the emergence of naturalism, and it is noteworthy that after 1908 Japanese prose fiction was written almost exclusively in the *genbun itchi* style. Naturalist writing, with its concern for detailed observation and ordinariness, has been linked with the preference of many Japanese twentieth-century writers for the confessional mode, or for the *shishōsetsu*.

Japanese Romanticists (*Nihon Roman-ha*). Critics and poets affiliated with the journal of the same name, published between 1935 and 1938. Yasuda Yojūrō, a student of German aesthetics and romantic poetry, was a leading critic of the group, whose nationalistic essays articulated themes of critique of modernity and nostalgia for a lost past. Other members were critic

Kamei Katsuichirō, former Marxist theorist who recanted and embraced the causes of Japanese colonialism and the war, and poets Jimbo Kōtarō and Itō Shizuo.

Japanese Romanticism (*Romanshugi*). Term loosely applied to writers affiliated with the journal *Bungakkai* (*Literary World*), published between 1893 and 1898. Many had been converts to or students of Christianity as youths. The most important writers were Kitamura Tōkoku, who founded the journal, and Shimazaki Tōson, who published his influential *shintaishi* ("new style poems") there. *Tanka* by the celebrated female poet Yosano Akiko, who absorbed and transformed stylistic elements of *Bungakkai* poetry into the verses of her *Midaregami* (*Tangled Hair*, 1901), have also been associated with Japanese romanticism.

People's Rights movement (*jiyū minken undō*). Movement launched in 1874 by Itagaki Taisuke and other samurai disaffected with the policies of the Meiji oligarchy. Agricultural depression and popular opposition to the new uniform tax system swelled the ranks of the movement, broadening its base to include village leaders, wealthy farmers and merchants and, by the 1880s, women. In 1880, the Osaka Congress of People's Rights called for the immediate establishment of a national assembly. The government quickly rejected this demand and imposed severe restrictions on the convening of public meetings. Itagaki's Liberal Party was dissolved in 1884.

Shasei. Term translated as "sketching" or "copying." It was adopted by Masaoka Shiki from the vocabulary of Meiji Western-style painting, and advocated by him as an essential compositional technique for modern practitioners of poetry in the *tanka* and *haiku* forms. Although Shiki defined and redefined his notions of *shasei* over the years, the following is one early example featured in the newspaper *Nippon* on January 8, 1900:

> In writing a poem it will not do to borrow from classical tanka and use cliche phrases like "a legendary forest" or a "sacred forest." The poem would better depict a scene or express a feeling as actually seen or felt by a person passing through a forest. If you have the time to sit at a desk and read a book on tanka, you should instead pick up a cane and go for a leisurely walk along a path in the woods. When you are in the actual setting, look for some specific part of the landscape (such as a house, a village, a stream, a hill, a field, a tower, a bird, a paper kite, etc.) that you might combine with the forest in your poem. Observe also many other less conspicuous features of the forest. . . . When you have completely captured the "feel" of the forest, you can return home. There you should begin composing many poems, bringing back the scenery in your mind's eye and focussing on one or another aspect

of it. (Makoto Ueda, *Modern Japanese Poets and the Nature of Literature*, Stanford University Press, 1983, p. 19.)

Early experiments of prose writers with the technique of *shasei* were called *shaseibun* (literally, "sketching writing" or "sketching literature").

Shiga Naoya (1883–1971). Member of the *Shirakaba* (White Birch) Society, admired as one of the "purest" *shishōsetsu* writers and a preeminent modern stylist.

Shikitei Samba (1776–1822). Writer. Best known as author of two works of comic fiction (a genre given the name *kokkeibon* in the 1820s): *Ukiyoburo* (1809–1813) and *Ukiyodoko* (1813–1814), describing scenes from Edo's public baths and barbershops.

Shimazaki Tōson (1872–1943). Writer. The publication of *Wakanashū* (*Young Leaves*, 1896) established Tōson as a leading Japanese Romantic poet, but by 1899 when he moved to Komoro, on the edge of the Shinshū mountains, Tōson had become interested in *shasei* and naturalist theories of description. His first long prose narrative, *Hakai* (*The Broken Commandment*, 1906) described the struggle of its young protagonist to publicly avow his identity as member of the outcaste or *eta* group. Tōson continued to produce semi-autobiographical works—some based on his experiences with the *Bungakkai* group, others exploring relationships in the nuclear and extended family. *Ie* (*The Family*, 1910–1911), and *Yoake mae* (*Before the Dawn*, 1929–1935) depict, with careful attention to historical detail, the impact of Meiji economic and political development as well as the forces of urbanization on branches of the Shimazaki family that had lived for generations in the Shinshū mountains.

Shishōsetsu (also, *watakushi-shōsetsu*). Form of modern Japanese prose narrative, narrated in the first or third person, that purports to represent (with varying degrees of distance or "purity," i.e. faithfulness) the experiences of the author. As an autobiographical form, the *shishōsetsu* has sometimes been compared with the German *Ich roman* or *bildungsroman*, and it has commonly been translated into English as "I-novel." Some scholars locate the first emergence of the pure *shishōsetsu* in 1913, with the publication of Kasai Zenzō's *Giwaku* (*Suspicion*), while Tayama Katai's 1907 *The Quilt* is seen as the general prototype for the confessional mode. In addition to Masao Miyoshi's article cited herein in chapter 3, recent extensive reassessments of the debate over self, subjectivity, *shōsetsu*, and *shishōsetsu* in modern Japanese literature are Edward Fowler's *The Rhetoric of Confession* (University of California Press, 1988) and James Fujii's *Complicit Fictions: The Subject in the Modern Japanese Prose Fiction* (University of California Press,

1993). An earlier, but important, English study is Janet Walker's *The Japanese Novel of the Meiji Period and the Idea of Individualism* (Princeton University Press, 1979).

Takizawa Bakin (1767–1848). Writer. Author of highly popular late Edo prose fiction, widely read into the early Meiji period. Bakin's best-known work was the long historical romance *Nansō Satomi Hakkenden* (*Satomi and the Eight Dogs*, 1814–1842).

Taisho period (1916–1928).

Tanizaki Junichirō (1886–1965). Prolific and widely translated author. English translations include *Some Prefer Nettles*, *The Makioka Sisters*, and *The Key*.

Tayama Katai (1872–1930). Writer. Author of *The Quilt* (*Futon*, 1907), a prose narrative describing a married writer's platonic infatuation with a young woman for whom he served as literary mentor. *The Quilt* has been seen as establishing the "confessional" mode as the typical pattern of Japanese naturalist fiction. Known for his concept of *heimen byōsha* ("flat" or "ordinary" description), Katai produced the anti-militarist "Ippesotsu" ("One Soldier", 1908), based on his observations as correspondent in China during the Russo-Japanese War. Other prose narratives include *Inaka Kyōshi* (*A Country Schoolteacher*, 1909) and *Toki wa Sugiyuku* (*Time Passes*, 1916).

Tokugawa period. See Edo period.

Tsubouchi Shōyō (1859–1935). Playwright, novelist, and literary theorist. His treatise, *Shōsetsu Shinzui* (*The Essence of the Novel*, 1885), elaborated a sustained critique of late Edo prose and advocated the adoption of conventions of Western realism. Tsubouchi claimed that Motoori Norinaga had affirmed certain principles of modern psychological realism in the latter's celebration of Heian court writing (particularly *The Tale of Genji*) in its difference from Chinese Confucian texts.

Uchimura Kanzō (1861–1930). Influential Meiji Christian thinker. His extensive writings were read by many young Meiji intellectuals. After studying Christian theology in the United States, he eventually became critical of the colonialist attitudes of missionaries in Japan. He organized *Mu-kyōkai* or "the Churchless Church."

Yanagita Kunio (1875–1962). Ethnologist. As a young man, he wrote poetry and was involved with the intellectual ferment surrounding the emergence of Japanese naturalism. As an official of the Ministry of Agriculture, Yanagita recorded details of the agricultural life which had begun to be irrevocably transformed under the onslaught of modernization. Credited with "founding" Japanese ethnology, Yanagita has remained an influential figure throughout the twentieth century.

Yosa Buson (1716–1784). Leading late Edo *haikai* poet and accomplished master of *bunjinga* (literati) painting. He developed a form of unconventional, abstract brush-painting known as the *haiga* ("haiku-painting"). In his writings on poetry, Masaoka Shiki harshly attacked Basho and praised the works of Buson.

Yoshimoto Takaaki (1924–). Poet and literary critic. His ideas were widely influential in the 1960s, following the defeat of the struggle against renewal of the Japan-U.S. Security Treaty. His work has been particularly concerned with theorizing the nature of the collective imaginary in postwar Japan.

Watakushi-shōsetsu. See *Shishōsetsu*.

Index

Karatani Kōjin is Professor
of Literature at Hosei University.
Brett de Bary is Associate Professor
of Japanese Literature at Cornell
University.

Library of Congress Cataloging-in-Publication Data

Karatani, Kōjin, 1941–
[Nihon kindai bungaku no kigen. English]
Origins of modern Japanese literature / Karatani Kōjin ;
translation edited by Brett de Bary.
p. cm.—(Post-contemporary interventions)
Includes index.
ISBN 0-8223-1312-X. — ISBN 0-8223-1323-5 (pbk.)
1. Japanese literature—Meiji period, 1868–1912—History and
criticism. I. Title. II. Series.
PL726.6.K2813 1993
895.6'090042—dc20   92-33670
CIP